The
Chefs Collaborative
Cookbook

The
Chefs Collaborative
Local, Sustainable, Delicious
Recipes from America's Great Chefs Cookbook

Chefs Collaborative & Ellen Jackson

Photography by Gentl & Hyers

The Taunton Press

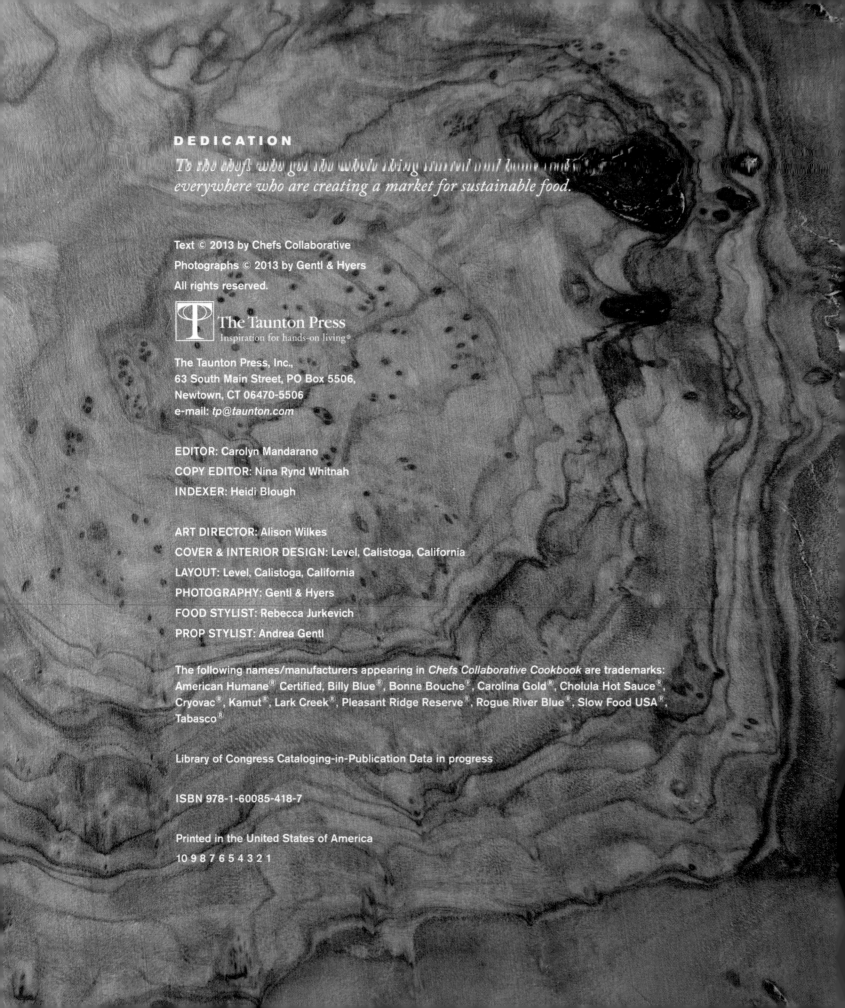

DEDICATION

To the chefs who get the whole thing started and bank and
everywhere who are creating a market for sustainable food.

The Taunton Press
Inspiration for hands-on living®

The Taunton Press, Inc.,
63 South Main Street, PO Box 5506,
Newtown, CT 06470-5506
e-mail: *tp@taunton.com*

EDITOR: Carolyn Mandarano
COPY EDITOR: Nina Rynd Whitnah
INDEXER: Heidi Blough

ART DIRECTOR: Alison Wilkes
COVER & INTERIOR DESIGN: Level, Calistoga, California
LAYOUT: Level, Calistoga, California
PHOTOGRAPHY: Gentl & Hyers
FOOD STYLIST: Rebecca Jurkevich
PROP STYLIST: Andrea Gentl

The following names/manufacturers appearing in *Chefs Collaborative Cookbook* are trademarks:
American Humane® Certified, Billy Blue®, Bonne Bouche®, Carolina Gold®, Cholula Hot Sauce®,
Cryovac®, Kamut®, Lark Creek®, Pleasant Ridge Reserve®, Rogue River Blue®, Slow Food USA®,
Tabasco®

Library of Congress Cataloging-in-Publication Data in progress

ISBN 978-1-60085-418-7

Printed in the United States of America

10 9 8 7 6 5 4 3 2 1

ACKNOWLEDGMENTS FROM CHEFS COLLABORATIVE

A book of this scope and depth—one that pairs the love of cooking and uncommonly good recipes with the wisdom of chefs and other experts for making sustainable choices—takes a lot of people to get right. We owe a debt of gratitude to so many.

First, this book could not have been written without the tremendous support, enthusiasm and skill of our editor, Carolyn Mandarano. Nor could it have been written without Ellen Jackson, a talented chef and writer with a depth of knowledge about sustainable cooking. She—remarkably—turned our vision into a great book. It was a pleasure to work with both of them, and we'll miss the weekly meetings to keep the book on track. Thanks also go out to the entire Taunton team, including Art Director Alison Wilkes. Thank you also to Angela Miller, our agent who believed in the project from the beginning.

There would be no book without Chefs Collaborative Board members past and present, especially John Ash, Michael Leviton, Andrea Reusing, and Bruce Sherman, who provided the vision for the book, made regular decisions about the content, and made sure that it stayed true to the mission of Chefs Collaborative. Thanks also to Amy Bodiker and Megan Westmeyer, who played important roles in developing the book.

The staff of Chefs Collaborative, Leigh Belanger, Rob Booz, Jen Ede, and Melissa Kogut, made valuable contributions to the book throughout the project and kept the organization running during such a consuming endeavor.

Special thanks to intern Lisa Kamer, who spent countless hours testing recipes and supporting the development of the book.

Francine Jeffrey, Pam Kogut, Pam Nourse, Lisa Smith, and Bob Van Meter—all avid home cooks—gave thoughtful feedback on sections of the book and re-tested recipes. And, many stepped in at crucial moments, including Mark Palicki of Fortune Fish in Chicago, who supplied us with soft shell crabs when none were to be found in New York during the photo shoot, and William Kingsland.

Finally, thanks are owed to Joanne Lamb Hayes and Lori Stein for their inspiration to write the book and their work to make the dream a reality.

ACKNOWLEDGMENTS FROM ELLEN JACKSON

I feel incredibly fortunate to have had the opportunity to work with Chefs Collaborative on this project; it's difficult to imagine a better vehicle for the expression of my passion—advocating for a sustainable food system through cooking and writing. I received the perfect balance of guidance and freedom from our editor, Carolyn Mandarano, and Chefs Collaborative Executive Director Melissa Kogut; both supported me every step of the way. The cookbook committee and board members were a wealth of expertise, always willing to share; I hope we've realized their vision for this book. Ann Colonna, Tim Daly, Jen Ede, Blake Esco, Lisa Kamer, and Bill Stephenson helped to test and re-test the recipes until they were right. Megan Westmeyer's insights were invaluable in helping me to shape the seafood chapter. Cory Carman and Piper Davis shared wisdom that made its way into the meat and poultry chapter. Andrea Reusing's careful eye kept it all on track and true to our collective vision. And my sweet husband, Steven Jackson, kept me on track through it all. I certainly couldn't have done it without him, or any of the rest of these individuals. Thank you all.

Contents

> **"It is the strength of our unified message as chefs that can continue to influence and change our food community for the better."**
>
> JOHN ASH, visionary chef and James Beard award-winning author

Chefs Collaborative:
John Ash
The Beginning

In the summer of 1993, a group of chefs got together on the big island of Hawaii to talk about environmental issues around food production. This began as an Oldways gathering; Oldways, founded by visionary K. Dun Gifford, is probably best known for introducing the Mediterranean Diet and its pyramid back in the early 1990s.

The year 1993 was an interesting time for food in America. The average cost of a loaf of bread was just over $1.50. E. coli and other deadly food-borne illness outbreaks were on the rise, and research on the impact of food processing plants on the United States' food supply was finally becoming part of the national conversation.

The understanding and use of terms like "organic" and "sustainable" were not part of the general conversation, as hard as that might be to imagine today. Topics like GMOs (genetically modified organisms) were unknown or not really understood to any extent by most of us. The National Organic Program administered by the United States Department of Agriculture (USDA) did not become law until December of 2000. Prior to that, "organic" was often seen as something "hippy dippy" and not really a part of mainstream thinking.

I was lucky enough to have grown up on a cattle ranch with my grandparents in Colorado; they pounded into me some sense of what it meant to take care of both the animals that we raised and the land that they roamed. Although there were many of us chefs that recognized the importance of creating a sustainable food system and supporting traditional food practices and local suppliers, we didn't have a unified voice. There was a sense among many chefs around the country that these issues were only things we talked about with our local like-minded growers and suppliers. There was no larger framework or organization that could help us define and spread the word until that serendipitous gathering in Hawaii.

Present at the gathering in Hawaii were a "Who's Who" of the culinary world at that time and still today. This group included myself, Paul Bartolotta, Rick Bayless, Catherine Brandel, Kathleen Daelemans, Gary Danko, Robert Del Grande, Mark Ellman, Susan Feniger, Amy Ferguson-Ota, Larry Forgione, Joyce Goldstein, Madhur Jaffrey, Jean-Marie Josselin, Mo Kanner, Matthew Kenney, Deborah Madison, Zarela Martinez, Nobu Matsuhisa, George Mavrothalassitis, Peter Merriman, Mark Miller, Mary Sue Milliken, Bradley Ogden, Phillipe Padovani, Nora Pouillon, Michael Romano, Oliver Saucy, Jimmy Schmidt, RoxSand Scocos, Allen Susser, Alan Wong, and Roy Yamaguchi, among others.

The day-long conversation focused on many things, but one big topic was the changing role of chefs in the public eye. Though the *Food Network* was not yet on the air, many chefs in America were being elevated to celebrity status. With that celebrity came the first real understanding that chefs could have an important role in educating not only their restaurant guests and employees but also the larger community about food, including influencing food policy. We knew that food-buying decisions chefs made for their restaurants could make an impact locally, but we wanted to do more. Could we apply sustainable and what I call "ethical" food choices collectively and on a national level to make a more dramatic impact? The answer was yes, and the decision was made to create an organization that united chefs in creating what we hoped could be a truly sustainable food landscape. In 2000, Chefs Collaborative was launched to help bring attention to national and global food issues.

The Collaborative was one of the first organizations to become involved in school lunch programs, where member chefs took an active role teaching elementary-school administrators and students the principles of sustainable food. Chefs Collaborative has partnered over the years with other stakeholders in the sustainable seafood arena. The first "Seafood Solutions" chefs' guide was issued by the Collaborative in 2000, aimed at educating and helping chefs to make good buying decisions. Monterey Bay Aquarium with Chefs Collaborative at the table, launched its successful Seafood Watch program. These initiatives, along with education forums and communiqués, have helped chefs understand the implications of subjects as diverse as grass-fed vs. natural vs. conventional beef; distribution issues and opportunities for local and regional food systems; and even make sense of eco-labels and green washing practices.

As one of the founding members of Chefs Collaborative, I've been impressed at the impact the organization has made over the years. I've learned so much from my association, as I know other chefs have, too. While we chose to stay focused on chefs and the community we're committed to serving, now is the time to broaden our audience. It is the strength of our unified message as chefs that can continue to influence and change our food community for the better.

At the gathering in Hawaii in 1993, including: John Ash, Paul Bartolotta, Rick Bayless, Catherine Brandel, Sam Choy, Gary Danko, Robert del Grande, Mark Ellman, Larry Forgione, Joyce Goldstein, Tim Keating, Deborah Madison, Zarela Martinez, George Mavrothalassitis, Peter Merriman, Mary Sue Milliken, Bradley Ogden, Philippe Pordavani, Nora Pouillon, Michael Romano, Jimmy Schmidt, RoxSand Scocos, Allen Susser, Roy Yamaguchi

Chefs Collaborative:
Michael Leviton
20 Years Later

In the late 1980s, I was a cook at Square One in San Francisco, California, where the food revolution was already under way. While the word "sustainability" did not exist in our vocabulary as chefs, there was an overarching belief that to be the best chef—and to make the best meals—you needed to start with great ingredients. It was not uncommon for chefs in that area to search out the best farmers, ranchers, bread bakers and cheesemakers because we knew that they put just as much care into their work as we did.

When I returned to New England in 1996, I found a much different culture. The area was not as robust with farmers, fishers, and other food artisans who shared a commitment to grow and produce great food, and it was a struggle to find the caliber of ingredients I was used to working with.

By then, Chefs Collaborative had a presence in Boston, and the organization connected me to like-minded chefs and food producers. Through my participation in Chefs Collaborative, I had an epiphany that flavor, healthfulness, and quality of ingredients are intricately linked to the care that is shown to the environment during production. From there, it wasn't a huge leap to becoming an avid supporter of local fishermen using methods of fishing that didn't deplete the supply of fish, farmers who needed chefs' support if they were to afford to stay on their land, and ranchers concerned with how they treated their animals and handled waste.

Thinking back about the chefs who founded Chefs Collaborative, I am struck by both their passion and their vision. But I doubt that even they could have predicted the monumental changes in our food system over the past two decades. I would like to believe that, as chefs, we have done them proud by remaining on the movement's leading edge—pushing the conversation (and the market) forward while celebrating all of the progress that has been made.

From the rise of farmer's markets and community-supported agriculture (CSA) programs to organic produce sold at Walmart and sustainable seafood pledges at grocery chains and big-box stores, we're looking at an utterly different food landscape than we were 20 years ago—even 5 years ago. But food safety scares, ocean dead zones, routine mistreatment of farm animals, and rising obesity rates still remind us how much work remains to be done.

We chefs are blessed with the capacity to influence the public's food choices. And our purchasing power is equally as influential among producers and purveyors. We will continue to push for ingredients produced and harvested with a passion for quality that matches our own; and we will continue to share the stories behind these ingredients with our customers, schoolchildren, public health professionals, the media—anyone, in fact, who will listen. With these and other efforts, we hope to keep this conversation—this movement—progressing.

With this book, we start where we always have—with a mixture of flavor and community. These two values have anchored us to our mission and principles since we began our work 20 years ago, and we have no doubt they will carry us into the decades to come. The community at our core is reflected in these pages—from the chefs who have provided recipes and information about our food to the farmers, ranchers, fishers, cheesemakers, foragers, and others who have brought the food into our kitchens and given us the tools and the context to understand how great flavor is created.

This cookbook is certainly a source of inspired recipes, but it goes deeper than that. The book is a blueprint for cooking like a sustainably minded chef. You'll find delicious dishes that feature less familiar cuts of meat, like Beef Shin and Farro Soup (page 161) and Pork Heart and Sausage Ragoût over Pasta (page 133). Lesser-known seafood species show up in Whey-Poached Triggerfish with Asparagus (page 205) and Coconut Black Drum Seviche (page 201). And seasonal showpieces like Goat Cheese Gnocchi with Spring Peas and Tarragon (page 250) and Autumn Pear "Ravioli" with Chanterelle and Shaved Pear Salad (page 34) will inspire you to cook in the rhythm of the seasons. The recipes will make you want to head straight to the kitchen (with a quick stop at the farmer's market first, of course). Beyond the recipes, though, practical sidebars help you sort through the intricacies of choosing ingredients responsibly; and stories from chefs explain why we cook the way we do.

Sustainable cuisine is not about dry statistics and dire predictions for the future. It's about an approach to sourcing and cooking predicated on flavor, quality, and sharing our passion and knowledge. The pleasures of the table—that mix of flavor and community—enrich us in mind, body, and soul and inspire us to do our best work. Cheers!

"Sustainable cuisine is about an approach to sourcing and cooking predicated on flavor, quality, and the pleasures of the table."

Christmas lima beans. Arkansas Black apples. Jimmy Nardello peppers. Gillfeather turnips. Pencil Cob grits. Eating your vegetables—and fruits, beans, grains, and seeds—has never been so appealing. Across the country, we are rediscovering "new" old plant varieties. These heirlooms, handed down through generations of gardeners and farmers, offer eaters more flavorful versions of everything from plums to potatoes, with as much nutrition as their names have personality. Old varieties are helping to preserve crop diversity and revive regional food cultures across the United States. They tell stories of our past, not only of those who grew them but also of the people who cooked and ate them. But the real reason we're eating more edible plants is because they're versatile and downright delicious.

A Reward Like No Other

Bulbs, flowers, fruit, fungi, grains, herbs, leaves, roots, and seeds. The world of edible plants is enormous, and growing and purchasing them rewards in endless ways. Some plants have multiple edible parts (garlic offers green garlic, scapes, and mature bulbs), others two growing seasons (for example, Tulameen raspberries come on in early summer, Caroline in fall). Picking a small patch of spinach sown just weeks before may inspire a home gardener to devote more space to growing food, but a half-dozen terra cotta pots planted with herbs for infusing meals with fresh flavor equally satisfies. Handing money directly to the grower at a farmstand or farmer's market ensures their livelihood; the anticipation of a weekly community-supported agriculture (CSA) share, full of familiar staples like onions, snap peas, and carrots, plus Kentucky Wonder beans or Green Zebra tomatoes (heirloom varieties the farmer grew last season), inspires creativity. The challenge and reward of growing food can be as great for the farmer as is the pleasure and possibility of a basket of newly harvested vegetables for a cook.

> "Food grown near to us is not only fresher but also offers us the opportunity to explore and eat from the regional edible plants available to us."

Vegetables, Fruits, and Other Edible Plants

Like shopping for meat and fish, choosing vegetables, fruits, and other food from plants requires us to ask questions in order to make informed purchases. Is it in season? Grown locally? Organic? Recent changes in both attitude and access, like the proliferation of farmer's markets across the country and the addition of gardens to schoolyards and fresh vegetables to lunch programs, illustrate a paradigm shift away from monocultures and centralized food production and toward greater variety, better flavor, and healthier choices. Food grown near to us is not only fresher but also offers us the opportunity to explore and eat from the huge catalog of regional edible plants available to each of us.

Shifting Seasons, New Plants

As chefs and home cooks alike embrace new vegetable varieties and cooking techniques, searching for fresh ways to preserve and extend the seasons is a natural evolution. We can savor each perfectly ripe ingredient—the too-brief appearance of sour cherries or fava beans—reassured that it will return next year and that this year's bounty can be preserved and unleashed later, to summon that particular week in July when the raspberry bushes were heavy with fruit and the air was filled with their perfume. Then we turn our attention to the crop that's just around the corner, ready to test us in our kitchens and tempt us at our tables.

The shift in seasons is most dramatic in the world of edible plants. One summer day's challenge to utilize the fruit of an over-productive zucchini vine quickly turns to cooler weather and an occasion to reacquaint ourselves with roasting, braising, and the best methods for preparing acorn squash. Rather than consulting lists of rules and ingredients, cooks are learning to experiment with different varieties and look for cues from the food, like "What grows together goes together" (think ratatouille, with its eggplant, peppers, and tomatoes, or a succotash of corn and shell beans). Developing those instincts and maintaining a larder filled with beans, grains, nuts, seeds, and spices—ingredients that are gaining in popularity as the foundations for our meals—multiplies the bounty of a plant-centric diet and makes cooking and eating a joy.

Wendell Berry taught us "Eating is an agricultural act." It has also become a political act. Three times a day, we have the opportunity to feed ourselves well without contributing to the long list of environmental and ethical problems connected to food production. Bringing balance to our diets with the vibrant colors and flavors of local, seasonal plants illustrates our hunger for food with a history and sense of place, food that ensures a delicious, diverse, and healthy future for the planet and its inhabitants.

"The challenge and reward of growing food can be as great for the farmer as is the pleasure for a cook."

BARRY MAIDEN

Hungry Mother | Cambridge, Massachusetts

Available from late fall to early spring, upland cress is a more pungent version of watercress, a better-known salad green. Similar in appearance to watercress and also a member of the mustard family, "creasy greens," as they're known in the South, deliver a sharp peppery punch more akin to horseradish and can stand up to stewing with ham hocks. SERVES 6

Heirloom Beet and Upland Cress Salad with Apples, Grapefruit, and Fennel-Buttermilk Dressing

2 pounds heirloom beets
(about 6 small or 3 medium)
3 cups upland cress or watercress
Fennel-Buttermilk Dressing
(recipe on the following page)
1 firm tart apple, such as Newtown
Pippin or Granny Smith, skin on,
julienned
1 pink grapefruit, segmented
Candied Walnuts (recipe on the
following page)

Heat the oven to 400°F. Leaving the tails and an inch of the stems on the beets, rinse them well and put them in a baking pan with ¼ inch of water. Cover the pan with aluminum foil and bake until the beets are tender when pierced with a knife, 25 to 40 minutes, depending on size. When they are cool enough to handle, peel the beets, slice in half, and cut into wedges.

Put the cress in a large bowl, add several tablespoons of dressing, and toss, using your hands to coat the greens. Add the beets, apples, and grapefruit segments to the bowl and gently toss to evenly distribute and coat the ingredients with the dressing. Add additional dressing as needed. Divide the salad between six plates and garnish with candied walnuts.

>>>

"Root vegetables are the ingredients I look forward to most; anything grown underground just seems to taste better."

PETER DAVIS

*Henrietta's Table in The Charles Hotel,
Cambridge, Massachusetts*

Fennel-Buttermilk Dressing

MAKES ABOUT 2 CUPS

1 egg yolk

1½ teaspoons Dijon mustard

1 clove garlic

2 tablespoons freshly squeezed
   lemon juice

1½ teaspoons Worcestershire sauce

½ cup buttermilk, preferably organic

1½ teaspoons toasted fennel seed

1 cup canola oil

½ cup extra-virgin olive oil

½ cup finely chopped chives

Kosher salt and freshly ground black pepper

Combine the egg yolk, mustard, garlic, lemon juice, and Worcestershire sauce in a blender or food processor. Pulse several times to mince the garlic. Add the buttermilk and fennel seeds and pulse to combine. With the machine running, drizzle the oils in slowly to emulsify. The dressing will be thick enough to coat the back of a spoon. Fold the chives in by hand and season to taste with salt and black pepper.

Candied Walnuts

MAKES 2 CUPS

⅓ cup granulated sugar

1 teaspoon freshly ground black pepper

⅛ teaspoon cayenne pepper

½ teaspoon kosher salt

2 cups (7 ounces) walnuts

Make a simple syrup by combining the sugar with ¼ cup water in a small saucepan over medium heat. Bring the mixture to a boil to dissolve the sugar. Remove the simple syrup from the heat.

Heat the oven to 300°F. In a large bowl, combine 2 tablespoons of the simple syrup, the black and cayenne peppers, and salt. Add the walnuts and toss to coat evenly. Lay on a baking sheet in a single layer and cook until dry and lightly toasted, about 20 minutes.

Appreciating Root Vegetables

On first glance, root vegetables don't seem to have much to recommend them. Hardy and decidedly unglamorous, these "fruits" from the soil hide an unexpected sweet side beneath skins riddled with bumps and warts, dirt-filled crevices, and hairy tendrils—and incredible keeping qualities. In fact, turnips, rutabaga, and parsnips, along with potatoes and other cheap and nutritious vegetables that grow below the earth, inspired the root cellar, an underground structure built for storing food supplies (vegetables, fruits, and nuts, mostly) at low temperature and steady humidity. Cool temps convert their starches to sugars so root vegetables are sweetest and tastiest in the winter months.

Like carrots, sweet potatoes, beets, and radishes, the colorful members of the family, the more neutral-toned root vegetables are nutritional storehouses. They're packed with flavor and fiber, low in fat and calories, high in antioxidants and complex carbs, and inexpensive to boot. Roasting brings out their best qualities, but don't stop there. Try mashing or braising root vegetables, adding them to soups (see Turnip Soup on page 46), layering them in a gratin, or making chips.

KENNETH MACDONALD

Sleeping Lady | Leavenworth, Washington

Everyone loves a classic done right. However, Caesar salad is one of those classics that people are opinionated and stubborn about. If you start with crisp lettuces, fresh buttery croutons, and this dressing, with just the right amount of garlic and anchovies, anything else you add will turn this salad into Caesar your way. **SERVES 4**

Classic Caesar Salad with Anchovies and Lemon

FOR THE CROUTONS

1 loaf rustic Italian bread (0 to 10 ounces), crusts removed, cut into ½-inch cubes

4 tablespoons (½ stick) unsalted butter, melted

Kosher salt and freshly ground black pepper

FOR THE CAESAR DRESSING

1 egg

2 anchovies, minced

1 clove garlic, crushed

2 teaspoons Dijon mustard

4 tablespoons coarsely chopped fresh herbs (parsley, thyme, chives, chervil)

¼ cup champagne vinegar

3 tablespoons freshly squeezed lemon juice

⅛ teaspoon Worcestershire sauce

2 ounces grated Parmesan

½ cup plus 2 tablespoons extra-virgin olive oil

Kosher salt and freshly ground black pepper

FOR THE SALAD

4 small heads romaine or assorted leaf lettuces, chopped

Freshly ground black pepper

FOR GARNISH (OPTIONAL)

4 slices thick-sliced bacon, crisped and crumbled

Shaved Parmesan

Microgreens and/or chervil leaves

Roasted red or sweet onion slices

Finely diced preserved lemon

MAKE THE CROUTONS

Heat the oven to 400°F. Toss the bread cubes with the melted butter to coat evenly. Sprinkle with salt and pepper, spread in a single layer on a baking sheet with a rim, and bake until golden brown, about 10 minutes. Set aside.

MAKE THE DRESSING

Coddle the egg by pouring boiling water over it to cover completely. Set aside for 10 minutes.

Place the coddled egg, anchovies, garlic, mustard, herbs, champagne vinegar, lemon juice, Worcestershire, and Parmesan in a blender or food processer and blend until smooth and creamy. With the motor running, drizzle the olive oil in slowly, until all of it is incorporated and the dressing is emulsified. Season to taste with salt and black pepper.

ASSEMBLE THE SALAD

Put the lettuce in a bowl and add enough dressing to coat. Add as many of the optional garnishes as desired, along with the croutons and freshly ground pepper and serve immediately.

JEREMY BARLOW

Tayst | Nashville, Tennessee

The flavors of late spring come to life in this starter, which easily becomes a main course when served with a small piece of fish or grilled chicken on the side. Or spoon the fiddleheads over a bed of ricotta or gnocchi and drizzle with the balsamic glaze. **SERVES 4 AS A STARTER**

Crispy Tofu with Fiddleheads and Strawberry Relish

1 pound firm tofu

½ cup balsamic vinegar

Kosher salt

1 cup fiddlehead ferns, cleaned
   and trimmed (about 6 ounces after
   trimming)

1 cup diced fresh strawberries

2 tablespoons chopped fresh mint

1 cup chopped green garlic cloves or
   ½ cup chopped garlic

½ cup olive oil

Freshly ground black pepper

The day before you plan to serve it, cut the tofu crosswise in half and place in a single layer in a shallow baking dish. Cover the tofu with waxed paper or parchment and place a small, flat pan or board that fits inside the baking dish directly on the paper. Put a couple of cans on top, to weigh the board down, and cover the dish with plastic wrap. Refrigerate overnight.

Bring the balsamic vinegar to a boil in a large, nonreactive frying pan. Reduce the heat to medium low and simmer until the vinegar has reduced to 2 tablespoons, about 20 minutes. Set aside for the following day.

On the day that you plan to serve the tofu, bring a large pot of salted water to a boil. Add the fiddleheads and cook until almost tender, 3 to 5 minutes, then remove to an ice bath to stop the cooking.

Combine the diced strawberries and mint and a pinch of salt for the strawberry relish. Set aside.

Cook the green garlic in oil in a frying pan over low heat until very tender, about 5 minutes. With a slotted spoon, remove the garlic to a small bowl and set aside, reserving the pan and garlic oil.

Pat the tofu dry and cut each piece into 6 squares. Add the tofu squares to the hot garlic oil, turning occasionally, until they are crispy on all sides, about 20 minutes. Remove the tofu from the oil to drain on a paper-towel-lined plate. Reheat the fiddleheads and green garlic in the same pan, and season to taste with salt and black pepper. Arrange 3 pieces of tofu in a line on each of four serving plates. Spoon the fiddleheads and garlic around the tofu, drizzle with the balsamic glaze, and spoon strawberry relish over the top.

Why Organic Costs More

In an ideal world, everyone would have access to food grown locally and sustainably 365 days a year. Realistically, certain regions of the country will never experience that security, regardless of economics and politics. But it's possible to make good choices at the supermarket, where organically grown food gets more shelf space every year. If you've ever wondered why organic products are often much more expensive than their conventionally produced equivalents, read on.

■ **Fewer inputs.** Conventional farmers use chemicals and synthetic pesticides (also known as inputs) to increase productivity and reduce labor costs. Organic farmers must hire workers for tasks like weeding and pest control; intensive land management including manual cultivation, crop diversity, and rotation; and managing soil fertility.

■ **No subsidies.** Government subsidies to industrial agriculture reduce the overall cost of crops and dwarf the amount dedicated to local and organic programs by billions of dollars.

■ **Certification.** USDA certification is expensive. Qualification requires farm facilities and production methods to comply with standards that can require costly modification of facilities. Annual inspection and certification fees run from $400 to $2,000, depending on the size of the operation. And additional employees must be hired to keep the strict daily records that are required to be available for inspection at all times.

■ **Higher fertilizer costs.** Organic farmers use compost and animal manure as an alternative to the cheap chemicals and fertilizers used by conventional farmers. Natural solutions are labor intensive and expensive to ship when they aren't available locally.

■ **Organic = slower growth.** Fertilizers are used on conventional farms to ensure that plants absorb nutrients easily, causing them to grow large quickly, without extending their roots. Furthermore, conventional farmers lose significantly fewer crops to pests and disease by using synthetic pesticides. Organic farmers eschew the use of chemicals, choosing to focus on the quality of the soil rather than rapid growth. Edible plants chosen for flavor, suitability for a particular climate, and environmental stewardship grow more slowly using organic methods, which allow them to extend their roots to absorb nutrients.

■ **Demand overwhelms supply.** Retail sales of organic food continue to increase sharply every year. However, organic farmland accounts for less than 1 percent of total farmland worldwide, and organic farms generally produce less volume than conventional. Conventional farmers have the land to produce more efficiently and in larger quantities, creating the supply to keep the costs to the consumer low.

■ **Crop rotation.** Organic farming depends on customizing a crop rotation to complement the climate, land, and season to return nutrients to the soil, maintain its quality, and prevent weed growth. After a crop is harvested, the area is often planted with a cover crop and allowed to "rest" and to replenish its nitrogen stores. Conventional farming uses every acre of land continuously to grow the most profitable crops, but there are hidden environmental costs (including degradation of soils) to growing without interruption.

■ **Handling costs.** After it is harvested, organic produce must be kept separate from conventional in order to prevent cross-contamination. Because they are handled and shipped in smaller quantities and because organic operations are usually located at a greater distance from major cities, organic crops cost more to transport.

NORA POUILLON

Restaurant Nora | *Washington, D.C.*

When they are grilled, eggplant and sweet red peppers, the main ingredients for this salad, take on slightly smoky notes that contrast beautifully with the salty olives and cheese and peppery basil or arugula. Arranged on a large platter, the various shapes and colors make for a dramatic impression that is second only to the salad's wonderful flavors. **SERVES 6 AS A STARTER OR 4 AS A MAIN COURSE**

Grilled Eggplant with Roasted Red Pepper and Black Olive Salad

3 tablespoons extra-virgin olive oil

1 tablespoon tamari

2 tablespoons balsamic or red-wine vinegar

1 tablespoon finely minced garlic

1 teaspoon dried oregano, preferably Greek

Kosher salt and freshly ground black pepper

1 large eggplant (about 1 to 1¼ pounds), cut lengthwise into ½-inch slices

2 large red peppers

3 tablespoons coarsely chopped fresh basil

8 ounces feta cheese, cubed

12 to 15 kalamata olives, pitted

Fresh basil leaves and/or arugula, for garnish

Heat a grill to high. Make the vinaigrette by whisking the olive oil, tamari, vinegar, garlic, and oregano in a small bowl. Season to taste with salt and black pepper.

Brush the eggplant slices generously with the vinaigrette and grill on each side for 2 to 4 minutes, or until tender and slightly collapsed. Remove and set aside. Grill the peppers, turning until blistered and charred on all sides. Put the peppers in a bowl, cover tightly with plastic wrap, and steam for 10 minutes.

When the peppers are cool enough to handle, peel off the charred outer skin and remove the seeds. If necessary, rinse quickly to remove stray seeds and skin. Cut the peppers into ½-inch-wide strips. Combine with the basil, feta, and olives and toss with the remaining vinaigrette.

Serve the red pepper-black olive salad on top of the room temperature eggplant steaks garnished with torn basil leaves and/or arugula.

HUGH ACHESON

Five & Ten Restaurant | Athens, Georgia

Tender melted leeks and homemade farmer cheese have found their ideal companions in the fall flavors of fresh figs and frisée tossed with a concentrated, tart apple cider vinaigrette. Boiled peanuts add crunch plus another layer of salty flavor as well as a nod to the chef's culinary leanings, firmly rooted in Southern ingredients and traditions. **SERVES 4**

Composed Salad of Poached Leeks, Fresh Figs, and Farmer Cheese

1 tablespoon unsalted butter

2 large leeks (about 1 pound), white portions only, halved and washed with root intact

1 cup chicken stock (homemade or store-bought)

½ teaspoon kosher salt

½ cup Simple Farmer Cheese (recipe on the facing page)

8 large fresh figs, stems removed and cut into quarters

2 cups frisée

1 cup shelled Boiled Peanuts (recipe on the facing page)

¼ cup Cider Vinaigrette (recipe on the facing page)

Melt the butter in a pan wide enough to accommodate the length of the leeks, probably 10 to 12 inches. Place the leeks in the butter, cut side down, and cook over medium heat for 10 minutes. Add the stock and salt and bring to a gentle boil. Cover and simmer over very low heat for 20 minutes. Remove from the heat and reserve.

Smear 2 tablespoons of farmer cheese on each of four plates. Put a braised leek half on top of each smear of cheese. In a medium bowl, combine the figs, frisée, and peanuts. Add about 2 tablespoons of the vinaigrette and toss well. Arrange the ingredients equally over the braised leeks and drizzle with the remaining vinaigrette.

Save the whey from the farmer cheese for Whey-Poached Trigger Fish with Asparagus (see page 205).

"I wait all year for the fruit from a local farm that has two special Black Mission fig trees that produce—in my opinion—some of the best figs on the East Coast."

WILLIAM DISSEN

The Market Place Restaurant, Asheville, North Carolina

Simple Farmer Cheese

MAKES ABOUT 1½ CUPS

½ gallon fresh whole milk

½ packet fromage blanc culture

1 tablespoon kosher salt

In a clean, nonreactive pot, heat the milk to 85°F over medium heat. Add the culture, stir, and cover. Leave at room temperature for 12 hours, after which time curds will have formed.

Using a long, thin knife, cut the curds into 1-inch cubes. Slowly ladle the curds into a colander lined with cheesecloth and drain at room temperature for 1 hour, reserving the whey for later use. Chill the curds overnight.

Using a stand mixer with the paddle attachment, mix the cheese with the salt, adding back a small amount of whey to achieve the desired texture.

Boiled Peanuts

MAKES ABOUT 2¼ CUPS

2 cups (7 ounces) peanuts

½ teaspoon kosher salt

Rinse the unshelled peanuts in cold water until the water runs clear. Drain and put the peanuts and salt in a large pot. Cover completely with fresh cold water. Bring the water to a boil over medium-high heat, reduce to a simmer, and cook for at least 1 hour or as long as 3 hours. (The variety and maturity of the peanuts determines the cooking time. Taste them throughout the cooking process to determine if they're done.) To check doneness, pull a peanut from the pot and crack it open. If the nuts are soft, they're done. If they're still crunchy, let the peanuts continue to simmer until they're soft. If the nuts are ready but aren't salty enough, turn off the heat and let them sit in the salted water. Drain completely when ready.

Store any leftover peanuts in their shells in the refrigerator for up to 1 week.

Cider Vinaigrette

MAKES ABOUT ⅔ CUP

1 cup fresh apple cider

1 teaspoon Dijon mustard

⅓ cup extra-virgin olive oil

2 tablespoons cider vinegar

¼ teaspoon kosher salt

In a small, nonreactive pot, heat the cider on medium-high heat and cook until the cider is reduced to about ¼ cup, 12 to 15 minutes; set aside to cool. Put the cooled cider in a blender with the mustard and slowly drizzle in the olive oil with the motor running. Add the vinegar and salt. Thin slightly with water if necessary.

The Well-Stocked Pantry

A pantry stocked with the bare essentials has the potential to turn "nothing" into dinner. We all have certain foods in our cupboards and refrigerators that we try never to be without. And once they are used, they are restocked immediately. Maybe you've wondered what ingredients chefs make sure to have on hand when they're not in their well-stocked restaurant kitchens. You'll see lots of similarities in these lists and gain some fun insights into the creative process that leads to getting dinner on the table when the cupboard is otherwise bare.

MARY SUE MILIKEN

Border Grill, Santa Monica, California
1. Canned sardines from Portugal
2. Basmati rice
3. Steel-cut oats
4. Sushi rice
5. Beluga lentils
6. Polenta
7. Barley
8. Dried shiitake mushrooms
9. Anchovies
10. Assorted seaweed

TONY MAWS

Craigie on Main, Cambridge, Massachusetts
1. Fish sauce
2. Good Dijon mustard
3. Banyuls vinegar
4. Pepper mill (filled with Tellicherry peppercorns)
5. Good sea salt
6. Mázi piri piri sauce
7. Good-quality extra-virgin olive oil
8. Yellow miso
9. Butter
10. Good soy sauce

BILL TELEPAN

Telepan, New York, New York
1. Extra-virgin olive oil
2. Parmesan/Romano cheese
3. Yogurt
4. Apples
5. Pasta
6. Beans
7. Eggs
8. Tequila
9. Bread flour
10. Crushed red pepper flakes

TORY MILLER

L'Etoile, Madison, Wisconsin
1. Mayonnaise
2. Crispy chili oil
3. Rice vinegar
4. Cholula Hot Sauce®
5. Rice
6. Giuseppe Cocco pasta
7. Dark chocolate bars
8. Chewy sweetarts
9. Potato chips
10. Fish sauce

CAROLYN FIDANZA

Saltie, Brooklyn, New York
1. Sea salt, preferably sel gris
2. Good olive oil
3. Sherry vinegar
4. Lemons
5. Garlic
6. Sesame seeds
7. Pasta
8. Sardines
9. Some sort of grain
10. Avocado

ROB CORLISS

ATE (All Things Epicurean),
Nixa, Missouri
1. Salt, both Celtic sea salt and pink Himalayan
2. Lemons (or ground sumac for lemony brightness)
3. Chiles (dried whole and/or ground)
4. Sichuan peppercorns
5. Olive oil
6. Farm fresh eggs
7. Local Greek-style yogurt
8. Stone-ground mustard
9. Agave nectar
10. Tamari or low-sodium soy sauce

ANN COOPER

Food Family Farming Foundation | Boulder, Colorado

Feta cheese and a lemony vinaigrette spiked with fresh oregano give this salad extra flavor, while the addition of chickpeas makes it hearty enough for a summertime lunch. It is especially good with thick slices of fresh tomato and grilled zucchini on the side. SERVES 6 TO 8

Mediterranean Couscous Salad

1⅓ cups whole-wheat couscous

5 tablespoons extra-virgin olive oil

6 tablespoons freshly squeezed lemon juice

2 teaspoons finely chopped fresh oregano

2 teaspoons kosher salt; more as needed

¼ teaspoon freshly ground black pepper; more as needed

2 scallions, white and 1 inch of green parts, thinly sliced (about ¼ cup)

1 cup sliced Greek olives

3½ cups chickpeas, cooked, or two 15-ounce cans, rinsed and drained

1½ cups crumbled feta cheese

Bring 1⅔ cups water to a boil over medium heat in a saucepan. Stir in the couscous, remove from the heat, cover, and let stand for 5 minutes. Put in a large bowl and set aside to cool slightly.

Whisk together the olive oil, lemon juice, oregano, salt, and black pepper.

Add the scallions, olives, and chickpeas to the cooled couscous and toss to combine. Pour the vinaigrette over the top of the salad and combine well, evenly distributing the vinaigrette and coating all of the ingredients. Add the cheese, toss again, and refrigerate until well chilled. Check the seasoning, adding more salt and pepper as needed, and serve cold.

"Couscous is a delicious and healthy tradition that goes with almost everything. Whole-grain couscous is easy to find, perfect for today's modern kitchen."

SARA BAER-SINNOTT

Oldways, Boston, Massachusetts

MICHAEL SCHWARTZ

Michael's Genuine Food & Drink | Miami, Florida

French feta cheese is typically made with sheep milk and tends to be milder and creamier than Greek feta. Its understated flavor nicely complements the sweetness of the peaches and the bright, peppery notes of the basil and radishes. Cheesemakers across the country are making a wide range of sheep milk cheeses, including French-style feta. Look for your own local source. SERVES 6

Peach and Radish Salad with French Feta and Almonds

½ small red onion

3 to 4 Easter Egg or French Breakfast
　radishes

4 or 5 ripe peaches
　(about 2 pounds)

¼ cup extra-virgin olive oil

2 tablespoons champagne vinegar

Kosher salt and freshly ground
　black pepper

½ cup fresh basil leaves, torn

1 cup French feta cheese, crumbled

¼ cup sliced almonds, lightly toasted

Thinly slice the onions on a mandoline or with a very sharp knife. You should end up with about ¼ cup. Fill a small bowl with cold water and a few ice cubes and soak the onions for 5 minutes; this mellows the sharp bite typical of raw onions and makes them crisp. Drain the onions and pat dry with paper towels. Thinly slice the radishes on the mandoline.

Halve and pit the peaches. Cut each half into quarters and slice the quarters into thin wedges. Combine the oil and vinegar in a bowl with some salt and black pepper and whisk to combine. Add the peaches, onions, radishes, and basil, tossing gently to evenly coat the ingredients. Season to taste with additional salt and pepper if desired.

Divide the salad equally among six plates and top with the crumbled feta and toasted almonds.

BRUCE WALLIS

At Sara's Table Chester Creek Café | Duluth, Minnesota

The winning formula for this salad is simple: combine seasonal greens—preferably one that's mild and one that's more assertive—with two seasonal fruits. Add salty cheese, spicy almonds, and sweet-tangy miso dressing to tie the whole thing together any time of year. In midsummer, when berries are plentiful, it's easy to overlook good partners like plums, peaches, nectarines, cherries, and melon. Don't miss out on these wonderful combinations. SERVES 4

Fruit Fusion Salad

FOR THE SPICED ALMONDS

1 tablespoon vegetable oil

½ teaspoon cayenne pepper

½ teaspoon freshly ground black pepper

1 teaspoon ground five-spice powder

1 cup raw almonds

1 teaspoon toasted sesame oil

½ teaspoon kosher salt

FOR THE MISO-HONEY DRESSING

¾ teaspoon Sichuan peppercorns

¼ cup white miso

5 tablespoons honey

¼ cup rice vinegar

¼ cup freshly squeezed lime juice

2 teaspoons toasted sesame oil

MAKE THE SPICED ALMONDS

Warm the oil in a large frying pan over medium heat. Stir in the cayenne pepper, black pepper, and five-spice powder. Add the almonds and stir to coat. Continue to cook, stirring frequently, until the almonds begin to darken slightly and become fragrant, 5 to 7 minutes. Remove from the heat and stir in the sesame oil. Transfer the almonds to a baking sheet with a rim, sprinkle with the salt, and allow to cool completely.

MAKE THE DRESSING

Grind the Sichuan peppercorns in a blender until crushed. Add 1 tablespoon of water along with the miso, honey, rice vinegar, and lime juice. Blend until smooth. Add the sesame oil and blend until emulsified. Refrigerate until ready to use.

FOR THE GREENS AND FRUIT

SUMMER

4 cups mixed baby Romaine and red oak
   lettuces, plus purslane, dandelion
   greens, and/or arugula
2⅔ cups mixed fresh berries,
   including raspberries, blueberries,
   and blackberries

FALL

4 cups fresh spinach and mixed young
   braising greens, plus arugula
2⅔ cups diced figs and pears

WINTER

4 cups torn or thinly sliced kale or
   cabbage, plus spinach
2⅔ cups roasted squash and apples

SPRING

4 cups baby lettuces, plus young chard
   and kale leaves, pea shoots, and fava
   greens, or arugula
2⅔ cup strawberries

FOR ANY-SEASON SALAD

4 ounces ricotta salata, cut into
   8 thin wedges

TO SERVE

Arrange 1 cup of greens on each plate with one-quarter of the fruit
(⅔ cup), 2 pieces of cheese, and some spiced almonds. Drizzle with the
miso-honey dressing and serve.

> "Sometimes a recipe is a template—a perfect
> balance of flavors and textures—that seasonal
> ingredients can be plugged into to capitalize on
> the peak freshness of each season's bounty."

EVAN MALLETT

Black Trumpet, Portsmouth, New Hampshire

STEVEN SATTERFIELD

Miller Union | *Atlanta, Georgia*

Famously prolific, zucchini are capable of overwhelming a home garden of modest size, as well as the gardener who cooks from it. These fritters are a great way to make a dent in the bounty and are equally at home on a plate with sausage and over-easy eggs or with something from the grill. Don't skip the yogurt sauce, which is the perfect finishing touch. (It's also good made with basil or a combination of mint and basil.)

MAKES ABOUT SIXTEEN 2½-INCH FRITTERS; SERVES 6 TO 8

Zucchini and Vidalia Fritters with Minted Yogurt Sauce

½ cup finely ground cornmeal

½ cup unbleached all-purpose flour

1 teaspoon kosher salt, divided; more as needed

¼ teaspoon freshly ground black pepper

⅛ teaspoon freshly grated nutmeg

1 teaspoon baking powder

1 medium onion, preferably Vidalia

3 medium zucchini (about 1 pound)

1 egg, lightly beaten

½ cup olive oil for frying; more as needed

Minted Yogurt Sauce (recipe on the facing page)

Whisk together the cornmeal, flour, ½ teaspoon salt, the pepper, nutmeg, and baking powder in a small bowl and set aside.

Grate the onion on the large holes of a box grater into a stainless-steel bowl. Transfer the grated onions to a piece of cheesecloth or a clean kitchen towel and squeeze out the excess liquid. Add the squeezed onions to another bowl; you should have about ½ cup. Grate the zucchini on the large holes of the box grater into the bowl with the onions. You should end up adding about 3½ cups of grated zucchini. Add the remaining ½ teaspoon of salt, toss to combine, and let the mixture stand for 10 minutes before transferring it to a piece of cheesecloth or clean kitchen towel. Wring out as much of the liquid as possible.

Put the mixture back into the bowl and add a little bit more salt if desired (most of it gets squeezed out). Add the beaten egg to the zucchini and onions, stir to combine, and add the dry ingredients.

Heat the oven to 200°F. Warm 2 tablespoons of oil in a cast-iron skillet or heavy pan over medium-high heat. Drop heaping tablespoons of the batter into the oil a few at a time, being careful not to overcrowd the pan. Use the back of a spoon to lightly flatten the batter. Cook for 3 to 4 minutes, or until light golden brown, then flip and fry for 2 to 3 minutes on the other side. Transfer to a paper-towel-lined plate to drain and then to a baking sheet to keep warm in the oven until all the fritters are cooked. Serve warm with Minted Yogurt Sauce on the side for dipping.

Minted Yogurt Sauce

MAKES 1 HEAPING CUP

¼ cup mayonnaise (homemade or
   store-bought)

1 small clove garlic, finely minced

1 cup Greek yogurt

2 teaspoons finely chopped lemon zest

1 teaspoon kosher salt; more as needed

2 teaspoons coarsely chopped fresh mint

Stir together the mayonnaise, garlic, yogurt, lemon zest, salt and 1½ teaspoons mint. Adjust the seasoning to taste and garnish with the remaining chopped mint.

"Summer yields inspiring vegetables, from the rainbow of heirloom tomatoes to the inevitable flood of summer squashes. The variety and contrast lend themselves to endless simple preparations."

ED DOYLE

Real Food Consulting, Cambridge, Massachusetts

Reading the Labels

s with meat, eggs, and dairy products, there are certain terms and claims used to promote and label vegetables, fruits, and other edible plants. Some are unique to produce items; others appear in multiple food categories.

The following list, which draws in part from a comprehensive list compiled by AWA (Animal Welfare Approved), includes terms and claims that are defined and controlled by the government—and many more that are not. Since common unregulated terms like "natural" and "locally grown" are widely used to attract buyers, understanding their value is key to making informed choices.

BEYOND ORGANIC/BETTER THAN ORGANIC/MORE THAN ORGANIC

No legal or regulated definition

All of these terms imply that the products described meet and exceed organic standards, though no verification of farming methods is defined or audited to ensure that this is the case.

BIODYNAMIC

No legal or regulated definition

"Biodynamic" agriculture goes beyond organic, envisioning the farm as a self-contained and self-sustaining organism. In addition to using organic practices such as crop rotation and composting, biodynamic farmers rely on special plant, animal, and mineral preparations and the rhythmic influences of the sun and moon.

CERTIFIED FARMER'S MARKET

No legal or regulated definition

A handful of states require their farmer's markets to be certified as a means of attempting to ensure that the farmers themselves produce the products being sold. Most markets establish their own rules for verifying product integrity at the local level.

CERTIFIED NATURALLY GROWN (CNG)

No legal or regulated definition

Certified Naturally Grown is a nonprofit organization offering certification programs tailored for small-scale, direct-to-market farmers and beekeepers using natural methods. CNG products are certified as having been produced in approximate accordance with national organic standard. The term is modeled on Participatory Guarantee Systems (PGS) programs that use a peer-review inspection process built on local networks.

CONVENTIONAL

No legal or regulated definition

"Conventional" refers to standard agricultural practices that are widespread in the industry. It may or may not include the use of pesticides, synthetic fertilizers, monocropping, and genetically modified organisms (GMOs).

FAIRTRADE

Defined by Fairtrade Foundation

The Fairtrade Foundation focuses on better prices, decent working conditions, local sustainability, and fair terms of trade for farmers and workers in the developing world. Most often used for coffee, the Fairtrade label indicates that the company has paid a sustainable price (that never falls below the market price) in an effort to address conventional trade's discrimination against the poorest, weakest producers.

FOOD ALLIANCE CERTIFIED

Defined by Food Alliance

This nonprofit organization certifies farms as well as food processors and distributors for sustainable agricultural and facility management practices. Purchase of Food Alliance Certified–products by consumers and commercial food buyers supports safe and fair working conditions and good environmental stewardship.

GENETICALLY MODIFIED ORGANISMS (GMOS)/GENETICALLY ENGINEERED

No legal or regulated definition

GMOs are plants and animals whose genetic make-up has been altered to exhibit traits that they would not normally have, like longer shelf life, an altered nutritional profile, a different color, or resistance to drought, certain chemicals, or pests. There are significant concerns about the potential environmental impact of genetically modified crops. Genetic modification is currently allowed in conventional farming, and foods that contain GMOs do not have to be labeled.

30 VEGETABLES, FRUITS, AND OTHER EDIBLE PLANTS

HEIRLOOM

No legal or regulated definition

"Heirloom" is used to describe unique plant varieties that are genetically distinct from the commercial varieties introduced by industrial agriculture. Heirloom varieties (sometimes also called antique, heritage, or traditional) are open-pollinated varieties with a long history (usually at least 50 years) of being cultivated, saved, and passed down by farmers within a family or group. They have evolved over time by natural or human selection. The term does not refer to specific farming practices or pesticide use.

LOCALLY GROWN

No legal or regulated definition

This term is used for food and other agricultural products that are produced, processed, and sold within a certain region. Eligibility might be subject to distance, state border, regional boundaries, or some other measure, and can be defined and regulated by individuals based on their specific mission and circumstances.

NON-GMO PROJECT

Defined by Non-GMO Project

Retailers and manufacturers who have chosen to take a proactive stance around the issue of genetically modified organisms (GMOs) can participate in the Non-GMO project, the first and only organization to offer independent verification for products made in the U.S. and Canada according to best practices for GMO avoidance. The nonprofit collaboration is committed to preserving and building sources of non-GMO products and consumer education and providing verified non-GMO choices by labeling products with a Non-GMO Project seal.

NO-TILL/MINIMUM-TILL/CONSERVATION TILLAGE

No legal or regulated definition

"No-till" describes a method at the core of agricultural sustainability practices. By directly seeding the next season's crops using little or no plowing, no-till operations reduce soil erosion and build valuable, nutrient-rich topsoil. In the absence of a technique for cultivating the soil, herbicides may be used to control weeds.

NO-SPRAY/PESTICIDE-FREE

No legal or regulated definition

Use of this term on a label or in marketing is not a guarantee that a farm or product is organic, but implies that no pesticides, herbicides, or fungicides have been applied.

ORGANIC/CERTIFIED ORGANIC

Defined by USDA

Products sold as "organic" must meet the USDA's National Organic Program production and handling standards. Generally speaking, organic production limits the use of chemicals, pesticides, and other inputs. It does not define production practices.

PESTICIDE-FREE

No legal or regulated definition

Used on its own, "pesticide-free" implies that no pesticide residue can be found on the crop. It does not address whether or not pesticides, herbicides, or fungicides were applied at other points in production.

SUSTAINABLE AGRICULTURE

No legal or regulated definition

Sustainable farming is socially just, economically viable, environmentally sound, and ensures animal welfare. The 1990 Farm Bill included this definition:
"The term sustainable agriculture means an integrated system of plant and animal production practices having a site-specific application that will, over the long term: satisfy human food and fiber needs; enhance environmental quality and the natural resource base upon which the agricultural economy depends; make the most efficient use of nonrenewable resources and on-farm resources and integrate, where appropriate, natural biological cycles and controls; sustain the economic viability of farm operations; and enhance the quality of life for farmers and society as a whole."

TRANSITIONAL

No legal or regulated definition

"Transitional" is an unofficial term implying that a farm is in the process of making the switch from conventional toward organic certification. (Products from that farm may also be labeled "transitional.") Organic methods must be practiced on the given area of land for three years before products harvested from it can be labeled as certified organic.

VINE-RIPENED/TREE-RIPENED

No legal or regulated definition

The term is used for fruit that has been allowed to ripen on the vine or tree. Many fruits are picked while still firm and unripe in order to ship long distances without damage, then treated with ethylene gas to soften when they arrive at their destination. "Vine-ripened" does not mean that the item is organic, non-GMO, pesticide free, or sustainably or family farmed.

Breaking It Down

EVAN MALLETT

Black Trumpet | Portsmouth, New Hampshire

Chef Evan Mallett gets a steady supply of pig heads. If you aren't quite as fortunate, ask your butcher or a local producer of cured meats for some guanciale, also known as "face bacon." Or you can use pancetta.

This salad joins all of the colors and flavors of autumn on one plate and features some of Evan's favorite heirloom root vegetable varieties. Serve it as a starter or as a main course accompanied by a crusty loaf of bread. **SERVES 8 AS A STARTER OR 6 AS A MAIN COURSE**

October Heirloom Salad

2 small, sweet red onions, preferably Wethersfield

1 cup cider vinegar, divided

2 teaspoons kosher salt, divided

1 small Long Island cheese pumpkin or butternut squash

1 Thelma Sanders or acorn squash

⅓ cup maple syrup

1 small celery root, peeled and cut into ½-inch dice (about 1 cup)

8 ounces Jerusalem artichokes, peeled and cut into ½-inch chunks

Freshly ground black pepper

12 Brussels sprouts, green outside leaves picked (save the hearts for another use)

8 ounces guanciale or pancetta, cut into small strips

1 bunch Lacinato (dinosaur) kale, cut into chiffonade

¼ cup extra-virgin olive oil

4 ounces Parmigiano-Reggiano, shaved with a vegetable peeler

8 large sage leaves, coarsely chopped

Shave or thinly slice the onions into a small ceramic bowl, cover with ½ cup cider vinegar, and sprinkle with ½ teaspoon salt. Mix well, cover with plastic wrap, and refrigerate overnight.

Peel and seed the squashes. Liberally salt the seeds and leave in a cold oven overnight to dry on a baking sheet. Meanwhile, dice the squashes into ½-inch cubes. Toss the squash in a bowl with the other ½ cup of cider vinegar, the maple syrup, and 1 teaspoon salt. Cover and refrigerate overnight.

The next day, take the onions and squash out of the refrigerator and remove the squash seeds from the oven. Heat the oven to 375°F and roast the seeds for about 25 minutes, or until they are dry and golden brown. Remove the seeds from the oven and increase the heat to 425°F.

Transfer the marinated squash to a roasting pan and add the diced celery root and Jerusalem artichokes along with ½ teaspoon salt and some black pepper. Roast for 20 to 30 minutes, stirring occasionally, until everything is caramelized but not too soft. Set aside to cool.

Meanwhile, blanch the Brussels sprouts leaves in boiling salted water for 20 seconds and then shock them in ice water to stop the cooking. Cook the guanciale or pancetta in a small pan, stirring occasionally, 10 to 12 minutes, or until it is crisp. Remove to a paper-towel-lined plate to drain.

In a large mixing bowl, combine the Brussels sprout leaves with the cooled squash, celery root, and Jerusalem artichokes, adding more salt and pepper to taste if desired. Add the kale ribbons, pickled onions and their liquid, and the olive oil. Toss well to coat all of the ingredients.

Divide the mixture among eight plates and sprinkle each one with guanciale or pancetta, Parmigiano shavings, chopped sage, and toasted squash seeds.

STEPHEN STRYJEWSKI

Cochon | *New Orleans, Louisiana*

Salty fried lemon slices, sweetly sharp shaved onions, crispy strips of beef jerky, and paper-thin slivers of earthy mushrooms come together with whole fresh mint and parsley leaves to create an unusually complementary and unbeatable combination of flavors and textures in this salad. SERVES 4

Shaved Mushroom and Onion Salad with Fried Lemons

2 lemons

Canola oil, for frying

Kosher salt and freshly ground black pepper

4 ounces good-quality beef jerky

8 ounces cremini mushrooms, thinly shaved

¼ cup fresh mint leaves

¼ cup fresh flat-leaf parsley leaves

½ small white onion, thinly sliced
(about ¼ cup)

Good-quality extra-virgin olive oil

Cut the lemons in half. Using a mandoline or a thin, sharp knife and beginning in the middle, cut 3 or 4 thin slices from each of the 4 lemon halves, for a total of about 12 to 16 slices.

In a shallow pan with straight sides, warm ½ to ¾ inch of canola oil over medium-high heat until hot, about 300°F (check with an instant-read thermometer). Add the lemon slices one at a time and fry in two batches of 6 or 8 slices until they are crisp and golden brown, 2 to 3 minutes. Remove the lemons from the oil with a strainer or slotted spoon onto a paper-towel-lined plate and season with salt.

Increase the heat of the oil to approximately 350°F. Cut the beef jerky in ¼-inch-wide strips and fry them quickly, about 10 seconds, or until they begin to soften and crisp at the edges. This happens quickly so watch carefully. If the jerky stays in the oil too long it becomes dry and chewy.

Toss the shaved mushrooms, herbs, onions, and jerky together, and season with the juice of the remaining lemon halves, a generous drizzle of olive oil, and salt and pepper to taste. Garnish with crispy fried lemon slices.

JIMMY SCHMIDT

Morgan's in the Desert | *La Quinta, California*

The rich colors and flavors of fall come together in this deconstructed "ravioli"/salad recipe, which makes an elegant start to a dinner party or festive meal, like Thanksgiving. It's a little bit of work, but the payoff is excellent: an usually impressive presentation that's fun to look at and even better to eat. SERVES 4

Autumn Pear "Ravioli" with Chanterelle and Shaved Pear Salad

1 small celery root, peeled, trimmed, and cut into 1-inch cubes (about 1 cup)

4 to 6 tablespoons (½ to ¾ stick) unsalted butter, divided

1 tablespoon finely minced shallots

1 cup fresh chanterelles, cleaned and thinly sliced (substitute firm wild mushrooms if chanterelles are unavailable)

Kosher salt and freshly ground black pepper

3 tablespoons finely grated Parmesan, divided

2 large underripe Bartlett or Anjou pears, peeled

1 tablespoon turbinado or granulated sugar

3 tablespoons cider vinegar; more as needed

½ cup porcini or extra-virgin olive oil

1 small firm but ripe red Bartlett or Anjou pear, julienned

1 cup arugula

1 teaspoon finely chopped fresh thyme

To make the filling, bring a pot of salted water to a boil over medium-high heat. Add the diced celery root and simmer until tender, about 20 minutes. (Determine by inserting a skewer or the top of a paring knife into one of the cubes; it should go in and out without resistance.) Drain and set aside to cool.

Meanwhile, melt 1 tablespoon of the butter in a nonstick pan over medium-high heat. Add the shallots, stir to coat with butter, and cook until opaque, 2 to 4 minutes. Add half of the mushrooms and a pinch of salt and continue cooking until they give up all of their liquid and begin to brown slightly, about 4 minutes. Remove the pan from the heat.

When the celery root is cool enough to handle, put it in the bowl of a food processor with 1 tablespoon of butter and purée until smooth. Add another tablespoon of butter if needed and salt and black pepper to taste. Add the sautéed mushrooms and shallots and pulse to coarsely chop. Add 2 tablespoons of Parmesan and pulse just to combine. Set aside.

Use a mandoline or sharp knife to slice the underripe pears across the widest part of their equators to make 16 round slices. Cut the remaining scraps into chunks and set aside.

Melt 1 tablespoon of butter in a large nonstick frying pan over medium-high heat. Lay pear slices in the pan, covering the bottom without overlapping. Sprinkle the tops with a little of the sugar. Cook until slightly browned and caramelized, about 2 minutes. Turn over for about 1 minute so the pears are cooked and tender, but not falling apart. Transfer the caramelized slices to a lightly oiled or buttered sheet of parchment paper on a baking sheet without overlapping. Repeat the process with the remaining slices.

When all 16 pear slices have been caramelized, add the pear scraps to the pan with the remaining sugar and cook until softened and well caramelized. Transfer the scraps to a blender and reserve.

Place 1 tablespoon of the celery root and mushroom filling in the center of 8 pear slices. Lay the remaining pear slices across the filling to form "ravioli." Reserve until ready to serve.

Add the vinegar to the pear scraps in the blender and purée until smooth. While the motor is running, drizzle in the porcini or olive oil until the mixture is emulsified. Season to taste with salt, pepper, and additional vinegar if necessary.

To serve, heat the oven to 400°F. Put the baking sheet with the "ravioli" on the top rack and heat thoroughly, about 10 minutes. Meanwhile, toss together the remaining raw mushrooms, julienned raw pears, arugula, and half of the thyme. Add enough of the emulsified vinaigrette to coat the salad and season to taste with salt and pepper.

Transfer 2 "ravioli" each to the center of four large, warm plates. Spoon a little vinaigrette over and around the "ravioli," and divide the salad among the plates, placing it on top of the "ravioli." Sprinkle each plate with some of the remaining Parmesan and thyme and serve immediately.

Understanding Genetically Modified Organisms (GMOs)

Want to avoid genetically modified organisms (GMOs)? It's not easy in the United States because our two most prolific crops—corn and soy—come almost entirely from GMO seeds. These two crops permeate the food systems—they provide sweeteners, fats, and other ingredients that end up in nearly all processed foods on the supermarket shelf, from breakfast cereals to snack foods to frozen meals. And they compose the feed for the animals on factory farms, meaning that GMOs have colonized the meat and dairy aisles, too. Not even produce is exempt—Hawaiian papaya and squash (yellow and zucchini) are also common GMOs.

Choosing organic is a good step toward avoiding GMOs, but an element of uncertainty remains since organic certification doesn't require GMO testing. When shopping in the produce section, you can tell if a fruit or vegetable has been genetically modified, organically grown, or produced conventionally with chemical fertilizers and pesticides by looking at the PLU (price look-up) code listed on the sticker. Conventionally grown items have a four digit code—a conventional banana is 4011. The PLU code for organically grown items is five digits beginning with "9". (An organic banana is 94011.) Genetically engineered produce has a five-digit code that begins with "8." (A GMO banana is 84011.)

Copying the genes from one organism that displays certain desired traits and transferring them into the genetic code of another organism creates GMOs. Genetically modified crops reinforce genetic homogeneity and promote large-scale monocultures. They contribute to the decline in biodiversity and the increased vulnerability of crops to disease, pests, and climate change. They've also led to an explosion in herbicide use, and they resort to ever more toxic herbicides.

GMO technology is still experimental; the benefits are as yet unproven and the long-term impacts on health, environment, and biodiversity have been subject to very little independent testing. For this reason, consumers have spoken out overwhelmingly in favor of labeling foods that contain GMOs. In this country, the current focus on GMOs is less about their long-term effects and more about consumer's right to know how food is grown and handled. As of 2012, 50 countries worldwide including Australia, Japan, and all of the countries in the European Union had some form of restriction on the production of GMOs. It's easy to eliminate an ingredient that's labeled, but GMOs aren't.

Non-GMO foods that are monitored for risk through cross contamination include chard, beets, brassicas (rutabagas, kale, bok choi, cabbage, turnips), squashes (acorn, delicata, patty pan), flax, and rice. Wheat, on the other hand, is the ingredient most commonly—and incorrectly—assumed to be genetically modified. As a key commodity crop, the biotech industry is pushing hard to bring GMO wheat varieties to the market.

GMOs have proven to be much more about selling agrichemicals than delivering tangible environmental or food-security benefits. The real farming of the future will come from innovative strategies for increasing biodiversity and building the health of soil.

TOM PHILPOTT

writer for Mother Jones

BARTON SEAVER

Chef and National Geographic Fellow | *Washington, D.C.*

For Barton Seaver, a great seafood dish is one that celebrates the beautiful and diverse flavors of the oceans without necessarily featuring the seafood at the center of the plate. In this recipe, the anchovies add unmistakable flavor—not to mention heart-healthy omega-3 fatty acids—without adding bulk. SERVES 4 TO 6

Broiled Kale Salad with Warm Walnut Anchovy Vinaigrette

1 large sweet potato, peeled and cut into
 ½-inch dice (about 1½ cups)

Kosher salt

2 bunches Lacinato (dinosaur) kale,
 stems removed

2 tablespoons olive oil

1 small red onion, thinly sliced
 (about ½ cup)

Two 2-ounce cans anchovy fillets packed
 in olive oil

1 cup toasted walnuts, roughly chopped

3 tablespoons freshly squeezed lemon juice

Place the potatoes in a small saucepan and cover with cold water. Season generously with salt and bring to a simmer. Cook just until tender, not but falling apart. Remove the potatoes from the cooking liquid and reserve.

Heat the broiler to high.

Tear the kale leaves into bite-size pieces and toss with 1 tablespoon of the olive oil. Place on a baking sheet and put it directly under the broiler. Cook the kale until it is charred and crispy. (Don't worry about burning it—the more char the kale has, the better). Remove from the broiler and reserve.

Heat the remaining 1 tablespoon of oil in a small frying pan. Add the onions and cook over medium-high heat until they begin to soften, about 5 minutes. Reduce the heat to medium. Add both cans of anchovies and their oil to the pan, using a spoon or spatula to gently mash them until the anchovies disintegrate into the sauce. Add the walnuts and cook for 1 minute more. Add the lemon juice and remove from the heat, stirring to combine.

To serve, place the kale on a large platter, sprinkle with the diced sweet potatoes, and spoon the vinaigrette over the top. Serve immediately.

MICHAEL SCELFO

Russell House Tavern | *Cambridge, Massachusetts*

This salad has much more than an assortment of flavors and textures. The beans and eggs can be cooked ahead, while the vinaigrette can be made several days in advance, leaving assembly of the salad for the last minute. It's lovely for lunch or as the anchor to dinner. Dress the beans in advance of eating to absorb the flavors of the vinaigrette. SERVES 4

Rustic White Bean Salad with Soft-Cooked Eggs, Olive Vinaigrette, and Grilled Bread

2 cups cooked white beans (navy or cannellini) or canned, rinsed and drained

½ fennel bulb, finely diced (about ¼ cup)

½ small sweet onion, finely diced (about ¼ cup)

½ rib celery, peeled and finely diced (about 3 tablespoons)

3 small cloves garlic, thinly sliced on a mandoline

¼ cup roughly chopped fresh flat-leaf parsley

1 teaspoon finely chopped fresh rosemary

1 tablespoon freshly squeezed lemon juice

Olive Vinaigrette (recipe below)

4 large eggs

Kosher salt and freshly ground black pepper

4 pieces rustic bread, brushed with olive oil and grilled

Extra-virgin olive oil, for drizzling

In a large bowl, combine the white beans, fennel, onions, celery, garlic, herbs, and lemon juice. Add about two-thirds of the vinaigrette and toss lightly. Let sit while you prepare the eggs.

Put the eggs in a small saucepan, cover with room temperature water, and bring to a boil. Reduce the heat, cover, and cook for exactly 5½ minutes. Pour off the hot water, transfer the eggs to a bowl filled with ice water, and leave to chill for 20 minutes.

To serve, season the beans to taste with salt and black pepper. Peel the eggs and cut them in half. Cut the grilled bread slices in half and arrange two halves on each plate. Spoon the bean salad over the bread and top with two egg halves. Drizzle some of the remaining vinaigrette around the plate and sprinkle the eggs with salt and pepper. Finish with a drizzle of olive oil over the eggs.

Olive Vinaigrette

1 cup oil-cured black olives, pitted

½ cup sherry vinegar

1 tablespoon Dijon mustard

2 anchovy fillets

1 shallot, cut in half

½ cup extra-virgin olive oil

Kosher salt and freshly ground black pepper

Put the olives, vinegar, mustard, anchovies, and shallots in a blender. Pulse a few times to combine, and then slowly drizzle in the olive oil with the machine running. Season to taste with salt and pepper, if needed.

Chefs' Favorite Beans

PETER DAVIS
Henrietta's Table

Maine yellow eyes (not to be confused with Stueben yellow eyes) are small white beans with a butterscotch-colored "eye." Substitute them for Great Northern or navy beans, classic but less interesting choices for baked beans. The remarkably creamy texture of yellow eyes is like a sponge for pork flavors. I also like to simmer them slowly in chicken stock with bay leaves and thyme plus onions, garlic, jalapeño, and bacon.

WILLIAM DISSEN
The Market Place Restaurant

I'm a fan of Sea Island red peas, also known as field peas or cowpeas. (I get mine from Anson Mills, where they're described this way: "Ruddy and diminutive, they represent the variety of field pea that informed early versions of Hoppin John in Coastal Carolina. They impart bold flavor, sweet creamy richness, and exceptional nutrition.") The flavor these peas impart to stews and sautéed dishes reminds me of my time living in Charleston, South Carolina.

DEBORAH SCARBOROUGH
Black Cat Bistro

I love rice beans and gigandes, which are large, flat white lima beans. I use them in garlicky bread soup with greens and shavings of Asiago cheese.

KIM MÜLLER
Foodcraft

Tepary beans are native to Central America but are indigenous to North America and were developed by Native Americans to be drought resistant. Still not widely known, they're more commonly found in the Southwest. I feature tepary beans in my South-western Heritage Bean Soup (see page 51), where their meaty, dense texture really shines.

TORY MILLER
L'Etoile

Cranberry beans are one of the mostly widely available and popular heirlooms. I like their texture and the way their rough exterior kind of melts away, leaving just the creamy, buttery bean.

JOSH LEWIN
Beacon Hill Bistro

I look forward to cranberry beans for two reasons: they're quite pretty, and shucking them for an hour with the dishwasher makes for a good change of pace. These beans are nice and buttery, and their velvety texture is easy to work into all types of dishes.

CHRISTOPHER EDWARDS

The Restaurant at Patowmack Farm | Lovettsville, Virginia

Wild purple nettles are also known as purple dead nettles, not because they'll kill you, but because they don't sting! An invasive weed and prized wild edible, nettles have high levels of antioxidants. If you're unable to find purple nettles, try the young tender tops of a mint or sage plant.

Inspired by a recipe for elderberry blossom fritters, this one calls for finishing the fritters with elderberry syrup. You can also substitute a good-quality aged balsamic vinegar. SERVES 6

Purple Nettle Fritters with Asparagus, Feta, and Elderberry Syrup

1 cup unbleached all-purpose flour

¼ cup cornstarch

2 tablespoons tapioca starch

¼ teaspoon ground nutmeg

½ teaspoon granulated sugar

1 teaspoon fine sea salt; more as needed

1¼ cups sparkling or seltzer water

30 wild purple nettles, cut fresh at the base of each stem

4 stalks asparagus

3 tablespoons extra-virgin olive oil

Freshly ground black pepper

Canola oil, for frying

1 lemon

¼ cup goat milk feta cheese

¼ cup elderberry syrup or aged balsamic vinegar

To prepare the tempura batter, combine the flour, cornstarch, tapioca starch, nutmeg, sugar, and salt in a medium bowl. Slowly add the sparkling water while whisking until it is well incorporated. Keep the batter cold until ready to use.

Rinse the nettles in a large bowl of cold water. Drain on paper towels and pat dry. Set aside until ready to fry.

Prepare the asparagus by peeling the bottoms of the stalks with a vegetable peeler, leaving the tip and about 2 inches below. Thinly slice the asparagus into small coins, about ¼ inch thick, and toss them with the olive oil. Season to taste with salt and black pepper and set aside.

Meanwhile, fill a large saucepan with deep sides with about 2 inches of canola oil and bring the oil to 350°F over medium-high heat (check the temperature with an instant-read thermometer). When the oil has come to temperature, begin dipping the nettles in the tempura batter individually, shaking off any excess batter before gently dropping them into the hot oil one at a time, taking care not to overcrowd the pan. Depending on the size of your pot, you may be able to fry 12 to 15 at a time. When the fritters are crispy and slightly golden, remove them from the oil with a strainer or slotted spoon. Allow them to drain on a paper-towel-lined plate in a warm spot and season immediately with salt. Continue to fry the nettles until all 30 have been cooked, drained, and seasoned.

Divide the asparagus among six plates and put about 5 fritters directly on top of each. Squeeze a little bit of lemon juice over the top of each plate and crumble some feta on top. Finish each plate with a drizzle of elderberry syrup or balsamic vinegar and serve immediately.

JUSTIN APRAHAMIAN

Sanford Restaurant | Milwaukee, Wisconsin

Nasturtium leaves lend depth—and gorgeous color—to this soup, which is full of subtle flavors. When nasturtium leaves aren't available, watercress or a combination of watercress and spinach are good substitutes.

The recipe can be made over 2 days because the nasturtium leaves are blended into the rest of the soup after it cools, so that they retain their color. SERVES 6

Nasturtium Soup with Braised Pistachios

3 tablespoons olive oil

1 pound onions, thinly sliced
   (about 2 medium or 3 small onions)

2 large bunches scallions, thinly sliced,
   including the greens

4 sprigs fresh thyme

2 bay leaves

12 black peppercorns

¾ cup dry white wine, such as Sauvignon
   Blanc or dry vermouth

10 cups vegetable stock

4 ounces fresh nasturtium leaves

¼ cup heavy cream

Kosher salt and freshly ground black pepper

Braised Pistachios, for garnish (recipe below)

Nasturtium flowers, for garnish (optional)

Warm the olive oil in a large pot over medium heat. Add the onions and cook, stirring occasionally, until they become translucent, about 7 minutes. Add the scallions, thyme, bay leaves, and peppercorns and stir to combine. Cook for 2 to 3 more minutes before adding the wine.

Increase the heat to medium high and use the wine to deglaze the pan, loosening any bits that have browned and stuck to the bottom with a wooden spoon. Continue to cook until the wine reduces by about half. Add the vegetable stock and reduce the volume by half again. You should have approximately 6 cups.

Remove the soup from the heat and chill until completely cold. Once the base is cold, add the nasturtium leaves in batches, using a blender or food processor to purée. Strain through a fine-mesh sieve, add the cream, and season to taste with salt and black pepper.

To serve, bring the soup to a gentle simmer over low heat. Season to taste with additional salt and pepper and serve immediately, garnished with braised pistachios and nasturtium flowers if you'd like.

Braised Pistachios

MAKES 2 CUPS

3 tablespoons extra-virgin olive oil

½ small onion, sliced

1 clove garlic, sliced

4 sprigs fresh thyme

2 bay leaves

½ teaspoon ground cardamom

½ cup white wine, such as Sauvignon Blanc

2 cups (9 ounces) shelled pistachios

1 cup vegetable stock

Kosher salt and freshly ground black pepper

Warm the olive oil in a sauté pan over medium heat and add the onions. Cook, stirring occasionally, until the onions are translucent, about 5 minutes. Add the garlic and sauté another 30 seconds. Add the thyme, bay leaves, and cardamom and sauté for 1 minute longer.

Deglaze the pan with the white wine and cook until nearly all of the liquid is gone and the onions are dry. Add the pistachios and cook, stirring, for a few minutes, to lightly toast and incorporate with the onions. Cover with the vegetable stock and bring to a gentle boil. Reduce the heat to low and continue to simmer slowly until the stock is nearly gone and the pistachios appear dry. Stir the mixture occasionally to prevent the onions and pistachios from sticking and to keep them moistened with stock. Season to taste with salt and pepper. The nuts can be made up to 3 days ahead and stored in an airtight container in the refrigerator.

JESSE ZIFF COOL

CoolEatz Restaurants | San Francisco, California

Make this soup when you can get perfectly ripe peaches—Elbertas are particularly good—or don't bother. Buy extra when they're at their most juicy and delicious, and freeze them for a taste of summer whenever the mood strikes. Fresh peaches require more water to get the right consistency, while frozen peaches add their own water. As a result, the amount of water indicated is not precise. SERVES 6 TO 8

Summer Peach Soup

3 tablespoons olive oil

2 medium onions, roughly chopped
    (about 2 cups)

1 to 3 teaspoons roughly chopped
    fresh thyme

4 medium peaches, frozen or fresh,
    peeled and pitted

1 bay leaf, preferably fresh

½ cup freshly squeezed orange juice

1 cup light or heavy cream

Kosher salt and freshly ground black pepper

Ground cayenne pepper (optional)

Granulated sugar, as needed

Chopped chives, for garnish

Crisp bacon or pork-belly pieces,
    for garnish (optional)

Warm the olive oil over medium heat in a large heavy-bottomed saucepan with a lid. Add the onions and cook slowly, covered, for about 10 minutes, or until they are soft and golden brown. Add the thyme for the last minute.

Coarsely chop the peaches and add to the saucepan along with the bay leaf. Add the orange juice and just enough water to cover all ingredients by about 1½ inches. Cover and simmer for about 15 minutes.

Remove the bay leaf and purée the mixture using a hand-held blender or food processor. Add the cream and thin to your desired thickness with water. Add salt, black pepper, and cayenne pepper to taste, if desired. Add sugar if necessary. Serve the soup warm or chilled, garnished with chopped chives and bacon or pork belly if you'd like.

TORY MILLER

L'Etoile | Madison, Wisconsin

The beauty of this soup, aside from it being delicious, is that it can be prepared and served in a variety of ways, depending on your skill level, how much time you have, and whether it's to be the elegant start to a meal or the meal itself. Tailor the ingredients and cooking methods and/ or shortcuts to your needs (i.e. purchase the duck stock and confit). SERVES 8 AS A MAIN COURSE

Hot-and-Sour Damson Plum Soup with Duck and Sushi Rice Crackers

1 tablespoon sesame oil

2 tablespoons rendered duck fat, divided

1 tablespoon finely minced fresh ginger

1 tablespoon finely minced garlic

1 large yellow onion, thinly sliced (about 1¼ cups)

3 ribs celery, thinly sliced (about 1½ cups)

2 small Thai chiles, thinly sliced, including the seeds

2 pounds Damson plums, halved and pitted

10 cups duck stock, homemade or purchased already prepared

2 tablespoons soy sauce

2 tablespoons mirin

2 tablespoons rice vinegar

1 tablespoon honey

3 small heads baby bok choy

4 legs Duck Confit (recipe on the facing page or purchased already prepared)

8 eggs (duck or chicken)

¼ cup white vinegar

Sushi Rice Crackers (recipe on the facing page)

4 scallions, thinly sliced, white and 1 inch of green parts

Radishes, for garnish (optional)

Spicy peanuts, for garnish (optional)

Warm the sesame oil and duck fat in a large pot over medium heat. Add the ginger and garlic and cook for 30 seconds while stirring. Add the onions, celery, and chiles and cook for 3 to 5 minutes, stirring occasionally. Add the plums, stir to combine, and cook for 3 minutes. Add the stock, soy sauce, mirin, rice vinegar, and honey; stir well to incorporate, and continue to cook until the volume has reduced by about one-fourth, about 45 minutes. Slice the bok choy and add during the last 10 minutes of cooking. Remove the skin from the duck legs and set aside. Pick the meat off the duck legs, add to the hot soup, and adjust the seasoning.

Just before serving, place the skin from the duck legs in a nonstick or cast-iron skillet. Add about a tablespoon of duck fat from the confit and crisp the skin over low heat. Although it may not appear to be crispy right out of the pan, the skin is ready when it's golden brown. Remove the crispy skin to a paper-towel-lined plate to drain.

When you are ready to serve the soup, bring 2 quarts of water and the white vinegar to a boil in a large, heavy saucepan. Swirl the water with a spoon and carefully slip in the eggs—crack them in a cup one at a time and tip the edge of the cup about ½ inch below the surface of the gently simmering water. Reduce the heat to medium. Use a spoon to lightly nudge the white toward the yolk and poach for 4 to 5 minutes, until the whites are set but the insides are still runny.

Place about 10 ounces of soup in each of eight deep bowls. Put a poached egg in each bowl along with a few rice crackers, some crispy duck skin, and scallions. Garnish with sliced radishes and/or peanuts if desired. Serve immediately.

Duck Confit

MAKES 4 DUCK LEGS

1 tablespoon allspice berries

1 tablespoons juniper berries

1 tablespoon coriander seeds

1 tablespoon Sichuan peppercorns

1 cup kosher salt

½ cup granulated sugar

4 cloves garlic, crushed

4 duck legs

3 to 4 cups rendered duck fat

Grind the allspice and juniper berries, coriander seeds, and peppercorns in a spice mill or coffee grinder. Add them to a bowl with the salt, sugar, and garlic and mix well to combine.

Arrange the duck legs in the bottom of a nonreactive dish or pan large enough to hold them in a single layer. Spread the spice mixture over the flesh, skin side down. Cover the pan with plastic wrap and refrigerate for 24 hours.

The next day, remove the duck legs from the refrigerator and heat the oven to 275°F. Meanwhile, melt the duck fat in a small saucepan over very low heat. Rinse and dry the duck legs, and arrange them in a single snug layer in a baking dish with high sides or in an ovenproof pan. Pour the melted fat over the legs (they should be covered) and place the pan in the oven. Cook the legs at a very slow simmer until the meat is fork-tender and can be pulled from the bone easily, about 3 hours. Remove the confit from the oven and cool the duck in the fat. It can be held in the fat until you're ready to use it or for up to several weeks.

Sushi Rice Crackers

MAKES ABOUT 36 CRACKERS

1 cup sushi rice

2 tablespoons rice vinegar

1 tablespoon mirin

Pinch of salt

Canola oil, for frying

Place the rice in a bowl filled with cold water. Swish it around, pour off the water, and repeat three more times, or until the water is clear. Place the rice in a small pan with a tight-fitting lid. Add 2 cups of water, cover, and bring to a boil over high heat. Reduce the heat and cook until the water is gone, about 20 minutes. Turn off the heat and let stand, covered, for 10 minutes.

Add the rice vinegar, mirin, and salt, and stir to incorporate the ingredients throughout the grains of rice. Remove the rice to a baking pan with sides. Pack it tightly into a corner and create a rectangular shape, about 9 by 4 inches, by pressing the rice firmly against the sides so that it comes to the top of the pan. Cool completely and, using a serrated knife, cut into ¼-inch-thick slices.

Heat a deep fryer to 350°F, or warm ½ inch to ¾ inch of canola oil in a shallow pan with straight sides over medium-high heat until it is hot, about 350°F. Fry the slices until they're golden brown on both sides, 3 to 4 minutes per side, then transfer to a paper-towel-lined plate to drain.

DAN BARBER

Blue Hill at Stone Barns | Pocantico Hills, New York

If you make this soup with turnips and parsnips harvested after the first freeze, it will be noticeably sweeter. When exposed to cold weather, root vegetables convert their starches to sugars to prevent the water in their cell structure from freezing. Their survival tactic is our reward.

Parsley root, also known as Hamburg parsley, is a pungent cross between celery and parsley. If you have trouble finding it, substitute 1 cup of peeled, thinly sliced celery root and an additional 2 tablespoons of parsley leaves. **SERVES 4 TO 6**

Turnip Soup

1 tablespoon unsalted butter

1 tablespoon vegetable oil

1 small onion, cut into ¼-inch dice
(about ½ cup)

1 small leek, white part only, finely chopped

2 medium purple-top turnips
(about ¾ pound), peeled, halved, and
thinly sliced

1 parsnip, peeled and thinly sliced

1 parsley root, peeled and thinly sliced

Kosher salt and freshly ground black pepper

4 cups vegetable stock
(homemade or store-bought)

1 cup fresh flat-leaf parsley leaves

½ cup picked fresh chervil leaves

¼ cup picked pale yellow celery leaves
(from the core)

Heat the butter and oil in a large heavy-bottomed pan over medium-low heat. Add the onions and leeks, reduce the heat to low, and cook slowly without browning, about 5 minutes.

Add the turnips, parsnips, and parsley root and season with salt and pepper. Stir to combine well with the leeks and onions, cover, and continue to cook slowly for 15 to 20 minutes, or until the vegetables become very soft. Be careful not to get any color on the vegetables.

Add the stock, bring the mixture to a simmer, and cook for 10 minutes. Allow to cool slightly, then purée in a blender in batches, adding some of the herbs each time. Make sure each batch is very smooth, then combine and strain the soup through a fine-mesh sieve. Chill in an ice bath to preserve the soup's bright color and fresh flavor. Reheat to serve, adjusting the seasoning as necessary.

ALISON COSTELLO

Capuchin Soup Kitchen | Detroit, Michigan

Uncommon in Western kitchens, pumpkin tips—the actual stem of the pumpkin—and leaves are important ingredients in southern Asia and many rural African regions. Not just another way of utilizing the whole plant and reducing waste, cooking with the entire pumpkin adds vitamin A, iron, and potassium to your diet. Collard greens, Swiss chard, chicory, and fresh spinach all make good substitutes. Some farmer's markets and Asian grocers carry pumpkin tips, or you can use 1 cup of diced, boiled pumpkin in their place. SERVES 4

Pumpkin Curry

4 tablespoons olive oil, divided

1 medium onion, cut into ¼-inch dice
  (about 1 cup)

1-inch piece fresh ginger, peeled and grated

3 cloves garlic, finely chopped

Spice Mix (recipe on page 50)

2 tablespoons tamarind paste or Tamarind
  Paste Substitute (recipe on page 50)

2 large waxy potatoes (about 1 pound),
  peeled, diced, and boiled until tender
  but firm

8 pumpkin tips (top 6 inches), cut into
  ½-inch pieces, boiled until tender but firm

1 cup peeled, diced pumpkin, boiled until
  tender but firm

2 pumpkin leaves, chopped

1 bunch collard greens, Swiss chard,
  chicory, or fresh spinach, washed,
  stemmed, and coarsely chopped

½ bunch fresh cilantro, coarsely chopped

2 teaspoons mustard seeds

In a large saucepan over medium-high heat, sauté the onions in the olive oil until soft and translucent. Add the ginger, garlic, and spice mix, stir well, and cook for 2 minutes before adding the tamarind paste, diced potatoes, pumpkin tips, and diced pumpkin cubes. Add water to cover and the chopped pumpkin greens and cook for 8 to 10 minutes over medium-high heat to reduce and thicken. Stir in the cilantro.

Sizzle the mustard seeds in the remaining oil; pour over the curry and serve immediately.

>>>

Spice Mix

MAKES 2 TABLESPOONS

3 whole cloves

2 small dried red peppers; more as needed

1 teaspoon cumin seed

1 teaspoon coriander seed

½ teaspoon black peppercorns

2 teaspoons sesame seeds

Crushed red pepper flakes (optional)

½ teaspoon ground cinnamon

½ teaspoon turmeric

Toast the cloves, peppers, cumin seed, coriander seed, peppercorns, and sesame seeds in a cast-iron skillet over medium-low heat until fragrant. Cool completely and grind with a mortar and pestle or spice grinder. Adjust the heat with red pepper flakes if desired, and then add the ground cinnamon and turmeric.

Tamarind Paste Substitute

MAKES ¼ CUP

1 tablespoon finely chopped prunes

1 tablespoon finely chopped dates

1 tablespoon finely chopped dried apricots

1 tablespoon freshly squeezed lemon juice

Soak the dates, prunes, and dried apricots in water. Drain; add lemon juice and purée in a food processor or blender until smooth.

Heirloom Beans

Heirloom bean varieties have been around for decades; their seeds produce the same variety every season without any manipulation by farmers or scientists. We eat some of the varieties all the time—kidney beans and pinto beans are heirlooms—but there are thousands of others, each with a unique appearance, texture, and flavor. Learning about their different characteristics is one way to introduce new flavors into a menu or onto your table inexpensively, while evoking a sense of place. Whether art, furniture, or food, heirlooms are items of value, passed down through the generations, often with stories.

An amazing array of shapes, sizes, colors, textures, and flavors make the world of heirloom beans exciting to explore. Meaty, creamy, sweet, nutty, herbaceous, mild, earthy: these are some of the qualities different beans exhibit, and yet the same bean grown in another area may taste completely different. Like wine grapes, grain, and pastured meat, beans express *terroir*, a broad term used to describe a site's attributes that help to define the character and flavor of what is grown there.

KIM MÜLLER

Foodcraft | Santa Fe, New Mexico

This recipe showcases heirloom ingredients unique to the Southwest, but given the wide variety of interesting beans available and the sources for them, feel free to substitute an alternative. Instead of tepary beans, use all pinto beans or any other interesting bean you find. And for the chicos, which can be hard to come by outside New Mexico, substitute hominy. Canned green chiles can stand in for the New Mexico green chile. MAKES ABOUT 3 QUARTS

Southwestern Heritage Bean Soup

1 cup pinto beans, picked through, rinsed, and soaked overnight

1 cup brown tepary beans, picked through, rinsed, and soaked overnight

1 cup chicos, soaked overnight

9 cups vegetable stock or water

2 ounces diced pancetta (optional)

¼ cup olive oil, if necessary

1 pound yellow onions (2 large or 3 medium), cut into ½-inch dice (about 2½ cups)

3 medium carrots, peeled and cut into ½-inch dice (about 1½ cups)

1 cup seeded, diced ripe tomatoes, or diced canned tomatoes with juice

1 New Mexico green chile, roasted, peeled, and diced into ¼-inch pieces (about ¼ cup)

1 tablespoon oregano, preferably Mexican

1 tablespoon ground toasted cumin seed

Kosher salt and freshly ground black pepper

Fresh cilantro, for garnish

Using three small pans, cook the beans and the chicos separately until tender. Start with 3 cups of vegetable stock or water in each pan and add more as needed to keep the beans covered. The tepary beans will take a bit longer to cook than the pintos, and the chicos will plump up but remain slightly chewy. The tepary beans and chicos should each take about 90 minutes, the pinto beans between 60 and 90 minutes. Do not drain the beans when they are done. Instead, set the pans aside and continue with the rest of the recipe.

Brown the pancetta, if using, in a heavy stockpot over medium heat. Remove about half of the rendered fat and save for another use. If you are omitting the pancetta, warm ¼ cup olive oil in a heavy stockpot. Add the diced onions and carrots to the fat and pancetta, or to the olive oil, and sauté over medium heat until tender, about 10 minutes.

Add the cooked beans and chicos to the pot, along with the stock, tomatoes, green chiles, oregano, and ground cumin seed. Simmer over low heat for about 1 hour to encourage the flavors to blend. Season to taste with salt and black pepper. Garnish with fresh cilantro and serve.

DAVID HIRSCH

Moosewood Restaurant | Ithaca, New York

Bright notes from fresh ginger punctuate the contrasting flavors of sweet squash, tangy miso, and earthy kombu in this colorful and comforting soup. Butternut squash is an all-round good choice, because it's easy to find and has a smooth skin that is less difficult to peel than ridged winter squashes. Kabocha and buttercup squash are also delicious, adding even sweeter, deeper flavor. Add cooked soba noodles to turn this soup into a satisfying meal. **SERVES 6 TO 8**

Winter Squash Soup

2 pieces of kombu seaweed (each 6 inches long and about ¼ ounce)

1 tablespoon vegetable oil

1 medium onion, cut into ¼-inch dice (about 1 cup)

2 teaspoons grated fresh ginger

1 medium butternut squash, cut into ½-inch cubes (about 4 cups)

½ teaspoon ground cinnamon

8 ounces tofu, cut into ½-inch cubes

4 cups lightly packed spinach leaves

⅓ cup white rice miso; more as needed

Cooked soba noodles (optional)

Put 8 cups of cold water in a medium saucepan and add the seaweed. Bring the mixture to a boil over medium-high heat, then reduce the heat to a simmer and cook, covered, for 15 minutes. After 15 minutes, drain and reserve the "stock." Discard the kombu.

In a 4- to 6-quart pot, warm the oil over medium-high heat before adding the onions, ginger, and squash. Sauté the ingredients, stirring often, for about 5 minutes. Add the cinnamon and continue to cook until the squash is tender when poked with a knife and the onions have softened, about 5 more minutes. Add the tofu and spinach and just heat through.

Place a ladleful of the kombu stock in a bowl and stir in the miso until it has mostly dissolved and there are no large chunks. Add the broth to the pot with the tofu and squash and heat until the soup is hot but not boiling (the healthful enzymes in miso break down at boiling temperatures).

Ladle soup into each serving bowl; add cooked soba noodles for a more substantial dish, if desired. Taste and add a bit more miso (dissolved in some of the soup) for saltier or more pronounced flavors.

Using Everything

Whether they're roots or fruits, most vegetables and many fruits come with something extra that's often discarded because it's not the part we're accustomed to eating, which isn't the same as it being inedible. Thrift is essential in a well-run restaurant kitchen, where food cost is closely tied to financial success. So you can enrich your compost pile, for benefits of one sort, or put these scraps to use in the kitchen, where they will make an obvious and very satisfying contribution to your abilities as a cook. The majority of these items can be combined to make a flavorful stock, but with so many other interesting and more substantial outcomes, it's a shame to stop there.

Stems and Stalks

These parts are routinely overlooked. Turn chard and collard stems into pickles, bake them in a gratin with cream and breadcrumbs (see Rainbow Chard Stem Gratin on page 77), or slowly simmer them in wine with lemon peel, then dress them with a simple vinaigrette. Herb stems add flavor to soups and stock, and cilantro stems belong anywhere the leaves do. Broccoli stems make stupendous hushpuppies (see Broccoli Hushpuppies on page 83), or can be peeled to reveal a tender core that makes an unusually delicious salad when thinly sliced, tossed with lemon juice and olive oil, and garnished with shavings of Parmesan.

Peels, Pits, and Pips

Fruit peels and pips (the small seeds of fleshy fruits like apples, grapes, and oranges) are often a rich source of pectin, especially in apples and quince, and should be included when making jellies and sauces. And the kernel inside apricot and cherry pits, called *noyaux* in French, can be cracked and used to infuse creams and custards with their delicate almond flavor. Citrus peel should always be saved for candying and marmalade, or popped in a low oven and dried for use in soups and stews.

Leaves and Greens

The greens from bunches of beets, young radishes, and turnips are tender and delicious when lightly sautéed or tossed into a salad. Or turn them into a filling for a savory tart for dinner (see Beets Greens and Legs Pie on page 73). Peach leaves steeped in cream make a lovely, delicate base for ice cream or panna cotta. And nasturtium leaves, like the flowers, are delicious in salad or as the base for a soup (see Nasturtium Soup with Braised Pistachios on page 42), while pickled nasturtium seeds make an unusual substitute for capers. Carrot tops, fennel fronds, and celery leaves are all attractive, flavorful garnishes.

Crusts and Rinds

Crusts and heels of bread should never be tossed. For a minimal amount of effort, you can make croutons or breadcrumbs for your freezer. With a bit more time and a few additional ingredients, leftover bread becomes a meal: Pappa al Pomodoro (see page 59); a panade, or savory bread pudding (see Blue Cheese Bread Pudding on page 265); or strata (see Wild Ramp and Farmstead Cheese Strata with Roasted Tomato Wine Butter on page 258). Parmesan cheese rinds added to a pot of beans or minestrone soup are pure magic. And watermelon rind makes a fine pickle (see page 56).

MARC MEYER

Cookshop | New York, New York

There are as many ways to make chutney as there are kinds of fruit to spotlight. An all-purpose base of vinegar, sweetened with honey and flavored with onion, garlic, and spices, can be adjusted to match the unique characteristics of whatever fruit is available or in season. EACH RECIPE MAKES ABOUT 1 QUART

Four-Season Chutney

FOR THE CHUTNEY BASE

¼ cup canola oil

1 medium onion, cut into ½-inch dice (about 1 cup)

5 cloves garlic, thinly sliced

1 teaspoon red pepper flakes

2 tablespoons yellow mustard seed

1 tablespoon fennel seeds

1½ tablespoons coriander seed

2 teaspoons turmeric

2 cinnamon sticks

4 bay leaves, fresh if available

¾ cup honey

½ cup apple-cider vinegar

1 teaspoon kosher salt

In a medium-sized nonreactive saucepan over medium heat, warm the canola oil. Add the onions, garlic, and red pepper flakes and sauté until the onions are translucent, about 5 minutes. Add the mustard seed, fennel seeds, coriander seed, turmeric, cinnamon sticks, and bay leaves and continue to cook for 5 more minutes. Add the honey, bring the mixture to a boil, and add the vinegar. Cook for another 5 to 7 minutes and add the salt.

FOR SPRING CHUTNEY

Add 2 cups of diced rhubarb and cook for an additional 3 to 5 minutes. Remove from the heat and allow to sit for 10 to 15 minutes. The rhubarb chutney is best used the following day, after the flavors have had time to develop.

FOR SUMMER CHUTNEY

Add 1½ cups (about 3 medium) of diced firm, ripe peaches and allow to sit for 10 to 15 minutes before refrigerating.

FOR FALL CHUTNEY

Add 1½ to 2 cups (about 4 to 5 medium) of diced tart apples, reduce the heat to low, and cook for 4 to 5 minutes. Remove from the heat and refrigerate.

FOR WINTER CHUTNEY

Add 2 cups of diced butternut squash and cook until tender, about 10 minutes. Remove from the heat and allow to cool slightly before refrigerating.

JAY PIERCE

Lucky 32 Southern Kitchen | *Greensboro, North Carolina*

Pickled watermelon rind is a Southern staple that takes the notion of ~~wasting nothing to an entirely new level by transforming a part of the~~ **fruit that is ordinarily discarded into a sweetly sharp, pleasingly tender pickle. The Christmas-y notes from the spices make these translucent, yellow-gold bites a must-have condiment with pork, though they also go down easily straight from the jar. MAKES ABOUT 1 QUART**

Watermelon Rind Pickles

8 pounds watermelon

3 tablespoons kosher salt

1 cup freshly squeezed lemon juice

2 cups granulated sugar

2 tablespoons grated fresh ginger

Peel of 1 lemon

2 tablespoons allspice berries

2 tablespoons whole cloves

Cut the watermelon pulp from the rind, leaving a thin layer of pink. Reserve the pulp for another use. Using a vegetable peeler, remove the green skin from the rind and discard. Cut enough rind into ½-inch by ½-inch pieces to make 8 cups.

In a large bowl, combine the salt and 4 cups of water. Soak the rind in the brine for 1 hour and drain.

In a large nonreactive pot, combine 1 cup water with the lemon juice, sugar, grated ginger, lemon peel, allspice, and cloves. Add the watermelon rind and bring to a boil over high heat. Reduce the heat to low, cover, and simmer for 50 minutes, or until the rind is translucent.

Using a slotted spoon, transfer the rind to a clean jar and cover with the strained pickling liquid. Store the pickles in the refrigerator for up to 6 months.

ODESSA PIPER

Roslindale, Massachusetts

Crab apples come in countless colors, shapes, and flavors. Bite-sized cultivars not much smaller than a nickel and no larger than a quarter in diameter are ideal for preserving. To hold up to the pickling process they should be firm and crisp, and fruit with red skins are the prettiest once processed. Look for the Dolgo, a brilliant red variety with dense flesh and tangy ripeness. Modern ornamental varieties rarely make good picklers because the fruit tends to be small, mealy, and bland. MAKES ABOUT 3 PINTS

Sweet-Sour Pickled Wild Crab Apples

1¼ pounds wild crab apples

1¼ cups high-quality cider vinegar

2 cups light brown sugar

1 whole star anise

½ teaspoon allspice berries

½ stick cinnamon

Wash the crab apples, leaving the stem and bud end intact. Prick each apple several times with a pin.

Combine the vinegar, brown sugar, star anise, allspice, and cinnamon in a large nonreactive pot and bring to a boil. Add the apples, return the mixture to a rolling boil, and reduce the heat to a bubbling simmer. Cook the fruit until it is soft all the way through, 10 to 20 minutes; times will vary widely depending on the size and firmness of the crab apples. Test one when they begin to look glossy.

Remove the fruit from the pot and, if necessary, reduce the pickling liquid to the consistency of light syrup, like maple syrup. Pack the still-warm fruit in pint-size sterilized jars and cover with the hot syrup, distributing the spices between the jars. Wipe the lips of the jars and screw on the lids.

The pickled crab apples will keep up in the refrigerator for up to 9 months. Serve them whole, on cheese plates with blue or salted, aged cow milk cheeses; or alongside lamb, pork, or spicy brats with mustard. The syrup has many uses, too, but is especially good in barbecue sauce, as a substitute for balsamic vinegar, or drizzled on pears, winter squash, or sweet potatoes before roasting.

> "What we choose or choose not to eat can either protect
> and enhance the biodiversity surrounding us,
> or as historically occurred, deplete it."

GARY NABHAN
Nature writer and sustainable agriculture activist

Biodiversity:
Out with the New,
In with the Old?

When it comes to plants, genetic diversity is threatened by "genetic erosion," or the loss of individual genes and combinations of genes like those found in heirloom varieties. The introduction of commercial strains into traditional farming systems often reduces the number of plant varieties, putting our food supply at risk. Genetic erosion is also caused by the emergence of new pests, weeds, and diseases; environmental degradation; urbanization; and land clearing through deforestation and bush fires.

Genetic diversity increases our ability to recover and thrive in the face of future adverse conditions, such as extreme and variable environments. According to Gary Nabhan, an internationally celebrated nature writer and sustainable agriculture activist, we have the power to help reverse the loss of biodiversity in agriculture by sampling the rich variety of foods nature provides.

Slow Food is one of several organizations committed to promoting biodiversity through consumption of regional foods in danger of becoming extinct. The Ark of Taste is an international catalog of rare foods threatened by industrial standardization, the regulations of large-scale distribution, and environmental damage. In an effort to cultivate consumer demand—key to agricultural conservation—only the best-tasting endangered foods make it onto the Ark.

SONJA J. FINN

Dinette | Pittsburgh, Pennsylvania

Pappa al Pomodoro is a Tuscan staple, a homey, porridge-like soup made from overripe tomatoes and yesterday's bread. La Pappa is traditionally served by itself, but it makes a delicious breakfast, with a fried egg on top, or a room temperature side dish for grilled meats.

Put together a big batch of the tomato mixture when you have too many ripe tomatoes and freeze in 4-cup portions. SERVES 4 TO 6

Pappa al Pomodoro

Kosher salt

4 pounds fresh tomatoes, or 4 cups home-canned tomatoes (or two 16-ounce cans plum tomatoes)

¼ cup extra-virgin olive oil, divided; more for garnish

½ teaspoon red pepper flakes

2 cloves garlic, finely minced

5 cups stale bread, torn into bite-size pieces

10 fresh basil leaves

½ cup grated Parmigiano-Reggiano

Bring a large pot of generously salted water to a boil over high heat. Fill a bowl with ice and cold water and set aside. Using a sharp paring knife, score the blossom end of the tomatoes with a shallow "X." When the water is boiling, drop the tomatoes in one at a time. Leave them for 15 seconds before transferring to the bowl of ice water. The skins should slip off easily. Remove the core and put the skinned tomatoes into a large bowl and crush well with your hands.

Heat 2 tablespoons of olive oil in a nonreactive pot. Add the red pepper flakes and garlic and quickly sauté over high heat until the garlic begins to sizzle; do not let it brown. Add the tomatoes and continue to cook over high heat, stirring frequently, until the mixture comes to a boil. Reduce the heat to a low simmer and cook for approximately 45 minutes, stirring often so the mixture does not stick to the bottom of the pan. The mixture should resemble a chunky tomato sauce.

Add the torn bread and stir well with a wooden spoon for a good 5 minutes to get the bread and tomato mixture fully incorporated. (Note: The pappa should be pinkish rather than bright red, and the tomato mixture should be fully absorbed by the bread. If there's extra loose tomato sauce, add more bread.)

Add the remaining 2 tablespoons of olive oil if needed; the mixture should glisten slightly. Tear the basil leaves and add to the tomato and bread mixture, stirring just until the basil is wilted. Add salt to taste; the amount will vary according to the variety of tomato.

To serve, spoon onto individual plates. Sprinkle with the grated Parmigiano-Reggiano and a good drizzle of extra-virgin olive oil.

GORDON HAMERSLEY

Hamersley's Bistro | Boston, Massachusetts

The ingredients for this freeform lasagna can be prepared ahead so that assembling and warming them and poaching the eggs are all that's standing between you and dinner. Serve these rich and delicious lasagnas—the very essence of spring—with a green salad, radishes, and warm bread for sopping up the creamy sauce and runny egg yolk.
SERVES 4

Asparagus, Spinach, and Spring Pea Lasagna

Kosher salt and freshly ground black pepper

4 small sheets fresh pasta (approximately 6 inches square)

3 tablespoons extra-virgin olive oil; more for the pan

2 cups loosely packed spinach, stemmed and washed

1 cup fresh shelled peas

4 medium-thick stalks asparagus, peeled, trimmed, and sliced into 1-inch pieces

½ cup ricotta

½ cup heavy cream

⅓ cup grated Parmesan

White truffle oil (optional)

¼ cup white vinegar

4 large eggs

¼ cup minced fresh chives

Bring a large pot of generously salted water to boil over medium-high heat. (It should hold enough water to cook the pasta sheets without crowding.) Add the pasta sheets and cook until al dente, 3 to 5 minutes. Carefully lift the pasta sheets out of the water and place them in a bowl of ice water to stop the cooking; use your fingers to keep the sheets separate, so they don't stick to one another. When the sheets have cooled, remove them from the ice water, drain, and transfer to a large bowl. Add the olive oil and toss the sheets to lightly coat, then cut each sheet on the diagonal to form two triangles. Lay the 8 triangles on a baking sheet and cover with a damp towel. Set aside or refrigerate for use the following day.

Bring a pot of generously salted water to a boil over medium-high heat. Put the spinach in a sieve and immerse the sieve in the water for 1 minute. Remove and immediately transfer the spinach to a bowl of ice water to stop the cooking. Once it is cool, drain the spinach and squeeze the excess water out of the leaves. Set aside.

Return the water to a boil, put the peas and asparagus in the sieve, and immerse the sieve in the boiling water for 3 minutes, or until the vegetables are just tender. Lift the sieve out of the water and immediately immerse in a bowl of ice water. When cool, lift out of the water and let drain.

When you're ready to assemble the lasagna, heat the oven to 400°F and lightly coat a baking sheet with olive oil. Bring 2 quarts of water to a boil in a large, heavy saucepan to poach the eggs.

To build the lasagnas, arrange 4 triangles of pasta on the baking sheet. Layer the ingredients on top of the pasta triangles: layer a generous tablespoon of ricotta, some spinach leaves, a few pieces of asparagus, and some peas. Add a tablespoon or two of heavy cream and a sprinkle of Parmesan. Lightly season with salt and pepper. Place the remaining triangles of pasta on top of each mound of the vegetables and repeat the layering of ingredients. On top of the top sheet of pasta place a few more asparagus and peas, 2 tablespoons more cream, and a light sprinkle more Parmesan. The lasagnas can be kept refrigerated for up to 3 hours until you are ready to cook them.

When ready to cook, place the sheet tray in the oven and bake for about 10 minutes, or until the cheese on the lasagna is golden brown. Remove the pan from the oven and lightly sprinkle each lasagna with white truffle oil, if desired.

Poach the eggs while the lasagnas are in the oven. Reduce the heat to low, so that the water maintains a slow simmer, and add the vinegar. Swirl the water with a spoon and carefully slip in the eggs—crack them in a cup one at a time and tip the edge of the cup about ½ inch below the surface of the gently simmering water. Use a spoon to lightly nudge the white toward the yolk and allow to poach for 4 to 5 minutes, until the whites are set but the insides are still runny. Remove from the water.

Using a spatula, carefully lift and slide a lasagna onto each of four plates. Top with a poached egg and pour any cream left on the tray around the base of the lasagna. Lightly drizzle with truffle oil, if using, sprinkle with chives, and serve immediately.

ANA SORTUN

Oleana | Cambridge, Massachusetts

"Dolma" comes from the Arabic word for "something stuffed." Grape leaves filled with ground lamb, rice, onions, and currants are among the most popular dolmas, but there are a variety of vessels for stuffing that include fruit, vegetables, and, in this recipe, sweet potatoes. Savory, well-seasoned fillings are added, and the dolmas are braised or baked, then served hot, cold, or at room temperature. SERVES 4

Sweet Potato-Chickpea Dolmas with Spinach and Crispy Mushrooms

4 small sweet potatoes (about 2 pounds)

2 tablespoons pine nuts or slivered almonds

½ pound king oyster or porcini mushrooms

2 tablespoons olive oil, divided

¼ teaspoon kosher salt; more as needed

¼ teaspoon freshly ground black pepper; more as needed

1½ to 2 tablespoons freshly squeezed lemon juice, divided

¾ cup cooked chickpeas or one 15-ounce can chickpeas, rinsed and drained

2 tablespoons tahini

1 small clove garlic, finely chopped

2 small shallots, thinly sliced

1 pound fresh spinach, rinsed and large stems removed

½ teaspoon ground cumin

¼ teaspoon cinnamon, preferably Vietnamese

⅛ teaspoon ground allspice

¼ cup chopped dried apples or currants

Tahini Sauce

(optional; see recipe on page 160)

Heat the oven to 350°F. Wrap the sweet potatoes in a double layer of aluminum foil and bake until tender, 45 to 60 minutes. Unwrap the potatoes and allow them to cool while you toast the nuts in the center of the oven until golden, 2 to 3 minutes.

Wipe the mushrooms with a damp paper towel, then trim and toss with 1 tablespoon olive oil, the salt, and black pepper and roast for 8 to 10 minutes, or until the mushrooms are golden brown with crispy edges. Cool to room temperature and toss them with 1½ to 2 teaspoons lemon juice.

Put a sweet potato into each of four large ramekins. Cut a slice horizontally from the top and gently spread out the sides of the sweet potatoes to fit the ramekins. Scoop out 3 to 4 tablespoons of flesh from each potato to create a space, and season the inside of each potato with a little salt. Set aside.

Transfer the scooped-out sweet potato to the bowl of a food processor and add the chickpeas, tahini, 1 to 1½ teaspoons lemon juice, and the garlic. Purée the mixture until it is the consistency of thick hummus and season to taste with salt and pepper.

In a large frying pan, heat 1 tablespoon olive oil over medium-low heat. Add the shallots and sauté until translucent, then stir in the spinach, cumin, cinnamon, and allspice. Cook until the spinach is wilted and tender. Add the dried apples or currants, toasted nuts, 1 to 1½ teaspoons lemon juice, and salt to taste.

Divide the sweet potato-chick pea purée among the four sweet potatoes and put an equal amount of the spinach mixture on top of each. Cover loosely with aluminum foil and bake for 15 minutes, or until the potatoes are hot all the way through. Reheat the mushrooms, spoon over the spinach, and drizzle each with tahini sauce, if desired.

>>>

Tahini Sauce

MAKES ABOUT ½ CUP

¼ cup tahini

¼ cup olive oil

2 cloves garlic, finely chopped

1 teaspoon ground cumin

Kosher salt and freshly ground black pepper

Combine all of the ingredients, except the salt and black pepper, in a blender or small food processor and blend until smooth. Season to taste with salt and pepper.

Community-Supported Agriculture

A full-blown local food movement has seen sales of local farm products soar, and subscriptions to community-supported agriculture (CSA) organizations with them. Some of the first CSAs in this country began in the mid 1980s, in the face of a farm crisis that was driving people off the land. Each year, the number of family farms dropped sharply while the hard work and risk inherent in food production continued to be shouldered by farmers whose costs of production were rarely covered by the prices they received. They definitely weren't earning a living wage. The CSA model invited local consumers to share in the harvest by paying in advance for an entire season and in doing so, experience a sense of ownership in the farm. In return, consumers would take whatever the farm could produce. Implicit in the concept is the idea that members also share the farmer's risk that some crops may do poorly based on weather, pests, and other forces out of his/her control.

This arrangement is beneficial for both farmer and consumer. Farmers spend time marketing and receive payment early in the season, which helps the farm's cash flow. Consumers develop a relationship with the people who grow their food, learn how it is grown, and have an opportunity to visit the farm. The food they receive is fresh from the field, flavorful, and full of nutrients; CSAs are no longer limited to produce. Some farmers include the option for shareholders to buy eggs, meat, cheese, flowers, or other food products along with their vegetables. Tens of thousands of families have joined CSAs; some areas of the country have more demand than there are farms. Regardless of where you live, there are likely to be several options available to participate in this unique shared experience of cooking and eating from a CSA (see Resources on page 291).

Kitchen Scrap Tips from the Pros

MARY SUE MILLIKEN
Border Grill

When we have fresh corn, I like to use the husks to wrap tamales and the cobs to make vegetable stock. I have yet to make corn silk tea, but the Koreans do it and it's delicious. Also, radish leaves are good in salads and in a green mole in Mexican cooking.

JOSH LEWIN
Beacon Hill Bistro

I use a lot of chard stems. We pickle them or slice them to add flavor to a base of shallots, peppers, and garlic for braising the leaves. They add beautiful color to the finished dish. We use herb stems and less-than-perfect leaves in purées and soups. Watercress trimmings make an awesome peppery soup, which is great garnished with oysters.

We use wood sorrel as a garnish and for salad greens. It has a long stem that isn't too fibrous and makes an amazing sauce if you blanch and purée it. Tons of flavor. Great with fish.

ANDREA REUSING
Lantern

As a cook it's very satisfying to use parts of plants that would otherwise go in the compost bin. We use coriander flowers and the bright green fresh seed on sashimi and the roots in curries; chestnut skins to smoke pork; fig leaves to wrap fish and chicken; tomato leaves to flavor soups and stews; and spicy, crunchy radish and broccoli seed pods in salads. We save most of our citrus rind to candy, dry, or turn into bitters.

DEBORAH SCARBOROUGH
Black Cat Bistro

We rarely throw anything away. We use a lot of shiitake mushrooms, and we save and dry the stems to flavor broth for mushroom risotto, to grind with sea salt for a meat seasoning, and to make mushroom consommé with black chanterelles and cauliflower custard. Chard stems get pickled for a pork dish that has hints of barbecue flavor, and carrot greens become pistou for drizzling on fish. Basically, we try not to throw anything away since most things can be used to at least flavor something. Apple peels and cores become a sauce for pheasant.

ED DOYLE
Real Food Consulting

Early training from some great European-trained chefs taught me that there should be no waste in the kitchen. Today, that same frugality combined with concern for the environment and wanting to show respect for farmers make us strive to use every morsel. Whether it's scraping a fish frame for tartare, using vegetable trimmings to make an intense broth, or using everything but the "squeal," we honor our ingredients and our craft by getting creative with what many folks see as fodder for the compost pile.

JONAH RHODEHAMEL

Oliveto Restaurant and Cafe | Oakland, California

Eggplant involtini are a popular vegetarian interpretation of the classic, but this version with farro and chard may become a new favorite. Divide the steps up between two days—make the risotto and roast the vegetables on day 1—to make the project more manageable. Assemble and reheat the involtini on the second day, sauté the greens and make the Parmesan Cream, which comes together quickly, when you're ready to serve. Save the chard stems for Rainbow Chard Stem Gratin (see page 77). SERVES 6 TO 8

Swiss Chard and Farro Involtini with Parmesan Cream

FOR THE INVOLTINI

4½ cups vegetable stock, divided

6 tablespoons extra-virgin olive oil, divided

4 cloves garlic, thinly sliced

1 medium onion, cut into ¼-inch dice (about 1 cup)

1 medium carrot, peeled and cut into ¼-inch dice (about ½ cup)

1 rib celery, cut into ¼-inch dice (about ½ cup)

1 cup farro

Kosher salt and freshly ground black pepper

1 cup cauliflower florets, about 1 inch in diameter

1 cardoon stalk or 2 celery ribs, cut into ½-inch pieces (about 1 cup)

½ teaspoon finely chopped fresh sage

½ teaspoon finely chopped fresh oregano

1 tablespoon coarsely chopped fresh flat-leaf parsley

½ teaspoon finely chopped lemon zest

2 tablespoons toasted pine nuts

16 large Swiss chard leaves, stems removed at base of leaf, blanched

2 cups fava greens or fresh spinach

MAKE THE INVOLTINI

Put the vegetable stock in a small pan, warm over medium heat, and hold warm over the lowest possible heat. Heat a pan with a heavy bottom over medium heat. Add 1 tablespoon of the olive oil and sauté the garlic until translucent. Add the onions, carrots, and celery and cook, stirring occasionally, until tender.

Add the farro to the vegetables and stir well to combine and coat the farro grains. Add the warm stock about ½ cup at a time, in the style of risotto. Continue to add stock to the farro, cooking and stirring until it absorbs almost all of the liquid each time before you add more stock. After about 35 minutes, or when the grains are al dente and still very slightly firm, season to taste with salt and black pepper; stir in 1 tablespoon of olive oil, then spread out on a baking sheet to allow the mixture to cool. Cover the pan with plastic wrap and refrigerate if not using immediately. About ½ cup of stock will remain in the saucepan; bring it to a boil.

While the farro is cooling, roast the cauliflower and braise the cardoons or celery. Heat the oven to 450°F. Toss the cauliflower with 1 tablespoon olive oil and season with salt. Add the florets to a sauté pan or small roasting pan. Put the cardoon or celery pieces in another pan, add the boiling stock, sprinkle with salt, and cover with aluminum foil. Place both pans in the oven for 15 to 20 minutes, or until the cauliflower is lightly browned and the cardoon or celery pieces are tender. Set both aside to cool.

Combine the cauliflower and cardoons with the herbs, lemon zest, and pine nuts. Add the farro, season to taste with salt and black pepper, and add a little bit of vegetable stock from braising the cardoons or olive oil if the mixture seems dry.

To assemble, spread the Swiss chard leaves out flat and put about ½ cup of filling close to the top. You may need more or less filling depending on the size of your chard leaves. Roll the leaves over the filling like burritos.

FOR THE PARMESAN CREAM

1 cup heavy cream

1 cup grated Parmigiano-Reggiano or Parmesan

Fruity olive oil such as Olio Nuovo

MAKE THE PARMESAN CREAM

Scald the cream, reduce the heat, and slowly add the cheese while whisking. Whisk until the mixture becomes glossy, then set aside in a warm spot.

TO SERVE

Put 1 inch of water and a steamer basket in a large pot with a lid. Bring the water to a simmer and steam the involtino for 5 minutes, or until they're hot in the middle. The involtino should be arranged in a single layer and may need to be steamed in batches. Lightly sauté the fava greens in the remaining olive oil, just until they wilt. Season with salt and pepper.

Spoon a pool of parmesan cream in the center of each plate. Divide the fava greens among the plates, placing some in the center of each one. Set 2 involtino on the greens and lightly drizzle with fruity olive oil.

CRAIG STOLL

Delfina | San Francisco, California

Make this pasta during the early summer months, when fava beans are starchier than the tender springtime variety. Guanciale is made by curing the meat from a pig's jowls and is similar in texture and flavor to pancetta. Substitute it, or good-quality bacon, if you can't find guanciale.

SERVES 4 AS A MAIN COURSE OR 6 AS A STARTER

Bucatini with Fava Beans and Guanciale

Kosher salt and freshly ground black pepper

5 pounds large, starchy fava beans, shucked (about 2 cups)

2 tablespoons extra-virgin olive oil; more for garnish

½ cup diced guanciale or pancetta

2 cloves garlic, smashed

2 teaspoons chopped fresh flat-leaf parsley, plus leaves for garnish

1 pound fresh or high-quality dried bucatini

¼ cup grated Parmigiano-Reggiano

Pecorino Romano, for grating at the table

Bring a large pan of generously salted water to a boil over medium-high heat and blanch the shucked fava beans for 30 seconds. Drain and transfer to a bowl filled with ice and cold water to stop the cooking. When they are cool enough to handle, peel the beans, removing the outer skin.

Refill the pot with water, generously salt, and bring back to a boil.

Warm the olive oil in a large heavy-bottomed sauté pan, add the diced guanciale and cook slowly over low heat until the fat is rendered and the guanciale is crispy and golden brown. Add the garlic and 1 teaspoon of the parsley, continuing to cook and stir for about 3 minutes. Add the shelled fava beans and 1 cup water. Season with a pinch each of salt and black pepper, increase the heat, and cook until the water begins to evaporate and the starchy beans begin to break down, about 10 minutes. Add more water to the pan if it starts to dry out.

Drop the pasta in the boiling water and cook until almost al dente. Reserve a cup of the pasta cooking water, then drain and transfer the pasta to the pan with the fava bean sauce. Add a few tablespoons of the reserved pasta water and the remaining teaspoon of parsley and continue cooking the pasta in the sauce until it is al dente and the sauce clings to the pasta. Add the Parmigiano and a drizzle of olive oil and transfer to serving plates.

Grate the Pecorino Romano over the pasta at the table, and finish with a few grinds of black pepper and a scattering of parsley leaves.

RICK BAYLESS

Frontera Grill | Chicago, Illinois

Filled with robust, flavorful greens like kale and chard, these tacos are earthy and rich, with a fresh citrusy punch from mojo made with green garlic. They come together quickly and are endlessly adaptable to whatever greens are in season, offering a refreshing change from the expected bean filling in many vegetarian tacos. Salty, tangy queso fresco is the perfect accent. MAKES 12 TACOS; SERVES 4

Tacos with Greens in Green Garlic Mojo

1 large bunch (about ½ pound) Lacinato or Russian kale, stems removed, sliced crosswise into ½-inch pieces

1 to 2 bunches (1 pound) Swiss chard, lower tough stems cut off, sliced crosswise into ½-inch pieces

½ cup Green Garlic Mojo (recipe below)

Kosher salt

12 small corn tortillas

4 ounces queso fresco, crumbled

¾ cup Roasted Tomato-Arbol Chile Salsa (recipe on page 72)

Edible flowers, for garnish (optional)

Put the greens (there should be about 8 cups) in a large frying pan over medium-high heat, and mix in the green garlic mojo, a large pinch of salt, and ½ cup water. Cook, stirring occasionally, until the greens are tender, about 15 minutes.

Meanwhile, warm the tortillas. Put a vegetable steamer in a large saucepan with ½ inch water in the bottom and bring to a boil. Wrap the tortillas in a heavy cotton kitchen towel, lay it in the steamer, and cover with a tight-fitting lid. Boil for 1 minute, remove from the heat, and let stand without removing the lid for 15 minutes. If you don't have a steamer, wrap the tortillas in 2 attached squares of lightly dampened paper towels. Microwave for 1 minute and immediately remove the tortillas from the towels. Store in an insulated warmer or small thermal chest for up to 1 hour. The tortillas will stay hot if the warmer isn't opened.

Spoon the greens into a warm serving dish, place the warm tortillas in a cloth-lined basket, and serve at the table with queso fresco, salsa, and edible flowers to garnish, if desired. Alternatively, spoon filling in the center of the tortillas and roll them up. Arrange 3 per plate with a spoonful of salsa across the middle and a sprinkle of queso fresco.

Green Garlic Mojo

MAKES 2 CUPS

5 to 6 whole green garlic stalks, about 6 ounces, washed and split in half lengthwise

1½ cups extra-virgin olive oil

¾ teaspoon kosher salt; more as needed

¼ cup freshly squeezed lime juice, preferably from key limes

1 tablespoon chopped fresh epazote, or 2 teaspoons dried

1 tablespoon lemon thyme leaves

Cut the green garlic crosswise into thin slices to make 1¼ cups and add to a medium sized nonreactive saucepan with the oil and salt. Stirring occasionally, bring the mixture barely to a simmer over medium-low heat; there should be just a hint of movement on the surface of the oil. Reduce the heat to the lowest possible setting and continue to cook gently, stirring occasionally, until the garlic is soft, 15 to 20 minutes. Add the lime juice, epazote, and lemon thyme and continue to simmer for 10 minutes to encourage the flavors to come together. Taste and add more salt if necessary.

>>>

Roasted Tomato-Arbol Chile Salsa

MAKES ABOUT 1½ CUPS

2 medium-small ripe red tomatoes (about 12 ounces)

12 dried arbol chiles, stemmed

4 cloves garlic, unpeeled

1 teaspoon kosher salt; more as needed

Put a rack 4 inches below the broiler and heat the broiler to high. Place the tomatoes in a pie tin or small rimmed baking sheet and roast until soft and splotchy black, about 6 minutes. Turn over and roast on the other side. Set aside to cool.

Toast the chiles in a small frying pan over medium heat, stirring constantly, until they are aromatic and have darkened slightly, 1½ to 2 minutes. Transfer to a blender. Roast the garlic cloves in the same frying pan, turning regularly until they are soft and black in places, about 15 minutes. Remove the skin and add to the blender. Add the tomatoes and salt and process until completely smooth.

Pour into a bowl and add enough water to give the salsa a spoonable consistency, 3 to 4 tablespoons. Season to taste with additional salt, if desired.

Living off the Land

Mushrooms. Huckleberries. Nettles. Fiddlehead ferns. Ramps. Truffles. Some of nature's most prized edible plants are those found in the wild.

As it gains in popularity, the act of hunting for wild edibles and medicinals—an activity widely referred to as foraging—has a new image. Wild crafting, as it is now sometimes called, describes the same act of harvesting plants from their natural—or wild—habitat, but with a greater emphasis on it being among the most pure form of revival of regional specialties and local offerings.

At its root, foraging, like hunting, is something we once relied on for sustenance and survival; it is the ultimate in bringing terroir to your kitchen. Herbalists and wild crafters observe certain rules so that resources are not damaged or depleted. Just as animals in the wild display restraint when hunting for food, taking only what they need, we should not harvest every last mushroom from the forest floor. Preserving the art of foraging is important to the revitalization of traditional foodways.

MARY SUE MILLIKEN

Border Grill | *Santa Monica, California*

Vegetables are the stars in this pie, sautéed with onions and garlic and seasoned with a salty cheese. Or try a combination of cheese and a little bit of flavorful meat like bacon, chorizo, anchovy, ham, guanciale, or salt cod. The possibilities are endless, but here are a few favorites to get you started: asparagus with prosciutto and Parmesan; zucchini with chorizo and cotija; and spinach, onions, and anchovies with black olives. MAKES ONE 10-INCH PIE; SERVES 6 TO 8

Beet Greens and Legs Pie

2 to 3 baking potatoes (about 1½ pounds)

¾ teaspoon kosher salt

Freshly ground black pepper

4 tablespoons (½ stick) unsalted butter, softened, for buttering the pie plate and brushing the crust

FOR THE FILLING

2 large bunches beet greens and stems

¼ cup extra-virgin olive oil

1 large onion, thinly sliced (about 1½ cups)

1¼ teaspoons kosher salt

Freshly ground black pepper

6 cloves garlic, sliced

½ teaspoon freshly grated lemon zest

1 cup whole milk

3 large eggs

6 ounces crumbled feta cheese

⅓ cup toasted pine nuts or slivered almonds

To make the crust, bake the potatoes several hours before serving. Heat the oven to 400°F, arrange the potatoes on a baking pan in the center of the oven, and bake until tender all the way through, about 45 to 55 minutes. Set the potatoes aside until they are cool enough to handle, then remove the flesh from the skin and mash it in a medium bowl with a fork. Add the salt and black pepper, cover, and chill until ready to use.

Heat the oven to 400°F. Spread a thick layer of soft butter all over a chilled 10-inch glass pie pan and press the mashed potato mixture into the pan to form a ⅜-inch-thick crust. Melt the remaining butter, brush it all over the crust and bake for 15 to 20 minutes, or until lightly browned. Remove the crust from the oven and set it on a rack to cool. Reduce the oven temperature to 350°F.

To make the filling, wash, dry, and separate the beet greens from the stems; dice the stems and coarsely chop the leaves. (You should end up with 1¼ to 1½ cups stems and 3 to 4 cups greens.) Heat the olive oil in a large frying pan over medium-high heat. Add the onions, salt, and black pepper and sauté until the onions are translucent and soft, 5 to 7 minutes. Add the garlic, lemon zest, and diced beet stems and continue to cook until the stems are soft, about 4 minutes. Add the greens and cook for a few more minutes, stirring frequently, until the liquid they produce has evaporated. Remove from the heat and transfer to a bowl to cool slightly.

Whisk together the milk and eggs. Add the cooled vegetable mixture and feta. Pour the mixture into the potato crust and bake for 20 minutes. Remove from the oven, sprinkle the top with the toasted pine nuts or almonds, and continue baking for another 20 minutes, or until the center has set. Serve hot or at room temperature.

DEBORAH MADISON

Santa Fe, New Mexico

When the summertime option of pairing green beans with tomatoes and onions is no longer possible, this combination of shallots, herbs, and pistachios is an equally delicious preparation for later-season beans.
SERVES 6

Blue Lake Green Beans with Shallots, Pistachios, and Herbs

1 pound fresh green beans, preferably Blue Lake or other pole beans

4 tablespoons (½ stick) unsalted butter

3 shallots, finely diced (about ½ cup)

2 tablespoons finely chopped fresh flat-leaf parsley

2 tablespoons finely chopped fresh marjoram

½ cup finely chopped pistachios

1 tablespoon kosher salt; more as needed

Freshly ground black pepper

Trim the green beans, unless they are very fresh and then you can leave the tips on. Bring a large pot of water to a boil over high heat.

Meanwhile, melt the butter in a large shallow sauté pan. Add the shallots, herbs, and pistachios and cook together over medium heat, seasoning with salt and pepper after several minutes.

When the water for the beans comes to a boil, add 1 tablespoon of salt to the water. Add the beans and cook until tender but still firm, about 5 minutes. Taste them as they are cooking to determine when they are ready. Drain and turn out onto a clean dry towel to soak up the excess water.

Put the beans in a bowl and toss them with the shallots, herbs, and nuts. Taste for salt, season with black pepper, and serve immediately.

Farmworkers' Conditions

The question that opened my eyes to the plight of farmworkers in this country was put to me by a tomato picker and community activist in Immokalee, Florida, who said: "How can you call food sustainable if the people who produce it do not make enough money to sustain themselves?"

The answer is you can't. Yet our entire food system rests on the shaky foundation of a labor force that is underpaid, ill-housed, often hungry, and illegal for the most part. Abuses such as sexual harassment and even abject slavery are all too common in agriculture. The average farmworker earns between $10,000 and $12,000 per year—and that includes those in higher-paid supervisory positions. By law, farmworkers are specifically excluded from receiving overtime pay, even when they put in more than 8 hours a day or 40 hours per week. They are not guaranteed collective bargaining rights. Children too young to work in other jobs routinely toil in fields. Half of the farmworker families in California's Central Valley, the most productive agricultural region in the United States, go hungry in the off-season. At a time when the average American can look forward to living 78 years, the average farmworker's life expectancy is 49.

We don't respect farmworkers, but we depend upon them. When the state of Georgia enacted a harsh law aimed at undocumented workers, the migrant laborers that the state's farmers rely on simply moved on, leaving $500 million of crops to rot in the fields. This example is a stark warning of what could happen anywhere in this country: the dairy farms of New England, the apple orchards of Michigan, the slaughterhouses of Iowa, the lettuce fields of California's Salinas Valley.

Unlike other problems facing society, the plight of farmworkers is easy to stop. All that is necessary is to (1) grant them the same rights that other workers enjoy and (2) find a way to give them legal status. Dinner depends on it.

BARRY ESTABROOK *is a former contributing editor to* Gourmet *magazine and is an award-winning writer and author of* Tomatoland, *a book that explores the cost of industrial agriculture—specifically the tomato industry—to humans and the environment.*

MONICA POPE

T'afia | Houston, Texas

Chard stems are frequently tossed into the compost pile, which is a mistake since they're sweet, tender, and tasty when cooked properly. The leaves can be steamed and served alongside the gratin or used in any number of ways including in the Tacos with Greens in Green Garlic Mojo (page 71), Swiss Chard and Farro Involtini with Parmesan Cream (page 66), or Pumpkin Curry (page 49). SERVES 6

Rainbow Chard Stem Gratin

2 large bunches rainbow chard (about 15 leaves each)

Kosher salt and freshly ground black pepper

2 cups heavy cream

3 sprigs fresh thyme

1 clove garlic

2 tablespoons unsalted butter

1 cup fresh breadcrumbs

½ cup grated Parmigiano-Reggiano

⅓ cup lightly toasted hazelnuts, coarsely chopped

Wash the chard and cut the leaves from the center ribs. Set the leaves aside for another use. Trim the tough ends of the stems and discard. Cut the stems crosswise into 3-inch lengths.

Bring a pot of generously salted water to a boil. Blanch the stems until crisp-tender, about 5 minutes. Drain and cool in an ice bath.

Heat the oven to 350°F and place a rack in the middle of the oven. Meanwhile, put the cream in a small saucepan with 2 thyme sprigs and the garlic clove and bring it to a simmer over medium-high heat. Reduce the heat to a simmer and continue to cook over very low heat until the cream is reduced by one-third to one-half. You want to end up with 1 to 1⅓ cups. Season to taste with salt and black pepper and set aside.

Use the butter to coat a shallow casserole or baking dish and arrange the drained chard stems on the bottom. Strain the cream through a fine-mesh sieve onto the stems. Finely chop the thyme from the remaining sprig and sprinkle on top. Cover with the breadcrumbs, grated cheese, and hazelnuts.

Bake the gratin for about 25 minutes, or until the cream has set.

BRADLEY OGDEN

Lark Creek® Restaurant Group | San Francisco, California

This soufflé recipe produces all of the show-stopping results that any self-respecting soufflé should, but with a minimum of fussiness. Little by little, it will deflate once it comes out of the oven, but there's no reason to tiptoe around while it's baking.

The flavors of spring in this dish are nicely complemented with a simple green salad, alongside some crispy bacon for breakfast or brunch, or with something more substantial to turn it into dinner. SERVES 6 TO 8

Corn Spoonbread Soufflé with Green Garlic and Asparagus

3 large eggs

1 cup whole milk

¼ cup (½ stick) unsalted butter; more for the dish

1 teaspoon kosher salt

½ teaspoon freshly ground black pepper

2 teaspoons finely minced red or green jalapeños

¾ cup yellow cornmeal

1 cup buttermilk

¼ cup finely sliced green garlic

2 cups ½-inch-long blanched asparagus pieces (from 10 to 12 stalks)

Heat the oven to 425°F. Butter a 2-quart soufflé or baking dish that is 3 inches deep and place it in a pan deep enough to hold it and several inches of water. Separate the eggs, dividing them into 3 yolks and 2 whites; save the remaining egg white for another use.

In a 2-quart saucepan, combine 1 cup water with the milk, butter, salt, black pepper, and jalapeños and bring to a simmer over medium heat. Slowly add the cornmeal, whisking vigorously to prevent lumps from forming. Cook for about 2 minutes, stirring constantly, until the mixture is very thick.

Slowly add the buttermilk, stir until blended, and remove from the heat. Allow the mixture to cool slightly, and then add the egg yolks, one at a time. Fold in the green garlic and asparagus.

In a clean dry mixing bowl, beat the egg whites until soft peaks form. Fold the egg whites into the cornmeal mixture. Pour the batter into the prepared baking dish, put the dish in the pan for the water, and fill the pan with water to come about a quarter of the way up the sides; bake for 20 minutes. When it is ready, the spoonbread will still be soft, not completely set, and light golden brown in color.

HUGO MATHESON

The Kitchen | *Boulder, Colorado*

Artichokes, like the best things in life, take a bit of work. The perennial plant wears an armor of leathery petals and prickly thorns to protect the prized, succulent heart. Working with an artichoke requires commitment and perseverance.

A little perseverance is in order when attempting this recipe as well, but it's worth the effort. Make the tomato sauce the day before you plan to serve the artichokes. The following day, clean and roast the artichokes, and make the quinoa while they're in the oven. SERVES 4

Roasted Artichokes with Quinoa

2 tablespoons extra-virgin olive oil, divided

1 medium onion, cut into ½-inch dice
(about 1 cup)

1 rib celery, cut into ¼-inch dice
(about ½ cup)

1 medium carrot, finely diced (about ½ cup)

4 cloves garlic, sliced

2 bay leaves, divided

1 teaspoon fresh thyme leaves

½ teaspoon ground coriander

¼ teaspoon freshly ground black pepper;
more as needed

4 cups vegetable broth, divided

1 cup white wine, such as Sauvignon Blanc
or Pinot Gris, divided

¼ cup freshly squeezed lemon juice

4 medium artichokes

12 shallots, finely minced

1 leek, well rinsed, halved, and sliced,
white part only

1⅓ cups quinoa, rinsed

½ cinnamon stick

3 whole cloves

½ cup cooked chickpeas or one 15-ounce
can chickpeas, rinsed and drained

¼ cup coarsely chopped piquillo peppers

12 kalamata olives, halved

Kosher salt

Tomato Sauce (recipe on the facing page)

Heat the oven to 425°F. Warm 1 tablespoon of olive oil in a large ovenproof frying pan over medium-low heat. Add the onions, celery, and carrots and cook, stirring frequently, until the vegetables are tender but not brown, about 7 minutes. Add half of the garlic, 1 bay leaf, the thyme, coriander, and black pepper and cook for 5 minutes longer. Add 2 cups of the vegetable broth and ⅓ cup white wine. Bring to a boil, stirring to loosen any browned bits on the bottom of the pan.

Meanwhile, put 2 tablespoons lemon juice and 2 cups water in a large bowl. Use a sharp serrated knife to cut 1 inch from the pointy tops of the artichokes and trim the stem even with the bottom leaves. Bend back and peel away the outermost layer of tough discolored leaves, and use kitchen scissors to snip off the tips of the remaining leaves. Cut the artichokes in half lengthwise, pull out the small purple interior leaves, and scrape out the fuzzy layer—the choke—with a small spoon. Rinse the artichoke halves and place them in the bowl of lemon water, turning to coat all sides.

Arrange the artichoke halves, cut side up, in a 9x13-inch baking dish or roasting pan and spoon the vegetables and broth from the frying pan over them. Set the frying pan aside for later. Cover the top of the baking pan with parchment and roast the artichokes until just tender, 20 to 25 minutes.

Warm the remaining 1 tablespoon of olive oil in the reserved pan, add the shallots and leeks, and sauté over medium heat until they begin to brown, about 5 minutes. Stir in the quinoa, the remaining garlic and bay leaf, the cinnamon stick, and cloves. Cook, stirring, until all are coated with oil. Stir in the remaining vegetable broth and wine and bring to a boil over high heat. Remove the pan from the heat, cover, and place in the oven until the quinoa is tender and most of liquid has been absorbed, about 15 minutes.

When the quinoa is ready, transfer the pan to the stovetop. Remove the bay leaf and stir in the chickpeas, peppers, and olives. Cook until everything is hot and any remaining liquid has been absorbed. Add salt and pepper to taste.

Drain the artichokes and grill or broil on the cut sides if desired. Divide the quinoa mixture among 4 plates. Spoon some tomato sauce onto the quinoa and top each serving with 2 artichoke halves. Pass the remaining sauce at the table.

Tomato Sauce

MAKES ABOUT 3 CUPS

1 tablespoon olive oil
½ cup finely chopped onions
1½ teaspoons sweet paprika
½ teaspoon hot smoked paprika
½ teaspoon dry mustard
½ teaspoon ground coriander
½ teaspoon ground cumin
¼ teaspoon caraway seeds
3 cups crushed tomatoes
Kosher salt and freshly ground black pepper

Warm the olive oil in a sauté pan over medium-high heat. Add the onions and cook until they begin to brown, about 5 minutes. Add the sweet and smoked paprika, dry mustard, coriander, cumin, and caraway seeds. Cook while stirring constantly until the ingredients are well combined and aromatic. Stir in the tomatoes and bring to a boil. Simmer for 5 minutes and keep the sauce warm until ready to serve. Season to taste with salt and pepper. This sauce can be made ahead and reheated just before serving.

> "It all comes down to grain....Yes, because it's delicious—a whole world of flavor that's been ignored for the past 50 years—but also because it's a critical missing link in any community's ability to feed itself."

DAN BARBER

chef/owner, Blue Hill at Stone Barns, Pocantico Hills, New York

Preserving Heritage Grains

Historically, grains have been central to European cuisines and throughout the Middle East and Asia. In the U.S., where meat is plentiful, grains have been pushed to the side of the plate until recently. Chefs and consumers who prioritize the purchase of local vegetables, meats, and seafood are beginning to see similar benefits in sourcing sustainably grown local grains. As demand grows, these heritage varieties are reappearing in local markets nationwide. And not a moment too soon, according to Dan Barber, chef/owner of Blue Hill at Stone Barns in New York, since 80 percent of agricultural production is devoted to raising grain to feed the animals that feed us. "We'll never achieve sustainability if we limit our focus to produce and proteins."

Across the country, farmers are starting to grow quality heritage varieties for chefs and bakers who are leading the movement to revitalize and preserve the flavor and diversity of grains once in danger of falling into obscurity. Eli Rogosa, a grain grower, seed saver, and baker from western Massachusetts, extols the unique and delicious flavors of heritage grains. "It knocks your socks off when you eat these ancient varieties." She likes to chalk it up to "grain terroir." "Grains have different textures, aromas, and flavors. Terroir has shaped the way we think about coffee and wine; it's time we start thinking about grain this way, too."

Sustainability of Grains

Commodity grains make up more than 99 percent of our grain supply. The majority of commodity grains are scientific hybrids, bred to thrive in industrial-scale conditions with the help of synthetic inputs—fertilizers, pesticides, and fungicides—and intensive irrigation. Heritage grains, on the other hand, self-maintain their genetic diversity and grow well in a range of specific climates and geographies. They require less water and fewer inputs, are genetically resistant to stress brought on by drought and disease, and produce higher yields in organic conditions. And their seeds can be saved and replanted.

Small-batch whole-grain flours usually retain the whole grain and are milled to order, offering a fresh, flavorful product with a higher nutritional content than commodity grains. "One of the greatest realizations for people tasting foods made with small-batch flour for the first time," says Clifford Hatch of Upinngil Farm in Gill, Massachusetts, "is that they can taste the whole grain—the germ, the bran, and the endosperm." Flavor is critical to the success of these products in the marketplace," says Glenn Roberts of Anson Mills in Columbia, South Carolina. "If the taste isn't remarkable, you won't get anyone's attention."

JOHN AND JULIE STEHLING

Early Girl Eatery | Asheville, North Carolina

Hushpuppies provide a more satisfying option for leftover broccoli stems than soup. Not only are these crispy cornmeal dumplings tasty, but they're also vegetarian, gluten free, and cost-effective to boot.

This recipe serves a crowd, but can easily be cut in half or thirds. For the eggs, use 3 for a half recipe or 2 for one-third. Look for cornmeal grown locally, especially in the southeastern United States.

This adaptable recipe can include everything from bacon and jalapeños to corn. MAKES 48 HUSHPUPPIES; SERVES 12 TO 16

Broccoli Hushpuppies

3 cups cornmeal

1½ teaspoons baking powder

1½ teaspoons kosher salt

½ teaspoon granulated sugar

¼ teaspoon baking soda

¼ teaspoon cayenne pepper

¼ teaspoon freshly ground black pepper

5 large eggs

½ cup buttermilk

2 cups grated broccoli stems

1 cup grated Cheddar

½ small yellow onion, grated (about ¼ cup)

¼ cup finely chopped fresh flat-leaf parsley

Vegetable oil, for frying

Combine the cornmeal, baking powder, salt, sugar, baking soda, cayenne, and black pepper in a large bowl.

In another bowl, whisk together the eggs and buttermilk. Add the broccoli stems, cheese, onions, and parsley. Stir to evenly distribute the ingredients and fold in the dry cornmeal mixture.

Heat 3 inches of oil in a medium saucepan until it reaches 325°F on a deep-fat thermometer. Gently drop the batter into the hot oil, 1 tablespoon at a time, adding only as many hushpuppies as will fit in one layer in the pan without touching. Fry until golden brown and cooked through, about 2 minutes. If they don't flip over by themselves, turn the hushpuppies once while frying. Drain on a paper-towel-lined plate and serve immediately with creamy garlic dressing or apple butter. (The hushpuppies can be made 30 minutes in advance and kept warm in the oven, though they won't be quite as crispy.)

> **"On any given day, emmer appears four or five times on my menu. I use both emmer and rye flours, sometimes in combination with other wheat flours, in house-made pastas, crackers, and biscuits for breakfast."**
>
> SETH CASWELL
> *chef/owner, emmer&rye, Seattle, Washington*

Going with the Grain

The selection of grains in the bulk bins just keeps growing. So much so that it's become challenging to keep the names and processing methods straight. Groats, grits, steel-cut, rolled, puffed, pearled, cracked, flakes, and flour all describe how a grain has been processed. The following list can help you sort out the facts and make choices about how and where to introduce more grains into your diet.

Several seeds are included below, too. These "psuedo-grains" or "pseudocereals" have a nutritional content similar to the grains among which they're included. Gluten-free grains and seeds are designated GF.

■ **Amaranth** (GF) is technically not a grain and, because it contains lysine, it is a complete protein. Amaranth seeds resemble little beige poppy seeds and have a grassy, haylike essence that mellows when paired with similarly bold flavors. Cook the seeds whole to make breakfast porridge or savory polenta, or combine amaranth flour with flour containing gluten for baking.

■ **Barley** has a tough hull, which is why pearled barley is easiest to find. It's delicious in soup or made like risotto, especially if you toast the grains first. Scotch barley (also called "pot barley") and barley groats are less refined and retain more of their bran. Barley flakes are good in granola, and barley flour has a soft texture that works well in dough and batters when combined with a source of gluten.

■ **Buckwheat** (GF) seeds (or berries) come from a flowering plant in the rhubarb family—buckwheat is not related to wheat and technically not a grain. Kasha are toasted buckwheat groats, often cooked into hot cereal; buckwheat flour has an assertive, winey flavor that's delicious in baked goods, particularly when combined with fall fruits. Buckwheat flour is also the primary ingredient in soba noodles.

■ **Bulgur** (also called cracked wheat) is precooked, dried, and cracked wheat kernels. The kernels are high in fiber, quick cooking, and have a mild wheat flavor and pleasant texture. Perhaps most famously used in the Mideastern salad tabouli, bulgur also makes a good pilaf or side dish and is a nice addition to soup or meatballs.

■ **Corn** is probably recognized as a vegetable first—kernels on a cob. But the list of derivatives from corn is long and varied: cornbread, tortillas, hominy, polenta, grits, popcorn. The main difference in the corn used in these preparations is how finely it is ground. Corn for polenta and grits is coarsely ground, while cornbread and tortillas use a finer grind and may come from white, yellow, or blue corn. Soft corn flour is a tasty addition to your baking when paired with flour containing gluten. Hominy and popcorn are the grain in its entirety (see Pork Shoulder and Hominy Stew on page 163).

■ **Couscous** is neither grain nor pasta. It is made from coarsely ground durum wheat and is a staple of the Mideastern kitchen. Like bulgur, it can be made quickly, by boiling or soaking, but the traditional preparation calls for steaming it twice in a couscousière.

■ **Farro,** also known as emmer and einkorn, is the term commonly used when referring to ancient wheat varieties still cultivated in Italy. Farro is thought to be the oldest species of wheat, and the one from which all wheat has evolved. The farro sold in the U.S. is typically the emmer variety, which is often semi-pearled, retaining some of its bran and nutrients but also cooking quickly. "Chefs cherish the nutty sweetness and delicate chew," says Maria Speck, author of *Ancient Grains for Modern Meals*.

- **Freekeh** (or frikeh) is green spelt, harvested before it ripens fully and then roasted. The resulting strong, smoky flavor has a meaty quality. Freekeh is traditionally used in grain cakes, soups, and pasta.

- **Kamut®** is a trademarked name for an organically grown ancient wheat variety called Khorasan. High in protein and vitamin E, with a sweet, buttery flavor and none of the bitterness of other wheat varieties, kamut is available in the same forms as wheat. It is especially versatile as flour, its fine texture well-suited to baked goods and pastries and recipes in which butter plays a starring role.

- **Millet** (GF) is a small-seeded cereal belonging to a family of grasses. Mild tasting, quick-cooking, and versatile, it can be prepared like polenta or couscous, eaten for breakfast like porridge, or used for texture in croquettes or terrines. Millet has a pleasing crunch when sprinkled on top of muffins and cookies or in a salad.

- **Oats** begin as groats, or hulled kernels. From there, they're steamed and rolled, steel-cut, or milled into flour. Because their germ and bran are rarely removed, oats are a whole grain that, compared to other grains, offer higher protein and beneficial fats, lots of B vitamins and beta-glucan, a soluble fiber said to have cholesterol-lowering properties. From porridge to granola to cookies, oats are sweet, nutty, and totally versatile. Oat flour has a nice chewiness, but it should be combined with flours containing gluten for structure.

- **Quinoa** (GF) is high in protein, easy to digest, and quick cooking. Pale beige or red, the tiny, round grain should be rinsed well before cooking to remove the saponin, its natural and bitter protective coating. Toast the seeds first and then cook them like pasta or rice. Make quinoa sweet or savory for breakfast; use it in baked goods, in its flour form, or whole, for crunch. Its assertive flavor, with hints of sesame, makes quinoa an excellent base for salads, polenta, or pilaf (see Heirloom Grain and Bean Salad on page 160).

- **Rye berries** are the source for pumpernickel and dark rye flours, both of which are milled from the whole berry. Light rye flour is what you get after removing the bran and germ. Whole-grain rye flour has a surprisingly mild flavor, with malty, caramel overtones that complement stone fruits and dried fruits. Cooked whole, rye berries are pleasingly tangy and chewy, good in all the same places as wheat berries, spelt, and the like.

- **Sorghum** (GF) makes most of us think of molasses, which is made from a nongrain variety of sorghum. The grain is similar in texture to millet and a good source of protein. It can be popped like popcorn, cooked into porridge, or ground into flour for baking. Sorghum tastes best when slightly toasted before cooking.

- **Spelt** is a protein-rich variety of hard wheat that can be interchanged with wheat berries or flour in most recipes. Distinguished by a mild natural sweetness and vaguely tart aroma, spelt flour behaves like a mild version of wheat flour, offering a satisfying soft and tender crumb with enough structure to hold other ingredients.

- **Teff** is a kind of millet that has more calcium and iron than other whole grains plus all eight essential amino acids. It's best in flour form and is the primary ingredient in injera, the spongy Ethiopian flatbread. Teff is pale cocoa colored and has a malty aroma; flour made from teff has a strong flavor and lacks gluten, requiring it to be mixed with whole-wheat or all-purpose flour. Whole teff can be used like millet or quinoa—in polenta and porridge, in side dishes, and added to baked goods.

- **Triticale** is a hybrid of rye and durum wheat that is easily grown without pesticides and fertilizers and boasts more protein and amino acids than either individual grain. The berries can be used in salads, soups, and stews, like wheat or rye berries; the rolled variety can be substituted for oats in granola, oatmeal, and the other usual suspects.

PATTIE TAAN

Farmhouse Inn | Forestville, California

Sweet and slightly floral when compared to a regular lemon, a Meyer lemon is a cross between a mandarin orange and lemon. Meyer lemons are widely available between November and March; gather extras at the end of the season for juicing and zesting. Freeze the spoils for use in the summertime with berries and stone fruit.

If you have the choice, coastal huckleberries have a fuller flavor—and shape—than their mountain cousins. Wild blueberries make a fine substitute. **SERVES 10**

Meyer Lemon Roulade with Huckleberry Compote

FOR THE LEMON MOUSSE FILLING

⅓ cup fresh Meyer lemon juice (about 3 lemons), strained

¾ cup plus 1 tablespoon granulated sugar, divided

6 tablespoons (¾ stick) unsalted butter

Pinch of kosher salt

1 large egg

4 large egg yolks

2 teaspoons gelatin

¼ cup cold water

¼ cup mascarpone

1 cup heavy cream

½ cup confectioners' sugar

FOR THE LEMON SPONGE CAKE

1 cup cake flour

½ teaspoon kosher salt

½ teaspoon baking powder

4 large eggs, separated

½ cup plus ⅓ cup granulated sugar

¼ cup canola oil

Zest of 1 Meyer lemon, finely chopped

>>>

MAKE THE FILLING

Combine the Meyer lemon juice, ½ cup sugar, the butter, and salt in a small nonreactive saucepan over medium heat. Bring the mixture to a boil to dissolve the sugar. Remove the lemon syrup from the heat.

In a nonreactive or glass bowl, whisk the egg and yolks with the remaining ¼ cup plus 1 tablespoon sugar until smooth. While whisking, drizzle a small amount of the warm lemon syrup into the eggs. Gradually add the remaining syrup until it's gone. Place the bowl over a pan of simmering water and stir constantly until the mixture has thickened slightly and coats the back of the spoon, about 15 minutes.

Soften the gelatin in the cold water. When it has dissolved, add the gelatin to the warm lemon-egg mixture, whisking to break apart, dissolve, and incorporate. Remove from the heat and set aside to cool slightly before adding the mascarpone. Whisk until smooth and set the mixture aside to come to room temperature.

When the entire mixture is room temperature, whip the heavy cream with the confectioners' sugar until it forms soft peaks. Whisk the curd until it's smooth and slightly looser, then gently fold in the cream and chill until set, 1 to 2 hours.

MAKE THE CAKE

Make the sponge cake while the filling is chilling. Position a rack in the center of the oven and heat the oven to 350°F. Line an 11x17-inch jelly roll pan or a 12x17½-inch sheet pan with parchment.

Sift together the flour, salt, and baking powder in a large bowl; set aside.

Add the egg yolks and ½ cup sugar to the bowl of a stand mixer. Using the whisk attachment, whip on medium-high speed until the mixture

>>>

3 cups fresh or frozen huckleberries, divided

⅓ cup granulated sugar

½ teaspoon ground cinnamon

2 teaspoons cornstarch

Zest and juice of ½ Meyer lemon

is pale in color. Add ¼ cup water and continue to whip on low speed. Once the water is well incorporated, slowly add the oil, continuing to whisk until blended. Add the lemon zest and gently fold in the sifted dry ingredients by hand. Set aside while you whip the eggs whites.

Using a clean, dry mixer bowl and the whisk attachment, whip the egg whites on high speed until foamy. Add the remaining ⅓ cup sugar gradually, continuing to whip until the whites form medium-soft peaks. Carefully fold the whites into the flour mixture in two additions.

Pour the batter onto the parchment-lined pan and smooth the top with an offset spatula to evenly distribute the batter. Bake for 10 to 12 minutes, or until the sponge in the center of the pan springs back slightly. Be careful not to overbake or the cake will split when it is rolled.

Allow the sponge to cool for 5 minutes before covering loosely with a piece of plastic wrap pressed directly on top of the cake. (Once cool, the wrap will remove the thin top layer of the cake when it is pulled off. Any remaining top layer can be pulled off carefully with your fingers.) Invert the cake onto a clean piece of parchment paper, remove the bottom piece of parchment, and invert right side up again. Cover.

ASSEMBLE THE ROULADE

To assemble, arrange the cake on a work surface with one long side facing you. Spread the cooled filling evenly over the cake, leaving 1 inch along the opposite long edge and ¼ inch on the other sides bare. Roll the cake away from you lengthwise, pressing against the parchment to make a tight spiral and gently peeling off the parchment as you roll the cake. Stop rolling at the far edge of the parchment and position a long piece of plastic wrap along the edge. Roll the roulade onto the plastic wrap and continue to roll using the plastic wrap to enclose the roulade. Twist the ends of the plastic wrap in opposite directions to tighten. Refrigerate until set, 4 hours or overnight.

MAKE THE COMPOTE

Heat 2 tablespoons water in a small nonreactive saucepan with 1 cup of the berries and cook until they begin to burst, 2 to 4 minutes.

Combine the sugar, cinnamon, cornstarch, lemon juice, and zest in a small bowl and whisk together before adding to the warm berries in the pan. Continue stirring over medium heat until the mixture thickens and turns from cloudy to clear. Remove from the heat and fold in the remaining berries. Chill until ready to serve.

TO SERVE

Unwrap the roulade, place seam side down on a large plate, and trim both ends. Cut into 1½-inch slices and serve with huckleberry compote.

PIPER DAVIS

Grand Central Baking Company | Portland, Oregon

A few cups of freshly milled whole-wheat flour from a neighbor inspired Piper Davis to experiment with the crust for this decadent tart. It turns out that whole wheat pastry flour makes a buttery and flaky crust if you follow a few important steps: Begin with very cold ingredients, add enough liquid to hold the dough together (more than you would with white flour), and refrigerate the dough overnight before rolling it out. This relaxes the gluten and allows the dough to fully absorb the moisture of the other ingredients, making it easier to roll and more tender.

In order to savor its individual rich flavors, serve slices of this tart adorned simply, with a dollop of freshly whipped cream.

MAKES ONE 10-INCH TART; SERVES 8 TO 10

Oregon Filbert and Honey Tart

FOR THE TART DOUGH

1 large egg

1 cup unbleached all-purpose flour;
   more for rolling

1 cup whole-wheat pastry flour

¼ cup granulated sugar

1 teaspoon kosher salt

½ teaspoon baking powder

¾ cup (1½ sticks) cold unsalted butter,
   diced into ½-inch cubes

FOR THE FILLING

2 cups hazelnuts

¾ cup honey

¼ cup brown sugar

¾ cup (1½ sticks) unsalted butter

½ cup heavy cream

2 large eggs

1 teaspoon pure vanilla extract

Freshly whipped cream, for serving
   (optional)

MAKE THE DOUGH

Break the egg into a small bowl and set aside. Combine the all-purpose and whole-wheat pastry flours, sugar, salt, and baking powder in a mixing bowl with high sides or the bowl of a stand mixer. Add the butter cubes and toss with the dry ingredients. Put the bowl in the refrigerator to chill for at least 10 minutes.

Pour ¼ cup of water over ice. Cut the butter into the dry ingredients using a stand mixer fitted with the paddle attachment or by rubbing the flour and butter together with your fingers. When the mixture resembles coarse cornmeal, add the ice water and egg, mixing just until the dough begins to come together. Turn the dough out onto a sheet of plastic wrap and use the heels and sides of your palms to gather and press the dough into a 1½-inch-tall disk. Wrap tightly and refrigerate for at least 2 hours.

MAKE THE FILLING

Heat the oven to 325°F. Toast the hazelnuts on a baking sheet for 20 to 30 minutes, or until they are a rich dark brown and their skins are beginning to fall off. Allow them to cool slightly and then use a clean, dry dishtowel to rub the nuts together to remove the remaining skin. Set the nuts aside.

Melt the honey, brown sugar, and butter together in a saucepan with high sides over medium-high heat. Bring the mixture to a hard boil, remove from the heat, and slowly and carefully whisk in the cream. Whisk in the eggs and vanilla when the caramel is just barely warm.

>>>

Lightly flour a work surface. Roll the dough out into a 14- to 15-inch circle about ¼ inch thick. Fold it in half and carefully lay the dough in a 10-inch tart pan with a false bottom and fluted edges. Press the dough into the corners and up the sides of the pan, then trim the edges with a rolling pin. Refrigerate for 15 minutes and heat the oven to 350°F.

Line the chilled tart shell with parchment paper and fill it with dried beans, rice, or pie weights. Bake for 25 minutes. Remove from the oven, reduce the heat to 325°F, and cover the bottom of the crust with the toasted hazelnuts. Pour the custard over the top and bake for 25 to 30 minutes, or until the custard has just set. Cool completely before serving and top with whipped cream if you'd like.

Baking with Whole Grains

Forget what you think you know about baking with whole grains. Lately, professional bakers and pastry chefs have become smitten with them, in part by disproving every unfavorable stereotype we've come to associate with them. (There's a reason baked goods made from whole wheat have a bad reputation.) When they are pure and fresh—and used creatively—whole grains taste incredible. In many cases, the addition of whole-grain flour improves the flavor and texture of familiar recipes (barley, spelt, or whole-wheat flour in pie crusts), and creates nuance and depth of flavor where refined flour cannot.

Baking is the best place to introduce more whole grains into your diet, and it doesn't involve trading pleasure for health and nutrition. Not only will they add subtle and unique nutty flavors to your baked goods, but whole grains also will impart a richness and complexity. Start by replacing 30 percent of the all-purpose flour in your favorite recipes with white whole-wheat flour. Or try adding 20 percent of another grain like barley or spelt. Adjust the percentages until the flavor and texture are to your liking. Cookies, muffins, pancakes, and quick breads are all good places to begin experimenting.

Good and Good for You

Most Americans don't eat enough whole grains. Unfortunately, their virtuous reputation hasn't been enough to convince us to eat more. We know that a fiber-rich diet has all kinds of benefits. Health experts and scientists agree that it reduces the risk of type-2 diabetes, heart disease, and stroke. It's high in antioxidants and lowers cholesterol. It diminishes the possibility for obesity and promotes better weight maintenance. And when it comes to nutrition, whole grains surpass their refined equivalent in every category. They also taste better.

That's the Way the Cookie Crumbles

Once you're familiar with the attributes of these grains, you'll be able to make changes to your regular recipes. Besides understanding differences in flavor, it's important to know how much gluten they contain. Gluten is the protein responsible for the formation of structure, which allows bread and baked goods to trap and hold air, causing them to rise. Too much gluten can cause undesirable chewiness; too little decreases structural integrity, meaning your cookie will crumble.

PETER MCCARTHY

EVOO | *Cambridge, Massachusetts*

Finding the right balance of fruit and crunch can be tricky when making a crisp, an otherwise simple but deeply satisfying dessert. This recipe gets it exactly right. A thick coating of buttery almond streusel tops the blueberries for the first half hour in the oven, then gets "refreshed" with another sprinkling that remains suspended, ensuring that each bite of blueberries has its own chunk of crunchy streusel. Tangy sour cream ice cream ties it all together in a decadent fashion. SERVES 10 TO 12

Blueberry Crisp with Almond-Oat Streusel and Sour Cream Ice Cream

FOR THE TOPPING

½ cup granulated sugar

½ cup light brown sugar

1 cup (2 sticks) unsalted butter, diced into
   ½-inch cubes, at room temperature

1 teaspoon pure vanilla extract

1 teaspoon ground cinnamon

½ teaspoon kosher salt

2 cups unbleached all-purpose flour

¾ cup old-fashioned rolled oats

1 cup toasted slivered almonds

FOR THE FILLING

Unsalted butter, for the pan

8 cups blueberries, fresh or frozen

1¼ cups granulated sugar

3 tablespoons brandy

3 tablespoons freshly squeezed lemon juice

2 teaspoons finely chopped lemon zest

½ teaspoon kosher salt

3 tablespoons cornstarch

Sour Cream Ice Cream (recipe on page 94),
   for serving

To make the topping, combine the granulated and brown sugars, butter, vanilla, cinnamon, and salt in the bowl of a stand mixer fitted with the paddle attachment. Mix on medium-low speed until smooth and creamy, about 3 minutes. Add the remaining ingredients and mix until just combined. Chill. The topping can be made up to 2 days in advance and kept in the refrigerator.

Heat the oven to 350°F and butter a 9x13x2-inch baking pan. In a large nonreactive bowl, toss the blueberries with the sugar, brandy, lemon juice, lemon zest, salt, and cornstarch. Pour into the prepared pan and crumble 4 cups of topping evenly over the berries. Bake for 25 minutes, then sprinkle with another 3 cups of topping and bake for 20 more minutes, or until the topping is golden brown and the filling is bubbling around the edges.

For individual portions, fill 10 to 12 lightly buttered 6-ounce ramekins or ovenproof bowls with the filling. Crumble ½ cup topping over the berries in each dish. Bake for 20 minutes, then sprinkle another 3 tablespoons of topping on each bowl and bake for 20 more minutes, or until the topping is golden brown and the filling is bubbling around the edges.

Serve warm with sour cream ice cream.

>>>

Sour Cream Ice Cream

MAKES 1 QUART

1 cup buttermilk

1 cup heavy cream

4 large egg yolks

¾ cup granulated sugar

¾ teaspoon kosher salt

1¼ cups sour cream

½ teaspoon pure vanilla extract

1½ tablespoons vodka

Scald the buttermilk and cream over medium heat in a nonreactive saucepan. Whisk together the egg yolks, sugar, and salt in a medium bowl until pale and smooth.

Slowly pour the scalded buttermilk mixture into the egg yolks, whisking constantly, and then add the warmed egg mixture back into the saucepan. Cook over medium-high heat, stirring constantly with a wooden spoon or heatproof spatula and scraping the bottom as you stir, until the mixture reaches 175°F and coats the spoon or spatula. Remove from the heat.

Add the sour cream, vanilla, and vodka, whisking to incorporate. Pour the custard through a fine-mesh sieve into a clean medium-sized bowl, cool in an ice bath, cover with plastic wrap and chill overnight.

Freeze the mixture in an ice cream maker according to the manufacturer's instructions.

Preserving Summer

One of the best things about summer—an embarrassment of riches, between the abundance and variety at the market and what might be growing in your backyard—can also become one of the most stressful. But preserving the season's bounty doesn't have to be time-consuming, equipment-intensive, or overly involved. It's not just about putting things in jars, but also drying, freezing, smoking, fermenting, and keeping ingredients that have a long shelf life, like squashes, potatoes, onions, and apples, in cold storage. If preserving seems like a project best left to those of previous generations, try pickling. Pickle peppers in vinegar or crab apples in vinegar and brown sugar (see Sweet-Sour Pickled Wild Crab Apples on page 57). Cauliflower, carrots, asparagus, pears, and cherries also make great pickles. Relishes and chutneys (see Four-Season Chutney on page 55) are prepared by pickling, too.

By taking some steps early in the season, like stocking up on sugar, vinegar, canning jars, and freezer bags, and by clearing space in your cupboards and freezer, extending the seasons becomes a matter of blanching some extra beans while preparing dinner to stash in the freezer, or drying a bumper crop of Roma tomatoes overnight in a low oven. Get in the habit of doubling recipes and soon you'll find yourself with enough tastes of summer to get you through to the next.

PETER HOFFMAN

Back Forty | *New York, New York*

Poached fruits are easy to prepare and are particularly good when served at the end of a large or elaborate meal. When combined, quinces and prunes offer an intriguing set of flavors that can be served with homemade or premium-quality vanilla ice cream or a dollop of crème fraîche. Reserve any extra poaching liquid for the next day's pancakes, waffles, or French toast. SERVES 6 TO 8

Poached Quinces and Armagnac-Soaked Prunes

1 cup granulated sugar

1 cup white wine, such as Riesling or Gewurztraminer

3 ripe quinces, about 1½ pounds

1 cup Armagnac

8 ounces dried prunes, with pits

Vanilla ice cream or lightly whipped crème fraîche

Put 1 cup of cold water in a large nonreactive saucepan with the sugar and white wine. Gently rub the quinces with your thumbs or a clean towel to remove the downy fuzz. Wash the fruit and use a sharp paring knife or a good vegetable peeler to remove the skin. Cut the quinces in half and remove the gnarly core with a melon baller. Be certain not to leave anything tough or fibrous behind. Cut the halves into quarters or thick wedges if they are very large.

Place the quartered quinces in the pot with the water, sugar, and wine and poach on very low heat for up to 2 hours. Do not allow the syrup to boil; quinces are delicate and will break down if there is too much activity in the pot. Although they may be ready after an hour, continue to simmer the quinces until they are deeply rosy and nearly translucent. Cool in the poaching liquid.

Pour the Armagnac over the prunes and add enough of the quince poaching liquid to cover the prunes. Cover with plastic wrap and leave overnight in the refrigerator.

The following day, combine the quinces and prunes. Spoon several prunes and quince wedges, along with some of the syrup, in each bowl. Top with a small scoop of ice cream or crème fraîche.

JENNIFER MCCOY

Cissé Trading Co. | *New York, New York*

Chestnut flour, which adds unique sweetness to these waffles, is available in specialty stores and is worth tracking down. A traditional substitute for wheat flour in Italy during the Middle Ages, chestnut flour is more like grain flours than nut flours. For a different but equally intriguing flavor, use ½ cup buckwheat flour in place of the chestnut flour and increase the amount of all-purpose flour to 1½ cups. SERVES 4 TO 6

Chestnut Waffles with Roasted Apples and Cream

FOR THE WAFFLES

2 tablespoons unsalted butter

1¼ cups unbleached all-purpose flour

¾ cup chestnut flour

1 tablespoon baking powder

½ teaspoon kosher salt

¼ cup light brown sugar

1¾ cups whole milk

2 large eggs, separated

½ teaspoon pure vanilla extract

FOR THE ROASTED APPLES

1 tablespoon unsalted butter, soft

3 medium apples, preferably Honeycrisp

2 tablespoons chestnut honey

Kosher salt

1 cup heavy cream, whipped to soft peaks (optional)

Maple syrup, for serving (optional)

MAKE THE WAFFLE BATTER

In a small saucepan, cook the butter over medium heat, stirring constantly to prevent it from burning. When it is deep golden brown, pour the butter and browned sediment into a bowl and let stand until just cooled.

In a large bowl, stir together the all-purpose and chestnut flours, baking powder, salt, and sugar until well combined. In another bowl, whisk together the milk, egg yolks, vanilla extract, and brown butter. Add the liquid ingredients to the dry ingredients and whisk smooth. Set the batter aside while you roast the apples.

MAKE THE APPLES

Position a rack in the center of the oven and heat to 450°F. Rub a baking sheet with the softened butter.

Peel, core, and quarter the apples, slicing each quarter into 2 or 3 wedges. Gently toss the apples with honey and a pinch of salt until evenly coated. Spread the wedges in a single layer on the baking sheet and roast until the edges begin to brown and the apples have softened, 15 to 20 minutes. Immediately transfer the apples to a small bowl to cool slightly.

MAKE THE WAFFLES

Heat a waffle iron. Whip the egg whites on high speed in the bowl of a stand mixer fitted with the whisk attachment for 2 to 3 minutes, or until thick, glossy, and quadrupled in volume. Gently fold the egg whites into the waffle batter.

Lightly coat the waffle iron with nonstick spray and cook the waffles according to the manufacturer's instructions. (For one 7-inch waffle, use ¾ to 1 cup of batter and cook until hardly any steam escapes from the waffle iron, 6 to 8 minutes.) Apply nonstick spray between waffles as needed.

TO SERVE

Serve the waffles warm, topped with roasted apples, whipped cream, and maple syrup, if desired.

I Wait All Year For...

JIMMY SCHMIDT

Morgan's in the Desert

Celery root is one of my favorites for its rich minerally flavor, nutritional profile, and versatility. I like to make a mock "risotto" from celery root by cutting the raw root into rice-shaped pieces, like grains, and cooking them for only 60 seconds to give them an "al dente" texture. I combine them with a silky celery root purée for the creamy texture. It looks and eats like rice-based risotto, but it delivers an amazing flavor and nutritional profile.

DEBORAH SCARBOROUGH

Black Cat Bistro

All varieties of stone fruit. We make stone fruit mustard, upside-down cakes, and blue cheese waffles with sautéed stone fruit. Anything that's left over or too ripe goes in the freezer. It's hard to keep up! We also make a stone fruit habanero jelly to serve with our cheese plate the rest of the year.

PAUL FEHRIBACH

Big Jones Café

I really look forward to morel mushrooms. Nothing reminds me of my youth, growing up in the forested hills of southern Indiana, quite like the earthy, sweet forest-floor smell of fresh mushrooms. Not only do they herald the arrival of spring, but they also take me home to the woods through the memory of smell every time.

JOSE DUARTE

Taranta

Heirloom tomatoes during the summer. They have incredible flavor. There's no need for anything but some salt and a little bit of extra-virgin olive oil. In season, tomatoes are just delicious.

WAYNE JOHNSON

Ray's Boathouse

It's all about the corn! I wait and wait for that sweet corn to come to its peak freshness. I like to grill it, shuck the kernels off, make stock out of the cob, and turn everything into sweet corn risotto.

ROB CORLISS

EAT

The raspberries in my home garden. When the raspberries start coming in, it is a fun challenge to compete with the birds (who steal them at every chance), my daughter (who picks and eats anything—everything!—that's bright red 24/7), and my wife (who loves, above all, never-refrigerated, fresh-from-the-vine raspberries). The handful I get to enjoy is pure heaven!

LENNY RUSSO

Heartland

Shell peas, asparagus, spring onions, morels, ramps, fiddlehead ferns, and spring-dug parsnips all signal the beginning of the growing season in Minnesota. Later, heirloom tomatoes, crab apples, and grapes mark the end of summer and the beginning of harvest season. And strawberries and pawpaws, which have very short seasons of about 3 weeks each.

ARIANA VITALE, KASK, AND DAVID SHENAUT, OREGON BARTENDERS GUILD

Portland, Oregon

Smooth, butterscotch notes from bourbon and a roasted barley simple syrup anchor this winter sipper. Look for barley in well-stocked tea shops and brewery supply stores. SERVES 1

Above the Grain

2 ounces bourbon, preferably Temperance
   Trader Bourbon Whiskey

½ ounce Toasted Barley Syrup
   (recipe below)

½ ounce fino dry sherry, preferably Lustau
   Puerto Fino Dry Sherry

1 dash Angostura bitters

2-inch piece orange peel, for garnish

Measure the ingredients into a mixing glass. Stir and strain into a double old-fashioned glass with a single large ice cube. Garnish with an orange twist.

Toasted Barley Syrup

MAKES ABOUT 3 CUPS

1½ cups hulled barley

4 cups demerara sugar

Spread the barley in a single layer in a dry frying pan and toast over medium-high heat until the kernels start popping and begin to brown. Add the toasted barley to a saucepan with 2 cups of water. Bring the mixture to a boil, remove from the heat, and add the sugar. Stir until the sugar has dissolved and allow to sit for 1 hour before straining. Cool completely before using.

GREG BEST

Holeman and Finch Public House | *Atlanta, Georgia*

This gin cocktail celebrates the end of summer with the unusual and delicious addition of juice from fresh cherry tomatoes. **SERVES 1**

Crush and Kiss

1 ounce gin, preferably Corsair Kentucky Gin

½ ounce St. Germain elderflower liqueur

½ ounce fresh squeezed lemon juice

Juice from 1 cherry tomato

½ ounce Kudzu honey syrup

1 sprig fresh spearmint, for garnish

In a shaker filled with ice, combine all of the ingredients and shake vigorously until well combined and chilled. Double strain into a cold cocktail glass with a stem. Garnish with a small sprig of spearmint.

Seasonal Sips

The best bartenders I know approach the composition of the cocktail like a chef conceives of a dish—by looking at the bones of a classic recipe or technique; considering the time of year, occasion, or food; and then tapping into his/her mind and the market to come up with the seasonal, regional, or gastronomic ingredients that will distinguish the drink. This approach also allows for concocting *à la minute* cocktails, when a bar chef is armed with both the proficiency and the prep: a well-curated collection of ingredients on hand for mixing customized cocktails to satisfy the taste of any given guest. A little imagination and confidence, as well as the mastery of the proper preparation (and balance!) of a dozen classic cocktails are all that's required, along with a bit of testing and tasting.

A new crop of artisan distilleries mean it's easy to stock your bar with an array of the cleaner, greener versions of modern and traditionally crafted spirits, liqueurs, and bitters. Paired with a pantry filled with a few top-notch ingredients, you have the foundation for creating a cocktail inspired by a perfectly ripe piece of fruit, a seasonal vegetable or herb, or a sauce, syrup, or vinegar. After all, a cocktail should be a manifestation of the season or reason: something refreshing for an afternoon picnic, a classic pre-feast aperitif, a festive sparkler for a fireside cocktail party, or a citrusy punch to celebrate the end of winter.

But why not go one step further. Use produce, spices, and botanicals to create house-infused spirits, seasonal simple syrups, sodas, and homemade bitters. Shrubs (also called "cellos," as in limoncello) are a traditional method for preserving fruit for year-round enjoyment. Try one with soda for a refreshing, alcohol-free treat or stirred into a cocktail to create the perfect balance. Vinegar-enhanced and alcohol-free, shrubs can be made with almost any combination of berry or stone fruit and aromatic: peach and ginger, cherry and cinnamon, loquat and mint, or strawberry and balsamic vinegar (see page 106).

ROBIN SCHEMPP *specializes in concept, product, and menu development for food and beverage clients. She speaks and writes about artisan cocktail development, among other topics, and is committed to regional, seasonal, and sustainable food and drink.*

Local or Organic?

The debate about local and organic—and which is better—continues to be a lively one, perhaps because there are no easy answers. When chefs find themselves in situations where they must choose one over the other, here are some of the issues they consider.

STEVE JOHNSON
Rendezvous in Central Square,
Cambridge, Massachusetts

Knowing your growers gives you the best chance to make an informed decision. And generally, if your growers are local, you're going to have a better opportunity to really "know" them. Ask questions about their growing practices; make physical visits to farms for firsthand information. Look at the plants in the fields, the setting, the equipment, their systems, compost, manure piles, water sources, and the aromas. There's nothing like seeing with your own eyes and smelling with your own nose. What matters is the grower's intent, the approach to stewardship, growing and handling practices, and quality of product. I choose local wherever and whenever I can if it contributes to moving the whole system in a positive direction.

RICHARD MCCARTHY
Market Umbrella, New Orleans, Louisiana

My preference is organic and local. Certification labels like organic are useful when the farmer isn't there (at a supermarket, for example). At farmer's markets, you have the opportunity to look the farmer in the eye, ask the tough questions, and choose to spend or not. Rigid concepts like organic and sustainable are put into context with economic and ecological realities. I've watched farmers evolve, as consumers grow more vocal and knowledgeable about their quest for sustainable products. So too have consumers grown in their understanding of rural needs, farm realities, and the like. Everyone learns.

DEREK WAGNER
Nick's On Broadway, Providence, Rhode Island

I always try to source locally first. I look to support someone in my local community, if it's at all possible. My team and I work tirelessly at finding farmers and producers in our area who we can work with and who will work, grow, and learn with us.

Given the costs involved with becoming certified organic, many small farmers/producers can't afford the certification process. But there are plenty out there who are doing the right things, using organic/sustainable methods. And there are others who are trying to do the right things by educating themselves and their customers and working toward being able to afford better equipment and materials to grow and harvest more. I believe they will never be able to do this if we don't support them financially and logistically. Local farmlands cannot be reclaimed, and farming cannot become a way to earn a living—or a desirable lifestyle—without our support.

DEBORAH MADISON
Santa Fe, New Mexico

I've always been on the "local" side of the fence, but I want organic, too, so really I think local-organic is best. Organically grown foods are very important to me, but I am always glad that my farmer's market isn't organic only. That leaves the door open for farmers to change their practices, and I've seen that happen. A conventional farmer looks around and sees that shoppers want organic, and bit by bit he or she drops the chemicals. I think that's great.

One thing I've noticed is that people mostly talk about the advantages of eating organically grown foods in terms of themselves and their health. But it's not just about us; it's also about how practices benefit soil, workers, and wildlife. It's an issue for other forms of life as well as our own.

ALAN WALTER

International House Hotel | New Orleans, Louisiana

Limoncino is limoncello with the addition of grappa. It can be made at home, but you'll want to plan ahead since it requires at least 2 months to extract. SERVES 1

Jinjin

1½ ounces Aperol

¾ ounce Limoncino (homemade—recipe below—or store-bought)

½ ounce cognac

Dash of bitters

¾ ounce Satsuma or similar mandarin orange juice

¾ ounce cucumber juice

2 teaspoons freshly squeezed Meyer lemon juice

2-inch piece lemon peel

1 sprig fresh dill

1 to 1½ ounces Belgian white beer, recarbonated in soda siphon if possible

In a shaker filled with ice, combine all the ingredients except the beer and shake vigorously until well chilled. Strain over new ice into a tall glass, like a hurricane or pilsner glass. Stir in the beer, leaving a layer of foam on top.

Limoncino

100-proof vodka

100-proof rum

Neutral (unflavored) eau du vie

Grappa

Zest from tangerines, navel oranges, grapefruit, kumquats, and Meyer lemons

Granulated sugar

Make a mixture of clear spirits that includes in descending proportions: vodka and rum (70 percent of the total), eau du vie (20 percent of total), and grappa (10 percent).

Add the zest from four pieces of fruit for every 6 ounces of alcohol. The zest should make up 10 percent to 15 percent of the volume when the spirits are added.

Pour the spirits and zest into a sealable glass container and store away from sunlight, agitating the contents every 4 days or so. Strain after 2 to 3 months and add sugar sparingly (about 1 cup sugar per 3 to 4 cups alcohol). Serve neat, chilled, as an after-dinner libation.

ADAM SEGER

Nacional 27 | Chicago, Illinois

Made with botanicals including hibiscus, fresh ginger, cardamom, and kaffir lime, Hum is the hand-crafted spirit behind this cocktail's striking crimson color and unique flavor. SERVES 1

Cool as a Cucumber

1 cucumber, sliced lengthwise into thin
   strips
1½ ounces Honey-Lavender Syrup
   (recipe below)
1½ ounces Hum botanical rum
Sparkling water
1 sprig fresh basil

Wrap the inside of a tall glass with a cucumber strip and fill with ice. Add the honey-lavender syrup and rum, and top with sparkling water. Place a basil sprig in the palm of your hand and slap it to release its fragrant oils. Add to the glass and serve.

Honey-Lavender Syrup

MAKES 1 CUP
1 cup honey
2 tablespoons water
3 long sprigs fresh lavender,
   or ½ ounce dried

Gently heat the honey with the water and lavender until it is the consistency of simple syrup. Cool and strain out the lavender. Refrigerate for up to 2 weeks.

ROBIN SCHEMPP

Waterbury, Vermont

A "shrub" is an acidulated beverage made with fruit, sugar, and vinegar. This combination preparation was traditionally used to preserve fruit for year-round enjoyment. Today, shrubs are a popular addition to cocktails and to sparkling water for refreshing non-alcoholic tonics.

MAKES 1 SCANT QUART

Strawberry Balsamic Shrub

3½ cups fresh strawberries, cleaned and stemmed

2½ cups raw sugar, preferably organic

1 cup white balsamic vinegar

1 cup aged balsamic vinegar

6 cracked allspice berries

12 cracked black peppercorns

Combine the strawberries and sugar in a wide-mouth glass jar. Use a muddler or wooden spoon to apply enough gentle—yet firm—pressure to break up the fruit. Cover the jar with a lid or plastic wrap and let it sit in a cool, dark place for 24 hours. Add the white and aged balsamic vinegars, allspice berries, and peppercorns. Stir until the sugar has dissolved, then cover and return to a cool, dark spot for a week or slightly longer, until the flavor is fully realized.

Press and strain the contents of the jar through cheesecloth or a fine-mesh sieve, pressing lightly to release all of the liquid from the fruit. Store in a clean container in the refrigerator.

JACKSON CANNON

The Hawthorne | *Boston, Massachusetts*

Bully Boy is Boston's first craft distillery. Their signature white rum, which is made with blackstrap molasses, has a smooth finish that combines beautifully with the warm, caramely flavors of Cardamaro and maple syrup. **SERVES 1**

Newton Old-Fashioned

½ ounce Cardamaro Amaro

¼ ounce Grade A maple syrup

Two dashes bitters, preferably Fee Bros.
  Barrel-Aged Bitters

Pinch of salt

2 ounces white rum, preferably Bully Boy
  Distillers White Rum

2-inch piece lemon peel

Combine the Cardamaro, maple syrup, bitters, and salt in a mixing glass and stir gently to combine. Add the white rum and ice and stir again. Strain into a double old-fashioned glass with a large handful of chopped ice. Twist a lemon peel over the drink, then discard the used peel.

"Given the growing interest in spirits produced using artisan methods, local grains, and carefully sourced ingredients, we use organic hard red wheat from Aurora Mills Farm in Linneus, Maine, for our un-aged whisky. The herbal flavors of the grain shine through in the absence of the barrel char, which overwhelms subtle flavor components in a traditional aged whisky."

WILL WILLIS

Bully Boy Distillers, Boston, Massachusetts

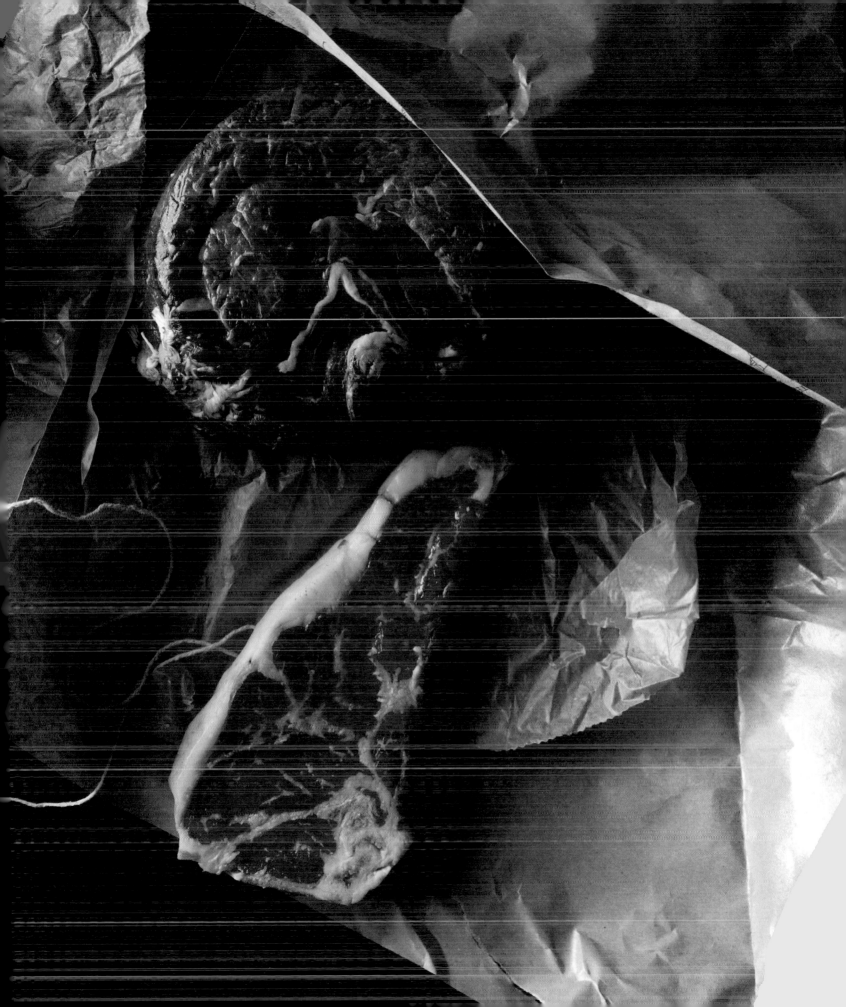

Meat and Poultry

"Choosing to eat animals raised on pasture and forage is better for the health of the planet and its inhabitants."

The sheer pleasure that comes from eating pastured meats isn't just in their honest and lively flavors. It's in knowing the story of how and where the animals were raised, what they ate, and who cared for them. It's in the realization that choosing to eat meat selectively represents a conscious contribution to the continued viability of local, sustainable farms and ranches. And for those old enough to remember, it's in the intense flavor memories summoned by the distinctive and complex flavors of grass-fed meat, of childhood meals and the way meat used to taste. Stephen Stryjewsjki, chef/co-owner of Cochon in New Orleans, Louisiana, recalls, "I distinctly remember the flavor of the pastured beef we ate when I was a kid. It's the flavor I've been pursuing throughout my culinary career."

The Changing Face of Meat Production

During the last decade, we've witnessed a gradual return to the cycle of growing, harvesting, and eating in sync with the seasons. What began as a slight shift in our interest in what we eat and how it gets to our tables has become a full-fledged movement that is undeniably shaping the future of food in this country—the way it's produced, marketed, purchased, and prepared. Nowhere is this more evident than in the growing supply of healthy, fairly priced meat available to consumers in every corner of the country. The fact that there are few places Americans can't find a small farmer or rancher raising cows, hogs, or chickens within a 100-mile radius is a hopeful sign that we're moving in the right direction, reviving what was commonplace as recently as three generations ago: local, sustainable supplies of food. We're again seeing excellence and ethics in meat production, where the quality of an animal's life has direct impact on its eating quality. Farmer's markets, butcher shops, local co-ops, and meat buying clubs can also tell you more about how the meat you're buying was produced.

With the availability of cheap commodity meat, there has been a cultural shift from thinking of meat as celebratory (Sunday roasts, Easter lamb, and Thanksgiving turkeys) to consuming it daily. This has proven to be an unsustainable strategy for our health and that of the environment, and it shows tacit approval for the inhumane treatment of animals that are raised in confined animal feeding operations (CAFOs) in order to meet our growing appetite for meat. The instinctive reaction of a conscientious eater might be to embrace a plant-based diet as the only answer. But the spectrum of sustainability offers options for every eater. The solution likely lies somewhere in the middle—eat a modest amount of good meat instead of eliminating it completely, and never stop asking if there's a better choice.

"Meat and dairy production have come under huge criticism in recent years, and rightly so," says Animal Welfare Approved Program Director Andrew Gunther. "But we mustn't tar all meat with the same brush. Indeed, pasture-raised livestock farming can offer real solutions to the health, welfare, and environmental issues we all care about. So by all means, let's reduce our intake of unsustainable, low-welfare, intensively reared meat. But let's make sure that the meat we do eat is always high-welfare, pasture-raised meat. For all our sakes."

Respecting the Animal, Appreciating the Flavor

Growing numbers of cooks and eaters are developing a deeper appreciation for plant-based foods while demanding a more humane approach to the rearing and processing of animals at the same time. We've come a long way from defining dinner as "meat and two veg," with the protein front and center, but we probably won't be taking meat off our plates entirely any time soon. And why should we? Meat is delicious, protein is essential to a balanced diet, and options for savoring high-quality meat in moderation abound. Instead, we can dramatically reduce the impact of what's on our plates by choosing to eat meat thoughtfully and respectfully. When we buy something, we support the system that produces it. Boycotting industrially raised animals may represent a vote against what has become an unhealthy, unsustainable system, but purchasing meat from a responsible producer who practices good animal husbandry is like casting a positive vote. The best way to change the system is to participate in it.

Rancher, environmental lawyer, and animal welfare activist Nicolette Hahn Niman explains, "When people learn about factory farms, they often—at least temporarily—cut back meat consumption. This is understandable. But buying beef from grass-based farms, which produce the tastiest, safest, and most nutritious food, and where farmers and animals can live good lives, is even more important. Real farms will only replace industrial animal operations when consumers support them with their daily food choices."

Choosing to eat animals raised on pasture and forage is better for the health of the planet and its inhabitants. And since the most environmentally sustainable animal farming is based on the rhythms of the seasons, the next logical step is to recognize certain meats as seasonal. Like all forms of vegetation, grass has a cycle of growth, reproduction, abundance, and retreat. Ruminants (cows, sheep, goats, bison, and game) in some regions graze most of the year on grass and forage. Others (chickens and pigs) get fewer of their nutrients from plants, but all pastured animals are at their peak when what they feed on is at its peak. In temperate areas of the country where animals can graze and root most of the year, the season is much longer. We stock our freezers with berries and line our pantries with jars of pickles and pears, attempting to set aside some of the bounty when it is most delicious. Why not do the same with pastured meat?

Today's sophisticated cooks and eaters agree that a ripe tomato is worth the wait, yet there's a disconnect when applying the same concept of seasonality to meat, an item we have come to expect will be available and consistent year-round. Eating sustainably is about the natural ebb and flow of supply and its relationship to the seasons. In the same way that we have adjusted our expectations, our palates, and our menus to the seasonality of vegetables and fruit, we can think about eating meat differently. Good meat is precious, and the process of finding and preparing it is one to be savored. Just as nothing says fall like a crisp apple, and sweet corn in August is a singular joy, the arrival of meat from pasture-raised animals when it is most plentiful should be anticipated with excitement, consumed with pleasure, and filed away as flavor memories to tide us over until the next season.

Good meat is precious, and the process of finding and preparing it is one to be savored.

GREG PERRAULT

June | Portland, Oregon

Nettles are a superfood masquerading as a belligerent weed. Among the first edible greens to sprout from the frozen ground in late February or early March, nettles are abundant in areas with significant annual rainfall. They're commonly found along roadsides, in vacant lots, and at farmer's markets, offering equal opportunity for urban foragers as well as suburban home cooks to benefit from their astonishing nutritional attributes and genuine palatability. The nettle's popularity as a found food is on the rise. SERVES 6

Lamb and Stinging Nettle Ravioli

3 large eggs, divided

2 egg yolks

2 cups 00 flour or unbleached
   all-purpose flour

½ teaspoon kosher salt; more for seasoning

3 cups raw young stinging nettle tops,
   divided

8 ounces ground lamb, preferably pastured

1 tablespoon mascarpone

¼ cup crumbled feta cheese

1 teaspoon toasted crushed coriander seed

Freshly ground black pepper

Semolina, for dusting

2 cups light caramel malt

8 tablespoons (1 stick) unsalted butter

Fresh nettles

Shaved Parmesan, for serving

Make the pasta dough by whisking 2 eggs and the egg yolks together. Sift the flour and salt onto a clean, dry work surface, preferably wood, and make a well in the center.

Add the eggs and yolks and, using a fork or your fingers, slowly incorporate the flour into the eggs. When the mixture begins to clump, add the water, 1 tablespoon at a time, until the mixture comes together in a ball. The dough should be firm and not sticky. Knead the dough for 8 to 10 minutes, or until smooth. Wrap tightly in plastic wrap and let rest in the refrigerator for 2 hours or overnight before rolling.

Make the filling while the dough is resting. Bring a pot of salted water to a boil over medium-high heat. Using tongs or gloves, add 1 cup of nettle tops to the water for 1 to 2 minutes. Drain immediately and place the greens in a bowl of ice water to stop the cooking. Cool, strain, and squeeze dry using a clean towel to remove as much moisture as possible. Coarsely chop the nettles to make about ¼ cup.

Mix the lamb, mascarpone, feta, blanched nettles, and coriander together and season with salt and black pepper. The filling can be made as much as a day ahead of assembling the raviolis.

Divide the dough into 4 equal pieces. Lightly dust a work surface with semolina and flatten the pieces into rectangles with your hands before rolling them, one at a time, through a pasta machine fixed at the widest setting. Continue feeding the dough through the rollers, narrowing the setting each time, until you have four 1⁄16-inch-thick strips (setting number 6 on a pasta machine) that measure approximately 4 inches wide by 16 inches long.

>>>

Place the pasta strips on a work surface lightly dusted with semolina. Using a teaspoon, place a spoonful of filling about 2 inches from the left edge of one strip. Be sure there is enough space to allow you to close and completely seal each dollop of filling. Place the next spoonful 2 inches to the right of the first and continue until the strip has about 8 dollops of filling. Prepare a second strip of pasta in the same way.

Whisk together the remaining egg and 2 tablespoons of water to make an egg wash. Using a pastry brush, lightly brush the egg wash on the outer edge and in between each mound of filling. This is the glue that will seal the raviolis. Completely brush a plain sheet of pasta with egg wash and place it, egg wash side down, over the filled pasta strip, stretching it over the filling. Working from the center of the strip out, press gently around each mound of filling, making sure there is no air trapped inside. Press the edges down for a tight seal. Repeat with the second filled pasta strip.

Have a platter or pan lightly dusted with semolina ready. Using a rolling cutter or a knife, cut the filled strips into individual raviolis, leaving a 1-inch margin of pasta around each one. If desired, trim the corners of the raviolis for a more uniform look. Arrange the raviolis in a single layer, dust with a bit more semolina, and refrigerate until ready to cook.

Make the wheat broth by steeping the malt in 2 quarts of water at 150°F for about 3 hours. After 3 hours, strain the water and malt through a fine-mesh sieve into a large nonreactive saucepan. Bring the liquid to a gentle simmer over medium heat and continue to cook and reduce until the flavor is rich and complex to your liking, about 45 minutes.

When ready to cook, bring a large pot of salted water to a boil over high heat. Gently brush the semolina off the raviolis and drop them in the rapidly boiling water. Cook for 4 to 6 minutes, or until they're tender but firm. Begin timing after the raviolis float to the surface.

Gently remove the raviolis with a spider or large slotted spoon to a colander (save some of the pasta cooking water for finishing). Add ½ cup pasta cooking water and 2 tablespoons butter to a wide shallow pan over medium heat. When the butter has melted, add the raviolis, warm through, and allow the sauce to thicken slightly.

To serve, bring about ⅓ cup of wheat broth per person to a boil. Add 1 tablespoon of butter for every ⅓ cup of broth and lightly season with salt and pepper. Transfer the raviolis to the wheat broth and add the remaining nettles. Cook for another minute before dividing among serving bowls. Sprinkle shaved Parmesan on top and serve.

"Years after flipping off my mountain bike into a tangle of itchy wild stinging nettles, now I tame them in preparations ranging from pastas and soups to sauces and sautés."

SETH CASWELL
emmer & rye, Seattle, Washington

HELENE KENNAN

Bon Appétit Management Company | *Mountain View, California*

Clean, vibrant Asian flavors paired with ground pork offer a twist on the classic mini hamburger. Topped with a crispy cucumber salad full of the traditional trio of Thai herbs—cilantro, basil, and mint—these sliders are especially good grilled. MAKES 12 SLIDERS; SERVES 4 TO 6

Thai Pork Sliders with Pickled Cucumbers

1 pound ground pork

1 clove garlic, finely minced

1 tablespoon finely minced fresh ginger

1 tablespoon sesame oil

½ teaspoon ground cinnamon

½ teaspoon crushed red pepper flakes

2 teaspoons soy sauce

¼ teaspoon white pepper

¼ cup seasoned rice vinegar

¼ cup honey (orange blossom works well with these flavors)

2 tablespoons freshly squeezed orange juice

2 cucumbers, peeled, seeded, and thinly sliced

½ bunch fresh cilantro, coarsely chopped

4 fresh basil leaves, coarsely chopped

8 fresh mint leaves, coarsely chopped

1 tablespoon vegetable oil

Sriracha (optional)

½ cup roasted salted peanuts, coarsely chopped (optional)

12 small rolls, split crosswise

Combine the pork with the garlic, ginger, sesame oil, cinnamon, red pepper flakes, soy sauce, and white pepper. Form twelve 2-inch patties and set aside.

Whisk the rice vinegar with the honey and orange juice until the honey has dissolved. Add the cucumbers, cilantro, basil, and mint, and toss to combine; set aside.

Lightly coat a griddle or large cast-iron pan with oil and warm over medium-high heat. Add the pork patties to the pan when hot, being careful not to crowd them (cook them in batches if needed). Cook for about 3 minutes on each side, or until firm to the touch.

Season the pickled cucumbers to taste with Sriracha chile sauce and chopped peanuts, if desired. Put one burger on each roll, top with pickled cucumbers, and serve the sliders.

MICHAEL LEVITON

Lumière | *Newton, Massachusetts*

A pâté de campagne, or country terrine, is a rustic preparation distinguished from smooth, mousselike pâtés made with chicken livers, for example, by the coarse grind of the meat and relatively small amount of liver. The panade, which is made with flour rather than bread, helps to enrich and bind the pâté.

Serve slices of terrine with seasonal fruit mostarda, Dijon or coarse mustard, cornichons, a parsley-shallot salad, and sourdough toasts. **MAKES ONE 3½-POUND TERRINE**

Country Pork Terrine

1¼ pounds lean boneless pork shoulder, cut into 1-inch cubes

1 pound pork fat back, diced

1 tablespoon unsalted butter

1 large white onion, finely diced (about ⅔ cup)

1 large clove garlic, finely minced

11 ounces pork liver (preferred) or chicken liver, cut into large pieces

2 tablespoons plus 1 teaspoon sea salt

½ teaspoon pink curing salt (instacure #1)

¾ teaspoon ground white pepper

¾ teaspoon Pâté Spice (recipe on page 118)

¼ cup plus 2 teaspoons heavy cream

2 small eggs

3 tablespoons unbleached all-purpose flour

4 tablespoons bourbon

⅓ cup chopped fresh flat-leaf parsley

1 teaspoon fresh thyme leaves

⅔ cup Bourbon-Soaked Fruit (recipe on page 118), drained and quartered

¼ cup pork stock (or chicken stock or cold water)

Freeze or thoroughly chill all grinder equipment and three medium bowls and chill the pork and fat; a few hours in the refrigerator for the equipment and pork should be sufficient. Assemble the grinder.

Working quickly and in small batches, grind the pork and the pork fat separately through the coarse die (about ½ inch diameter); place 1 pound of the pork into one of the bowls, ¼ pound pork into another bowl, and the pork fat into the remaining bowl. You can also have the butcher grind the pork and the fat for you and wrap them separately. Return the bowls to the freezer until well chilled.

Melt the butter in a small sauté pan and cook the onions with the garlic until slightly softened. Put the mixture in a bowl and refrigerate until completely cool.

Grind the ¼ pound coarsely ground pork, the coarsely ground pork fat, liver, sea salt, curing salt, white pepper, and pâté spice through the medium die (about ¼ inch diameter) into the chilled bowl of a stand mixer. Place in the freezer while you prepare the panade.

Combine the cream, eggs, flour, and bourbon in a small bowl and whisk until smooth (this is called the panade). Add it to the meat mixture in the mixing bowl and then add the pound of coarsely ground pork. Add the onion and garlic mixture, the parsley, thyme, and bourbon-soaked fruit and, using the paddle attachment, mix on low speed. With the machine running, drizzle in the pork stock on low speed and mix for 30 to 60 seconds, until sticky to the touch.

Lightly moisten a 1½-quart terrine mold (moistening it will help the plastic to adhere), then line with plastic wrap, leaving enough overhang on the long sides to fold over the top once it's filled. Fill the mold with the terrine mixture, packing it down to remove air pockets. Fold the plastic from each side over the top and cover with the lid. Refrigerate overnight.

>>>

The next day, remove the terrine from the refrigerator and let sit at room temperature for 1 hour. Heat the oven to 300°F. Put the mold in a roasting pan with high sides and add enough very hot tap water to come halfway up the sides of the mold. Bake for about 1 hour, or until the interior of the terrine reaches an internal temperature of 145°F (use an instant-read thermometer to check).

Remove the roasting pan from the oven and the mold from the water bath; let the terrine cool to room temperature, then refrigerate overnight.

To remove the terrine from the mold, use the plastic wrap to gently coax it out of the mold by pulling on it from both ends. The terrine will be quite sturdy when it is completely cold, so don't hesitate to be a bit aggressive if necessary. Remove the plastic wrap from the terrine, then slice and serve.

Pâté Spice

MAKES 1½ TABLESPOONS

½ teaspoon ground cloves

½ teaspoon ground nutmeg

½ teaspoon ground ginger

½ teaspoon ground coriander

1 teaspoon ground cinnamon

1½ teaspoons white pepper

Combine the ingredients and mix well. Store in a cool, dry place in an airtight container. The spice will keep for 6 months.

Bourbon-Soaked Fruit

MAKES 1¾ CUPS

1 cup bourbon, or enough to cover the fruit

1 cup prunes or dried figs, or a combination

Put the bourbon in a small saucepan and heat to 180°F. Put the fruit in a medium bowl. Pour the bourbon over the fruit and let sit until tender but not mushy, about 15 minutes. Store leftover fruit in the refrigerator for the next terrine or spoon over ice cream. It will keep indefinitely.

Choosing Pastured Pork

Over 90 percent of the pork produced in the United States comes from enormous, total-confinement operations where quality is not defined by flavor but by high yields, accelerated growth, and leanness. Unlike other conventionally raised meats, pork produced on an industrial scale has less fat. And since fat is flavor, and feedlot hogs are bred to be 50 percent leaner than they once were, their meat is bland.

Chefs in search of humanely raised, flavorful, well-marbled pork have been looking to small, traditional farms that have perpetuated older (heritage) breeds to supply their restaurants. The American Livestock Breeds Conservancy explains that pigs fit into small-scale farming operations more easily than cows or sheep, so small diversified farms are more likely to have these older breeds.

Berkshire was one of the first breeds to be rescued from obscurity by chefs, but it and other rare breeds are now widely available to consumers. Seek out regional heritage hogs including Red Wattle and Tamworth, also known as "bacon pigs." Ossabaw pigs thrive in woodland settings and make good cured ham, and Large White and Large Black are hardy hogs thought to have descended from Chinese breeds.

Pigs have complex needs and behavioral instincts, yet they are produced on a larger industrial level than any other mammal because of high demand. Pigs raised on pasture or in deep straw bedding have a higher quality of life, are environmentally healthy, and offer deep, nuanced flavors. Significant differences in production result in astounding differences in the flavor of their meat. Because they are omnivorous and on most farms can't live on what they forage alone, many pigs are fattened with grain diets that include either corn or soy. If it is important to you, seek out pig ranchers who give their animals feed that is free of genetically modified organisms (GMOs). Grain diets can be supplemented with extras, which could mean anything from scraps destined for the compost pile to fallen fruit on an orchard floor to acorns and nuts found when rooting in the wild. The flavor of pastured pork is often influenced by this finishing diet.

Cuts of Beef

A beef cow is divided into nine large sections known as primals, which are cut into individual roasts and steaks. Understanding how a carcass is divided provides an anatomical overview of which cuts come from what section of the animal, making it easy to see why certain cuts lend themselves to specific preparations and cooking methods. It's important to remember that each animal has a limited number of cuts, so there's only so much skirt steak and tenderloin to go around.

The **chuck** (shoulder and neck), **brisket** (chest), and **shank** (lower front leg) are tough, active muscles, full of flavor. Brisket, cross rib roast, chuck roll, and under blade are cuts from the chuck that are best suited to moist cooking methods like braising and stewing. With long, slow cooking, the collagen in these cuts converts to gelatin and the meat becomes soft and succulent.

Support muscles, like the **rib, loin,** and **sirloin,** are found along the animal's back and yield tender cuts, including the rib eye, tenderloin, and top loin. Dry-heat cooking methods like grilling, roasting, and pan-frying are the best way to prepare these cuts.

The **short plate** and **flank** account for less than 10 percent of the carcass weight and are located directly under the rib and sirloin. Popular cuts like the flank steak and skirt steak, of which there are just two per animal, are found in this under midsection.

The **round** makes up about 27 percent of the carcass weight and is the source of many lean, underutilized steaks and roasts. Round roasts including the bottom round, eye of round, sirloin tip, rump roast, and bottom round roast are usually very economical. A good recipe and moist heat are the only secrets to turning these budget cuts into delicious meals.

Sustainable ranchers have to sell every part of their animals to be economically viable, including **offal,** or **variety meats.** Heart, kidney, tongue, tripe (intestines), and oxtail are all considered delicacies when properly prepared. Nonorgan meat is best when prepared with moist heat or when added to soups and stews, while organs like the heart and liver are good pan-fried and sliced.

BILL TELEPAN

Telepan | *New York, New York*

Beef cheeks are the pockets of meat from the cheeks inside a cow's head. Because cows chew a lot, their cheeks are full of muscle, making this cut of meat succulent and full of rich flavor if prepared properly. You can special-order beef cheeks from most butchers, or buy them directly from a beef producer at your local farmer's market.

Long cooking is the key to breaking down the cheek muscles. Here, browning the meat reduces the cooking time without sacrificing flavor and tenderness. SERVES 6

Beef Cheek Goulash with Noodles

2 beef cheeks (about 2 pounds total)

Kosher salt and freshly ground black pepper

¼ cup vegetable oil

1 medium onion, cut into ¼-inch dice
(about 1 cup)

2 small green bell peppers or 3 small
Hungarian wax peppers, cut into ¼-inch
dice (about 1 cup)

2 cloves garlic, finely chopped

3 tablespoons Hungarian paprika

⅛ teaspoon caraway seeds

One 28-ounce can whole tomatoes, drained
and finely chopped

4 cups beef stock or water

4 cups cooked, buttered egg noodles,
for serving

½ cup sour cream, for serving

Season the beef cheeks with salt and black pepper. Heat the oil in a large frying pan over high heat until almost smoking, about 1 minute. Carefully add the cheeks to the pan and brown, 5 to 7 minutes per side. Transfer from the pan to a paper-towel-lined plate to drain.

Reduce the heat to medium high and add the onions, peppers, and garlic, cooking until tender, about 5 minutes. Stir in the paprika and caraway seeds and cook for 3 minutes, then add the tomatoes. Use a wooden spoon to break the tomatoes up a bit and scrape up any brown bits left on the bottom of the pan after browning the meat. Cook until the pan is almost dry, then stir in the stock or water, add the beef cheeks back to the pan, and bring to a boil over high heat. Reduce the heat to low and simmer, covered, until the meat is tender, 2½ to 3 hours.

Remove the meat from the sauce and set aside until cool enough to handle. Simmer the liquid, uncovered, until slightly thickened, about 20 minutes. Shred the meat, return it to the sauce, add salt and pepper, if necessary, and bring to a boil.

Serve over buttered noodles with a dollop of sour cream on each serving.

ASHLEY CHRISTENSEN

Poole's Diner | *Raleigh, North Carolina*

Brining is the secret to perfect fried chicken. It tenderizes and seasons the chicken inside and out, so the flavor you get when you bite into the crispy brown crust is what you taste when you get to the tender juicy chicken inside. A dip in buttermilk is the second half of the one-two punch. Shaking the chicken in a brown paper bag of seasoned flour might seem old-fashioned, but there's no arguing with tradition when it comes to fried chicken. SERVES 4 TO 6

Buttermilk Fried Chicken

6 tablespoons kosher salt

3 tablespoons granulated sugar

One whole chicken, about 4 pounds, cut into eighths, or chicken pieces totaling 4 pounds

2 cups buttermilk

3 cups unbleached all-purpose flour

1 tablespoon fine sea salt

1 tablespoon finely ground fresh black pepper

Canola oil

½ cup honey

One 4-inch sprig fresh rosemary; more for garnish

Three 4-inch sprigs fresh thyme; more for garnish

2 tablespoons cold unsalted butter

To make the brine, put 1 quart of water in a container with a tight-fitting lid. Add the salt and sugar; shake vigorously until they have dissolved, then add a second quart of water and set aside.

Arrange the chicken pieces in a single layer in a nonreactive baking dish (with sides) that fits comfortably in your refrigerator. Cover the chicken with the brine, making certain all pieces are completely submerged. Cover the dish with plastic wrap or a tight-fitting lid and refrigerate for 12 hours.

After 12 hours, remove the chicken pieces and lightly pat dry with a paper towel; transfer them to a large bowl containing the buttermilk. Use tongs or a fork to turn the chicken until all of the surfaces are coated.

Measure the flour, salt, and black pepper into a brown paper grocery bag, gather the top in your fist to seal it, and shake the bag to mix the seasoning into the flour.

Pour ¾ inch of canola oil in a large cast-iron skillet and heat over medium high.

While the oil is heating, dredge the chicken: Add four pieces of chicken to the grocery bag, lifting each one from the buttermilk and allowing the excess to drip off before placing it in the bag. Space the pieces out so they aren't touching one another to start. Gather the top of the bag, grasping it with your fist and shake vigorously to coat all of the surfaces with flour. Remove the chicken from the bag and place on a baking sheet in a single layer. Repeat with the remaining 4 pieces.

>>>

Use a deep-fry thermometer to check the temperature of the oil. (If you don't have a deep-fry thermometer, test the temperature by adding a pinch of flour to the pan. If the oil is hot enough, the flour will float and sizzle. To be certain, add one piece of chicken to the pan to see if it sizzles enthusiastically before adding more.) When the oil has reached 325°F, add the pieces to the pan one at a time, skin side down, without crowding or stacking them. Depending on the size of your pan, you may have to work in batches so that the chicken pieces don't touch one another. Allow each piece to brown and crisp on one side, and then carefully turn using tongs. Brown the second side like the first, using tongs to rotate the chicken pieces in the pan every few minutes, until each piece of chicken reaches an internal temperature of 165°F at its thickest point. The entire process should take between 18 and 22 minutes. Smaller cuts, like the wings, will be finished sooner and should be removed from the pan first. The temperature will carry over and continue to rise once you remove the chicken from the pan.

Place the fried chicken on a paper-towel-lined rimmed baking sheet and let rest for 15 minutes.

Meanwhile, warm the honey in a small saucepan over medium heat. Add the rosemary and thyme sprigs, bring to a simmer, and then remove from the heat. Whisk in the cold butter until the mixture is emulsified.

Arrange the chicken pieces on a platter and drizzle with the herb-infused honey. Garnish with additional sprigs of rosemary and thyme and serve hot.

"Not only for our health, but for the sake of our stressed planet, we need to start thinking about meat proteins as accompaniments to vegetables rather than vice versa."

EVAN MALLETT
Black Trumpet, Portsmouth, New Hampshire

LENNY RUSSO

Heartland | *Saint Paul, Minnesota*

Rabbit is most often prepared and eaten during the winter months, in braises and with rich sauces. But rabbit is actually most plentiful in spring and summer months, when it is available fresh from some butchers and meat counters. You can ask your butcher to remove the thigh bone, as called for in this recipe. SERVES 6

Pan-Roasted Rabbit with Barley and Morel Mushroom Risotto

FOR THE RISOTTO

4 tablespoons (½ stick) unsalted butter, divided

4 ounces morel mushrooms, cleaned and halved if large, or a combination of wild mushrooms

Kosher salt and freshly ground black pepper

2 teaspoons finely minced garlic, divided

4 cups vegetable stock

1 tablespoon grapeseed oil

1 medium white onion, cut into ⅛-inch dice

1 large carrot, peeled and cut into ⅛-inch dice

2 ribs celery, peeled and cut into ⅛-inch dice

1 bulb fennel, cut into ⅛-inch dice

8 ounces hulled barley

1 tablespoon fresh thyme leaves

FOR THE RABBIT

6 rabbit hind legs, thigh bone removed

1 teaspoon fine sea salt

½ teaspoon freshly ground black pepper

3 tablespoons coarsely chopped fresh rosemary leaves

2 tablespoons unsalted butter

MAKE THE RISOTTO

Heat a nonreactive pan over medium heat and add 2 tablespoons of butter. When it has melted, add the morels and season with a pinch of salt and black pepper. Sauté the mushrooms until tender and just cooked through, about 5 minutes, depending on the size of the mushrooms. Add 1 teaspoon of the garlic, cook for 1 more minute, and remove the pan from the heat. Set aside.

Bring the stock to a slow simmer in a nonreactive pot. Meanwhile, heat 1 tablespoon of butter with the oil in a shallow braising pan or saucepan over medium-low heat. Add the onions, carrots, celery, fennel, and the remaining teaspoon of garlic and sauté until tender and translucent. Add the barley, season with salt and pepper, and sauté with the vegetables, stirring occasionally until the barley begins to change color (this is called pearlizing).

Once the barley has pearlized, add the stock slowly, about ½ cup at a time. Continue to stir the barley as you add the stock. Wait until the stock is absorbed completely before adding the next ½ cup. Repeat this process until the stock is gone; the barley should be tender but not soft. Remove the pan from the heat and add the thyme and the reserved morels and their cooking liquid. Gently stir in the remaining 1 tablespoon of butter and season to taste with salt and pepper if necessary. Cover the risotto and reserve.

PREPARE THE RABBIT

Heat a large frying pan over medium-high heat. Season the rabbit on both sides with salt, pepper, and rosemary. Add the butter to the pan and when it stops foaming, add the rabbit. Brown the pieces well on both sides, cover the pan, and reduce the heat to low. Cook for 4 minutes.

TO SERVE

Divide the risotto among six shallow bowls. Place a rabbit leg on top of the risotto so that the leg bone is standing straight up and serve.

MATT JENNINGS

Farmstead | Providence, Rhode Island

A great porchetta is succulent inside, with a crispy, crackerlike skin outside. Here, the porchetta is tightly wrapped to ensure that the juice from the meat is preserved; as a result, it steams during the first few hours of cooking. When the plastic wrap and foil are removed, the oven temperature is increased to crisp up the belly on the outside. Once you've mastered this porchetta in the oven, try it on the grill for a smoky version.

Start this recipe 24 hours in advance, since the pork needs at least that long to marinate. The fully wrapped roast can sit in the refrigerator for up to 3 days (its flavors become even more intense and fully developed). **SERVES 8 TO 12**

Crispy Porchetta with Salsa Verde

One 5- to 7-pound skin-on pork belly

One 2- to 3-pound trimmed pork loin

3 tablespoons finely chopped lemon zest

2 tablespoons fennel pollen or toasted crushed fennel seed

6 cloves garlic, finely chopped

2 tablespoons coarsely chopped fresh rosemary

2 tablespoons coarsely chopped fresh thyme

1 tablespoon coarsely chopped fresh oregano

2 tablespoons extra-virgin olive oil

Kosher salt and freshly ground white pepper

Salsa Verde (recipe on the facing page)

Lay the pork belly, skin side down, on a clean surface with the long edge parallel to you. Arrange the pork loin in the center, widthwise, so that it is approximately the same as the belly in length. Trim away any overhanging ends of the loin and carefully fold the belly over the loin.

Trim the pork belly so that it can be wrapped snugly and completely around the pork loin, including a 2-inch overlap. Trim away the meat and fat—but not the skin—from the 2-inch overlap to create a thin flap of skin. (The flap will help seal the roast when it is rolled.) Remove the loin from the belly and set it aside. Using a sharp paring knife, "score" the belly all over by making ½-inch-deep incisions.

Combine the lemon zest, fennel pollen or seeds, garlic, rosemary, thyme, oregano, and olive oil in a small bowl and stir together to form a paste. Rub the belly and loin with the paste, working it into all of the cracks and crevices. Generously season the belly with salt and white pepper.

Return the loin to center of the belly and wrap the belly around it, sealing it with the skin flap. Using butcher's twine, tie the porchetta at 1-inch intervals, keeping the twine taut to make a compact roast. (The importance of neatly tying the porchetta will become apparent when it comes time to slice it.) Tightly wrap the porchetta in plastic wrap, then in foil, and refrigerate for at least 1 day and up to 3 days.

When you are ready to cook it, transfer the still-wrapped porchetta to a roasting pan fitted with a rack, to prevent the meat from sitting on the bottom of the pan. Leave the roast out for about 2 hours, until it comes to room temperature.

Arrange a rack in the bottom third of the oven and heat the oven to 325°F. Cook the porchetta for 3 to 4 hours, or until an instant-read thermometer inserted in the center of the roast reads 130°F. Remove the roast from the oven and increase the heat to 500°F.

Remove the foil and plastic wrap from the roast and pat dry. Return the porchetta to the oven and cook on the middle shelf, turning frequently, until the skin is crisp all over, about 20 minutes. When the exterior is crispy and golden brown, let the roast rest for approximately 15 minutes before slicing it with a very sharp knife. Remove the twine and arrange the slices on a platter, or place on individual plates. Serve with salsa verde at the table.

Salsa Verde

MAKES ABOUT 1 CUP

1 cup packed freshly picked parsley leaves

½ small red or yellow onion, cut into ½-inch dice (about ¼ cup)

2 anchovies

1 tablespoon white balsamic or white-wine vinegar

2 tablespoons capers

½ cup extra virgin olive oil

Place the ingredients in a food processor and pulse several times until they form a loose sauce.

> ## "A pasture-raised heritage breed pig
> ## is the best choice for porchetta, with its
> ## extra fatty belly, which balances the
> ## lean meat of the loin."
>
> **BOB PERRY**
> *University of Kentucky College of Agriculture*

ETHAN STOWELL

Staple and Fancy Mercantile | Seattle, Washington

Perfectly roasted chicken is the litmus test that separates good cooks from great cooks. Few items are easier to prepare or more satisfying to eat if you begin with a fresh pastured bird, season it well, and don't stray too far from the formula of olive oil or butter, lemon, garlic, and herbs. The accompanying stew of braised greens and tender white beans seasoned with pancetta round out this meal, tailor-made for a wintery Sunday evening. SERVES 4

Roasted Chicken with Controne Beans, Pancetta, and Lacinato Kale

FOR THE CHICKEN

1 whole chicken, about 3 pounds

1 head garlic, cut in half

1 lemon, cut in half

1 bunch fresh thyme

¼ cup extra-virgin olive oil

Kosher salt and freshly ground
  black pepper

**FOR THE BEAN AND
KALE STEW**

2 tablespoons extra-virgin olive oil

4 ounces pancetta, diced

2 cloves garlic, thinly sliced

2 tablespoons unsalted butter

2 bunches Lacinato kale, cut into
  1-inch pieces

2 cups Controne beans, cooked,
  with 1 cup of the cooking liquid
  reserved

Kosher salt and freshly ground
  black pepper

Position a rack in the center of the oven and heat the oven to 350°F. Wash the chicken inside and out and pat dry. Stuff the cavity with the garlic, lemon, and thyme. Rub the entire bird with the olive oil and season generously with salt and pepper.

Put the chicken on a V-shape rack in a large roasting pan and cook until it is golden brown all over, about 1½ hours. A thermometer inserted in the thigh joint should read 165°F, and the juices from the thickest part of the thigh should run clear when it is pierced with a knife. Remove the chicken from the oven and let it rest for at least 20 minutes.

While the chicken is resting, make the stew. In a medium-size pot, heat the olive oil and pancetta over medium heat and cook until the pancetta is brown and crispy, about 5 minutes. Add the garlic, butter, kale, beans, and bean liquid, using a wooden spoon to scrape up the browned bits from the bottom of the pot. Simmer until the kale is cooked thoroughly, 5 to 6 minutes. Add a little water if the stew appears dry. Season to taste with salt and pepper.

Cut the chicken into serving pieces and serve on a platter alongside the stew.

JOHN HALL

Canela Bistro | *Sonoita, Arizona*

Some of the authentic ingredients and flavors in this recipe are difficult to find outside the Southwest, but don't let that discourage you from trying this dish. Cabrito, or young goat, is readily available but can be replaced successfully with a leg of lamb. Ask the butcher to remove the femur and aitchbone of either and to butterfly it. **SERVES 6**

Roasted Leg of Goat with Bordal Beans

10 ounces Bordal beans or cannellini beans

½ cup plus 2 tablespoons olive oil, divided

1 medium white onion, cut into ½-inch dice
(about 1 cup)

2 fresh chile de arbol, roughly chopped

8 cups vegetable or chicken stock or water

1 head garlic

Kosher salt and freshly ground black pepper

8 ounces wild amaranth leaves or
fresh spinach

2 ounces chilhuacle negro chiles or ancho
or guajillo chiles

2 ounces chile negro or pasilla chiles

3 ounces dried prunes, soaked in hot water

One 4-pound leg young goat, butterflied

One 12-ounce lager-style Mexican beer

2 large bunches (about 8 ounces total)
winter greens (such as Lacinato kale,
Swiss chard, dandelion greens, or
spinach), roughly chopped

Cover the beans with cold water by 2 inches and soak overnight. The next day, drain the beans and set aside. Warm 3 tablespoons of olive oil in a large pot and cook the onions with the chile de arbol until slightly soft and translucent. Add the beans and stock or water and bring the mixture to a simmer over medium-high heat. Reduce the heat and cook until the beans are tender, about 2 hours.

Roast the garlic by heating the oven to 350°F. Cut off the top of the head to expose the cloves. Put the garlic in a small baking dish, drizzle with 2 tablespoons olive oil, and sprinkle with salt and black pepper. Cover the dish with aluminum foil and bake until the skin is toasty and the cloves are tender and golden brown, about 45 minutes.

When the garlic is cool enough to handle, warm 2 tablespoons of olive oil in a wide sauté pan over medium heat. Squeeze the roasted garlic cloves from the head and add to the pan with the amaranth or spinach. Cook over high heat until tender, about 5 minutes, then remove from the heat and set aside to cool.

Purée the chiles and drained soaked prunes in a blender to form a paste and season with 1 tablespoon of salt. Set aside.

Season the butterflied goat leg with salt and pepper. Fill the cavity with the cooled amaranth or spinach and garlic, roll up, and tie with butcher's twine. Warm the remaining 3 tablespoons of olive oil in a cast-iron skillet large enough to hold the goat leg and sear the outside of the leg until brown and crispy on all sides. Remove from the heat.

Heat the oven or a grill to 350°F. Smear the leg with the prune-chile purée and put the pan in the oven or the leg on the grill. Roast until the internal temperature of the meat is 130°F and a crust has formed all over, about 1 hour. Allow the meat to rest for 20 to 30 minutes before slicing.

While the meat is resting, add the beer and a large pinch of salt to the beans and bring to a simmer. Add the roughly chopped greens just prior to serving and season to taste once more. Put the beans and greens on a serving platter and arrange the sliced meat on top.

VITALY PALEY

Paley's Place | Portland, Oregon

Game is the seasonal category of meat that best satisfies our cravings for hearty, warming dishes that are absent from our summertime diets. Perfect for fall and the start of the season, quail is a small game bird that gently ushers in winter birds like ducks and geese.

Boneless quails, which have all but the leg bones removed, can be ordered from a butcher or specialty-foods purveyor. If you're short on time, roasted chestnuts are available peeled and vacuum-packed In upscale groceries. **SERVES 4**

Chestnut, Prune, and Bacon-Stuffed Quaiis

1 cup pitted prunes

1 cup cream sherry

¼ cup brandy

1 tablespoon canola or grapeseed oil; more if necessary

4 ounces smoked bacon, cut into ½-inch dice

8 ounces roasted chestnuts

3 tablespoons coarsely chopped fresh sage

Kosher salt and freshly ground black pepper

8 boneless quails

1 bunch fresh thyme

3 tablespoons Persillade (recipe on page 132)

Place the prunes in a small saucepan with straight sides. Add the sherry and brandy, and bring to a boil over high heat. Remove from the heat and set the pot aside to allow the prunes to plump and absorb the sherry mixture, about 30 minutes. Once they're completely cool, drain the prunes well, reserving the liquid for later use.

Heat 1 tablespoon of oil in a small frying pan over medium heat. Add the bacon and sauté until the fat is rendered and the bacon is browned and crispy, about 15 minutes. Remove to a paper-towel lined plate to drain and cool. Strain and save the fat for cooking the quails.

Place the drained prunes, bacon, chestnuts, and sage in the bowl of a food processor. Add 3 tablespoons of the prune poaching liquid, season with salt and black pepper, and pulse several times until the mixture just comes together. Divide the stuffing into eight equal portions and stuff each quail with a portion of the mixture. With a paring knife, pierce a small hole in the quail's skin between the body and thigh and thread an opposite leg through it all the way to help the stuffing stay in place. Repeat the process with the remaining quails.

Heat the oven to 400°F. Line a large rimmed baking sheet with whole branches of thyme. Season the quails all over with salt and pepper. Heat 4 tablespoons of bacon fat in a large frying pan over medium heat. Sauté the quails, 4 at a time, placing them breast side down into the hot bacon fat. Cook until golden brown, about 2 minutes, turn over and cook for 2 more minutes. Remove and place the birds on the bed of thyme in the baking sheet, breast side up. Discard the cooking fat and wipe the frying pan clean. Repeat the process with the remaining the 4 quails using the rest of the bacon fat. Augment with canola oil if there is not enough bacon fat to cook the quails.

>>>

Place the baking sheet in the oven and roast for about 15 minutes. Remove the pan from the oven and heat the broiler. Brush the tops of the quails with the prune poaching liquid and place under the broiler to glaze, about 2 minutes.

Transfer the quails to a platter, drizzle with the remaining prune poaching liquid, sprinkle with persillade, and serve.

Persillade

MAKES ABOUT 3 TABLESPOONS
½ bunch fresh flat-leaf parsley
2 small cloves garlic

Finely chop the parsley leaves on a cutting board and set to one side. Finely chop the garlic and add to the pile of chopped parsley. Chop the two together until well incorporated and very finely chopped. Transfer the persillade to an airtight container and refrigerate until ready to use.

"Historically, game has been a livelihood and staple for families. Nowadays, chefs who feature game on their menus are using some of the traditional preparations to highlight its unique flavors."

ERIC STENBERG
Jack Creek Grille at Moonlight Basin, Big Sky, Montana

TONY MAWS

Craigie On Main | *Cambridge, Massachusetts*

The offal and odd bits of pigs are the basis for well-loved dishes around the world. But even if you have half of a hog in your freezer, it probably didn't come with enough offal to make dinner. By adding pork sausage links, this slow-cooked ragoût stretches to feed a family when spooned over pasta. And chances are good that they won't know what's in this red sauce, unless you tell them. **SERVES 4 TO 6**

Pork Heart and Sausage Ragoût over Pasta

4 links pork sausage, coarsely chopped

2 pork hearts, coarsely ground or chopped

1 medium white onion, cut into ¼-inch dice (about 1 cup)

1 small fennel bulb, cut into ½-inch dice (about ½ cup)

1 medium carrot, cut into ¼-inch dice (about ½ cup)

½ cup fresh (or frozen) cèpes, cut into ¼-inch dice

½ small leek, white part only, cut into ¼-inch dice (about ¼ cup)

½ rib celery, cut into ¼-inch dice (about ¼ cup)

3 cloves garlic, finely chopped

1 salt-cured anchovy, soaked and dried

2 teaspoons crushed red pepper flakes

½ cup Armagnac

1 cup canned crushed tomatoes

1 cup dry white wine, such as Sauvignon Blanc or Pinot Gris

4 cups homemade chicken stock (or all-natural canned)

½ cup heavy cream

Kosher salt and freshly ground black pepper

1 pound fresh or dry pasta, cooked according to the package directions

1 tablespoon chopped fresh sage

1 tablespoon chopped fresh flat-leaf parsley

1 tablespoon extra-virgin olive oil

½ cup freshly grated pecorino-romano

Heat a large heavy frying pan over high heat until hot. Add the sausage links and hearts and sear, stirring until well browned, about 5 minutes. Remove the browned meat from the pan, pour the fat into another container, and return 1 tablespoon to the pan.

Add the onions, fennel, carrots, cèpes, leeks, celery, garlic, anchovy, and pepper flakes to the pan and cook over medium-low heat, stirring occasionally, until the vegetables are slightly softened, about 5 minutes.

Add the Armagnac, increase the heat slightly, and stir with a wooden spoon, loosening the brown bits stuck to the bottom of the pan. When the Armagnac has evaporated, add the tomatoes and wine and cook until reduced by half. Add 2 cups of the chicken stock and cook on medium-high heat until most of the liquid has disappeared.

Add the remaining 2 cups of chicken stock and the meat. Simmer, covered, until the meat is tender, about 30 minutes. Add the cream and simmer for another 15 minutes. Season to taste with salt and pepper.

Divide the pasta among individual plates and top with ragoût. Sprinkle each with sage and parsley, a drizzle of olive oil, and the cheese.

STEVE JOHNSON

Rendezvous in Central Square | Cambridge, Massachusetts

The key to really great roast chicken, beyond a good bird, is to keep the skin crispy and the meat underneath moist. Inspired by ras al hanout, the earthy, sweet Moroccan spice blend used across North Africa, the combination of spices used for this chicken turns its skin a beautiful mahogany brown and imparts a rich flavor. If cooking the chicken in the oven, use the juices left in the pan to make a sauce by adding a little bit of fresh rosemary and a few drops of sherry vinegar. SERVES 4

Smoke-Roasted Whole Chicken with Moroccan Spices

1 whole chicken, about 4 pounds

2 tablespoons Spice Rub
   (recipe on page 136)

2 tablespoons extra-virgin olive oil

Kosher salt

1 sprig fresh rosemary, for the sauce
   (if roasting chicken in the oven)

Sherry vinegar, for the sauce
   (if roasting chicken in the oven)

To grill the chicken, use a combination of hardwood logs and all-natural hardwood charcoal and build a small fire on one side of an outdoor kettle-style cooker. To roast the chicken in the oven, heat to 350°F.

Wash the chicken with cold water inside and out, drain, and pat dry. Rub the outside of the bird all over with about 2 tablespoons of the spice mixture followed by the olive oil. Sprinkle all over with salt and let the bird rest for about 20 minutes or until the grill or oven gets hot.

If grilling the chicken, when about one-third of the charcoal is lit, place the chicken on the grill on the opposite side of the cooker, away from the fire. Cover loosely with the lid and open the top vent so that the fire continues to smolder without burning bright. Allow the chicken to smoke-roast for about 1¼ hours, turning it every 15 or 20 minutes to insure even cooking all around. The bird is done when the thigh joints start to loosen, the juices in the cavity run clear, and the skin is a beautiful mahogany brown. An instant-read thermometer should register 165°F.

To roast the chicken in the oven, place it in a cast-iron skillet on the center rack and turn it every 20 minutes to crisp the skin all over. After about 1¼ hours, or when the thigh joints begin to loosen and the juices inside start to run clear, the chicken should be ready. An instant-read thermometer should register 165°F.

Let the chicken cool for about 10 minutes, then cut it into pieces suitable for serving. Use the juices left in the pan to make a sauce by adding a sprig of fresh rosemary, a few drops of sherry vinegar, and a pinch of salt, whisking to blend. Spoon over the chicken pieces and serve.

>>>

Spice Rub

MAKES ABOUT 3/4 CUP

¼ cup ground cumin

2 tablespoons ground coriander

1½ teaspoons hot chili powder

1½ teaspoons paprika

1½ teaspoons ground cinnamon

1½ teaspoons ground allspice

¾ teaspoon ground cloves

1½ teaspoons kosher salt

1½ teaspoons freshly ground black pepper

¾ teaspoon dried oregano

¾ teaspoon dried basil

½ teaspoon dried rosemary

½ teaspoon dried thyme

½ teaspoon dried sage

½ teaspoon cayenne pepper

¾ teaspoon ground anise seed

Mix the spices together in a small bowl and set aside. If you begin with fresh spices, this batch will keep for 6 months if stored in a tightly sealed container.

"Not all pastured chicken tastes the same. And it shouldn't. The only thing that is consistent is the greater texture and flavor of pastured chicken when compared to the chicken most Americans are used to eating."

JENNIFER SMALL
Flying Pigs Farm, Shushan, New York

Choosing Pastured Chicken

Some chickens are raised for meat (broilers), others for eggs (layers). The majority of both birds produced in the United States today are raised in continual confinement, in extremely dark, cramped conditions, surrounded by their own excrement. Factory-farmed chicken may be the darkest side of meat production; changing your chicken purchasing habits is an easy and meaningful first step in supporting sustainability. Because factory farming has reduced the genetic diversity of modern commercial chickens by breeding them for certain desirable traits, they are literally unfit for life outdoors. Birds labeled "antibiotic-free" mostly come from factory farms, too, and "free range" and "range-fed" are both loose definitions that don't necessarily mean the birds were on pasture, but just that they had access to the outdoors.

True pasture-raised chickens get sunlight, exercise, and access to an omnivorous diet of bugs and grubs. They are meaty and rich in flavor, with just the right amount of fat to make them succulent. However, since "pasture raised" has no legal definition, the best way to know what you're getting is to ask about the conditions—where the bird lived, what it ate, and how much time it spent outside. Unless the label specifically guarantees that it is a "pastured" bird, assume it is not. Heritage breeds raised on pasture are even better: Silver Laced Wyandotte, Barred Rock, and Cornish are a few you're likely to find.

Heritage birds are more nutritious and flavorful than the newer breeds, but they require different cooking techniques than supermarket chickens. Because their flavor is something that requires time and age to develop, historic breeds are butchered when the chickens are at least 12 weeks old. (Commercially produced broiler chickens are butchered after about 42 days.) By this age, the birds are well exercised, with big working thighs and legs and somewhat tougher skin that has acclimatized to life outdoors. The carcass is slender with flat, less meaty breasts, which means that one of the challenges of cooking a heritage bird is that the light and dark meat require different cooking times. When roasting a whole heritage chicken, it should be trussed, to maintain a compact shape that self-bastes. Be sure to save the carcass to make an unimaginably rich broth impossible to get from commercial chickens, which are too young to impart much flavor.

TODD HUDSON

The Wildflower Cafe & Coffee House | *Mason, Ohio*

Because it is often extra lean (with only 10 percent to 15 percent fat), grass-fed ground beef is more susceptible to overcooking than the 30 percent fat ground beef blend usually favored for burgers. Without the extra fat to baste the meat, you can insure against dryness with a pat of herby butter, though the grass-fed beef doesn't need any help in the flavor department. By following the cooking instructions here, you'll get juicy burgers every time, butter filled or not. **MAKES 6 BURGERS**

Grass-Fed Herb Burgers

¼ cup (½ stick) unsalted butter, softened

3 sprigs fresh basil, finely chopped

3 sprigs fresh flat-leaf parsley, finely chopped

1 sprig fresh oregano, finely chopped

1 clove garlic, finely chopped

2¼ teaspoons kosher salt, divided; more for seasoning

1¾ teaspoons freshly ground black pepper, divided; more for seasoning

2 pounds grass-fed ground beef

6 large rolls or English muffins, toasted

3 tablespoons mayonnaise

6 large fresh spinach leaves

Six ⅛-inch slices sweet onion, such as Vidalia

Six ¼-inch slices ripe tomato

Put the softened butter in a small bowl and add the basil, parsley, oregano, garlic, ¼ teaspoon salt, and ¼ teaspoon black pepper. Use a fork or the back of a spoon to break up the butter and incorporate the ingredients. Transfer the herb butter to a piece of plastic wrap, shaping it into a log about 1¼ inches in diameter. Roll the herb butter tightly in the plastic wrap and refrigerate until firm, about 30 minutes.

When the butter is firm, cut the log crosswise into 6 rounds. Combine the beef, 2 teaspoons salt, and 1½ teaspoons pepper in a large bowl. Divide the beef mixture into 12 equal pieces and pat each out to make a round wide enough to fit the bun, about 5 inches. Place a piece of butter on each of 6 rounds. Top each with another beef round and press the layers together to make a butter sandwich, about 1 inch thick. Pinch the edges of the beef together firmly so the butter will not leak out during cooking.

Meanwhile, heat a charcoal grill to 400° to 425°F or a gas grill on high.

Season the outside of the burgers with a sprinkle of salt and pepper and place them on the hottest part of the grill. Cook the burgers for 4 to 4½ minutes, then turn them over and cook for another 4 to 4½ minutes, for medium rare. For more well done, slide the burgers over to the coolest part of the grill, close the cover, and wait for 3 to 5 minutes, or until the burgers reach the desired doneness.

Let the burgers rest in a warm spot for at least 5 minutes. During this time, the hot juices that gravitate to the middle of the burger will redistribute themselves. At this point, toast the rolls or English muffins, then place a burger on one half and top each with mayonnaise, spinach, sweet onion, and tomato.

Just How Much Meat Is That?

It's tough to visualize how much freezer space a quarter of a cow might occupy. Consequently, there's a misconception that it's far more meat than one family could possibly store, let alone eat.

Actually, a quarter of beef will yield roughly 90 pounds of meat, or about the same amount as a small hog. A family of four can expect to get 50 to 60 meals a year from that quarter, or one meal per week featuring beef.

The meat will take up about 4.5 cubic feet in the top freezer of a standard home refrigerator, leaving little room for anything else. For a few hundred bucks, a stand-up or chest freezer guarantees extra space for your ice cubes, spoils of the abundant berry season, and a pint or two of ice cream.

Here's what a typical quarter of **beef** might look like:

Steaks (1 inch thick)

5 T-bone steaks
3 sirloin steaks
5 rib-eye steaks
3 round steaks
1 flank steak or tri-tip roast

Roasts (3 pounds each)

1 sirloin tip roast
2 arm roasts
1 rump roast
4 chuck roasts
1 brisket

Other Cuts

Two 1½-pound packages of
  short ribs
At least two 1½-pound
  packages of soup bones
40 to 50 pounds of ground beef
Organ and variety meat

Meat from a typical half **hog** consists of approximately these amounts:

12 to 14 pounds pork chops
Two 1½-pound packages of spare ribs
Three 4-pound shoulder roasts
Two 8- to 9-pound hams
8 to 10 pounds of ground pork and/or sausage
2 ham hocks
8 to 10 pounds of bacon
Organ and variety meats

DOLAN LANE

clarklewis | *Portland, Oregon*

Grilling grass-fed steaks isn't much different from grilling conventional beef if you stick to a few guidelines. Remove the steaks from the fridge at least 30 minutes before cooking and generously season them. Cook over high heat (450° to 475°F is ideal), turn the steaks just once, and don't pierce them to check for doneness.

A 5-minute rest is especially important for a grass-fed steak—it allows the juices to disperse through the muscle fibers so that every bite is juicy. SERVES 4

Grilled New York Steaks with Asparagus, Spring Onions, and Porcini Sauce

1 pound small new potatoes, washed

Kosher salt

1 large bunch asparagus (about 1 pound)

6 small spring onions

1 pound porcini mushrooms

¾ cup extra-virgin olive oil, divided

⅓ cup Madeira

3 cups beef or veal stock (homemade
   or store-bought)

6 sprigs fresh thyme, leaves only

1 bay leaf

½ cup (1 stick) unsalted butter,
   cut into ½-inch cubes and chilled

Four 10-ounce New York steaks,
   preferably grass fed, at room temperature

Freshly ground black pepper

Fleur de sel

Put the potatoes in a large pot, cover with cold water, add salt, and bring to a boil over medium-high heat. Lower the heat and simmer until tender, or a knife inserted in the widest part of a potato pierces it easily. Remove the potatoes from heat, drain, and briefly run cold water over them to stop the cooking. When the potatoes are cool enough to handle, cut them in half and thread on four 12-inch skewers. Set aside.

Wash the asparagus and snap off the woody, fibrous ends. Reserve until ready to grill. Wash and trim the onions, leaving 6 inches of the green tops. Clean and trim the root end, leaving enough intact to hold the halves together once the onions are split. Slice the onions in half lengthwise and set aside.

Clean the porcinis by wiping them with a warm, slightly damp cloth, then separate the caps from the stems. Peel the stems with a vegetable peeler and if fat, halve lengthwise before slicing crosswise ¼ inch thick. Slice the caps into a similar size and shape.

Add 2 tablespoons of olive oil to a wide sauté pan and warm over medium-high heat. When the oil is hot, add the sliced mushrooms, season with salt, and cook, making sure not to overfill the pan. You may have to sauté the mushrooms in two batches. Once the mushrooms are cooked, add them all back into the same pan and deglaze with the Madeira. Add the stock, thyme, and bay leaf and gently reduce the liquid by half. Remove the bay leaf and slowly whisk in the cold butter, bringing the sauce up to a slight boil each time more butter is added; this helps to emulsify the sauce. When all of the butter has been incorporated, hold the sauce in a warm spot.

>>>

Heat the grill to high. Generously season both sides of the steaks with salt and black pepper and brush lightly with olive oil. Set aside.

Toss the spring onions and the asparagus with 2 tablespoons of olive oil each in separate bowls. Season with salt and pepper. Put the onion halves on the hottest part of the grill to caramelize, about 2 minutes, before moving them to an area with lower heat to continue to cook and soften.

While the onions are cooking on the side, add the steaks to the hottest part of the grill for 3 to 3½ minutes, then use tongs to flip them and grill 3 to 3½ minutes on the other side for medium rare. Remove and let rest. Brush the potatoes with olive oil, sprinkle with salt, and place on the grill to brown and heat through when the steaks are cooked through halfway.

Put the asparagus on the grill after the steaks have been removed and are resting. Cook until tender (about 5 minutes), then divide among four plates. Remove the potatoes from the skewers and put some on each plate with a steak. Sprinkle the steaks with fleur de sel and pepper, then spoon porcini sauce over the top and drizzle everything on the plate with extra-virgin olive oil. Serve immediately.

"Contrary to conventional wisdom, grass-fed beef from an older animal (close to 30 months) has more flavor and is more tender."

MICHAEL LEVITON
Lumière, Boston, Massachusetts

Why Grass Fed

Animals that can be labeled "grass fed" are cattle and other ruminants including sheep, goats, and bison. In 2007, after decades of debate and discussion, the United States Department of Agriculture (USDA) set standards for what the label "grass (forage) fed" means: One hundred percent of the animal's diet must come from forage (grass and legumes in season, hay and silage during the winter months). The animal can never eat grain, soybeans, or cottonseed meal.

Companies that market using the USDA grass-fed distinction do so voluntarily, and their growing practices must be supported with documentation. The American Grassfed Association, which has created standards that exceed USDA requirements, has a seal certifying that the cow has spent its entire life on pasture or range. Other certifying agencies like Food Alliance, Certified Humane, and Animal Welfare Approved have originated their own standards for sustainability and animal welfare. They give the consumer a more comprehensive picture of the animal's quality of life and how it was raised, and they require ranch visits by an auditor for the purpose of verifying a producer's growing practices and claims. Because verification is independent, third-party certification can be expensive. Some agencies also charge an annual fee, based on a percentage of gross annual sales of the certified product.

The result of a forage-based diet is healthier meat with less fat and cholesterol and more flavor. Grass-fed meat is often described as meatier and purer, with a complex flavor and pleasant mineral qualities. It may also be more expensive. Because of the time, effort, and materials needed to raise animals humanely and sustainably, small producers have higher costs. And since fattening animals with grains is faster and cheaper and grass-fed animals don't get as big as feedlot animals, ranchers raising animals on grass have a larger investment in the animal, in terms of both dollars and time.

Good meat is more expensive than commodity meat. Government subsidies on grain have historically enabled large-scale commercial producers to sell meat at an otherwise unsustainably low price. There's nothing natural about factory farming—the food the animals eat, their living conditions, their rate of growth, and their behaviors and habits. These factors all contribute to a stressed and unnatural-tasting animal. Buying humanely raised meat supports a system that promotes different practices: growing animals slowly, choosing breeds for flavor and how well they're suited to the climate and pasture of a place, safe working conditions, environmental stewardship, and the preservation of open space.

Consumers choose grass-fed meat over grain-fed for a variety of other reasons.

- Studies show that grass-fed meat is lower in fat and higher in vitamins, minerals, omega-3 fatty acids, and linoleic acids.

- Animals raised on pasture are healthier than feedlot animals and so is the environment that nurtures them. Animals raised on grass increase soil fertility, help manage pests and weeds, and convert vegetation inedible to humans into a source of healthful, environmentally appropriate food.

- Grazed lands have been shown to slow global warming by removing carbon dioxide from the air and storing it in the soil. Grazing land in the Great Plains contains 40 tons of carbon dioxide per acre while cultivated soil contains just 26 tons of carbon dioxide per acre.

- Meat from grass-fed animals requires just 1 calorie of fossil fuel to produce 2 calories of food. Many grain and vegetable crops require between 5 and 10 calories of fossil fuel for each calorie of food or fiber produced.

- Grass-fed and pastured animals participate in a cycle that nourishes and gives back to the soil rather than taking from it. They improve diversity and are essential to sustainable farms that don't use chemicals and fossil fuels.

- Typically, grass-fed meats are sourced directly from small- and medium-size producers because large producers don't have the infrastructure to raise animals on pasture.

WILLIAM DISSEN

The Market Place Restaurant | Asheville, North Carolina

At the height of summer, when peaches and blackberries often end up together in cobblers and pies, try the combination in a savory chutney. Succulent slices of pork tenderloin with a crispy bacon crust, slathered with blackberry-peach chutney, will have you rethinking the role of summer's ripest stone fruit and juiciest berries on your menu. **SERVES 4**

Pork Tenderloin with Bacon and Blackberry-Peach Chutney

One 1½-pound pork tenderloin

Pork Brine (recipe on the facing page)

8 ounces thinly sliced smoked bacon
   (about 12 slices)

Kosher salt and freshly ground black pepper

2 tablespoons extra-virgin olive oil

Blackberry-Peach Chutney
   (recipe on the facing page)

Put the pork in a pan large enough to accommodate it and the brine solution. Cover the container and let the pork sit in the brine, refrigerated, for 2 hours. After 2 hours, remove the pork from the brine, rinse well with cold water, and pat dry.

Using a sharp knife, remove the layer of silver skin from the pork tenderloin. Gently slice the smaller tapered end of the tenderloin without going all the way through it. Tuck the butterflied end of the pork underneath, creating a tenderloin that's uniform in size and that will cook at the same rate.

Lay the bacon strips in the center of a large piece of plastic wrap, about 24 inches by 24 inches, overlapping them slightly. Place the tenderloin in the center of the bacon and use the plastic wrap to fold the bacon over the pork, like rolling sushi. Firmly roll forward, away from you, wrapping the bacon around the pork tenderloin while holding the sides of the plastic wrap, to create a tight cylinder. Tie the ends with butcher's twine and refrigerate overnight.

Heat the oven to 450°F. Remove the plastic wrap from the tenderloin and use several pieces of butcher's twine to secure the bacon. Season the pork with salt and black pepper. Warm the olive oil over medium-high heat in a large ovenproof sauté pan. When hot, add the pork to the pan and crisp the bacon on all sides. Place the pan in the oven for 10 to 12 minutes, or until an instant-read thermometer registers 140°F. Remove the pork from oven and rest for at least 5 minutes before slicing. Serve with blackberry-peach chutney.

Pork Brine

MAKES 2 QUARTS

½ cup kosher salt

½ cup granulated sugar

½ cup black peppercorns

½ bunch fresh thyme

2 bay leaves

3 cloves garlic, peeled

Place 2 cups of cold water in a small saucepan and bring to a boil. Remove the pan from the heat, add the salt and sugar, and stir to dissolve.

Add 6 cups of cold water, the peppercorns, thyme, bay leaves, and garlic cloves and cool at room temperature.

Blackberry-Peach Chutney

2 tablespoons extra-virgin olive oil

1 medium yellow onion, cut into
  ¼-inch dice (about 1 cup)

½ teaspoon finely minced garlic

1 jalapeño, finely minced

2 fresh peaches, skinned and cut into
  1-inch dice

2 tablespoons honey

3 tablespoons brown sugar

¼ cup apple-cider vinegar

1 cup fresh blackberries

Kosher salt and freshly ground black pepper

Heat the olive oil in a nonreactive pan. Add the onions and cook, stirring occasionally, until they are translucent. Stir in the garlic, jalapeño, peaches, honey, brown sugar, and cider vinegar.

Cook for 8 to 10 minutes, or until the peaches are soft but not falling apart. Add the blackberries to the pan and season with salt and black pepper. Continue to simmer for up to 10 more minutes, or until the mixture has thickened slightly. Remove from the heat and cool. Once it has cooled completely, taste the chutney again and add more salt and pepper before serving if necessary.

GREG LAPRAD

Quiessence | *Phoenix, Arizona*

The chuck roast comes from the front shoulder of a cow, a portion of the animal that's both hardworking and fatty; when cooked for a long period of time, it makes for the right combination of richness, flavor, and fall-apart tenderness. When it comes to braising, bone-in roasts take about the same amount of time as boneless, but add so much extra flavor and succulence that they're preferable. Look for a 7-bone roast, which comes from the chuck, or cross rib roast. SERVES 6

Red-Wine Braised Beef with Winter Squash Mash and Apple Gremolata

FOR THE BEEF

One 4½- to 5-pound bone-in beef chuck
   roast or similar cut

Kosher salt and freshly ground black pepper

¼ cup extra-virgin olive oil

3 large yellow onions, cut into 1-inch chunks

3 carrots, peeled and cut into 1-inch chunks

6 ribs celery, cut into 1-inch chunks

2 cups robust dry red wine, such as
   Zinfandel or Cabernet

4 cups beef stock (homemade or
   store-bought)

¼ cup red-wine vinegar

½ head garlic

2 bay leaves, preferably fresh

4 sprigs fresh thyme

2 sprigs fresh rosemary

FOR THE APPLE GREMOLATA

2 firm tart apples, such as Newton Pippin
   or Granny Smith

¼ cup coarsely chopped fresh
   flat-leaf parsley

Zest of 1 lemon, finely chopped

¼ cup extra-virgin olive oil

Kosher salt and freshly ground black pepper

>>>

Heat the oven to 325°F. Generously season the beef all over with salt and black pepper.

Heat the oil in a large ovenproof Dutch oven or braising pot (5 quarts is a good size) over medium-high heat. Brown the beef on all sides, turning it with tongs as you go, about 18 minutes total. Remove the beef and put it on a large plate to collect any juice that it releases.

Add the onions, carrots, and celery to the pot and cook over medium-high heat. Season with salt and pepper and cook, stirring often, until the vegetables begin to brown, about 7 minutes. Add the wine and scrape the bottom of the pan with a wooden spoon to remove any charred bits on the bottom. Bring to a boil and reduce the wine by half, then add the stock, vinegar, garlic, bay leaves, thyme, and rosemary. Bring to a boil, add the meat and any juice that has collected to the pot, cover, and transfer to the lower third of the oven.

Braise the meat at a gentle simmer until tender, about 3 hours, turning the meat every hour. Check after the first 15 minutes that the liquid isn't simmering too vigorously; reduce by 10° or 15°F if it is.

Make the gremolata while the beef is in the oven. Peel, core, and finely dice the apples. Toss with the parsley, lemon zest, and olive oil. Season to taste with salt and black pepper and set aside at room temperature.

>>>

FOR THE SQUASH MASH

1 medium butternut squash, about
 2½ pounds

1 medium acorn squash, about 2½ pounds

2 tablespoons olive oil

Kosher salt and freshly ground
 black pepper

6 tablespoons (¾ stick) unsalted butter

1 tablespoon white-wine vinegar

When the beef has about 1 hour of cooking time remaining, make the squash mash. Cut the butternut and acorn squash in half, remove the seeds, and brush the cut surfaces with olive oil. Season generously with salt and black pepper and place in a baking pan, cut side down. Roast in the oven, uncovered, with the beef for about 45 minutes, or until tender. When the squash is cool enough to handle, scoop the flesh from the skin and pass it through a ricer or a food mill, adding in the butter as you go, 1 tablespoon at a time. Stir in the vinegar, and season to taste with salt and pepper.

Remove the beef from the oven and cut the roast into rustic slices. To serve, place a spoonful of squash mash in the center of a plate or shallow bowl, top with a couple of slices of braised beef, and finish with a spoonful of gremolata on the side.

Defrost Tips for Beef

Water makes up a significant part of meat's structure. As meat freezes, water expands, forming ice crystals that push and make tiny imperceptible tears in the meat's fibers. For that reason, dry-aged beef is a better candidate than wet-aged or freshly cut beef for freezing and defrosting because it contains less moisture and its fibers are more elastic and able to fight against the expanding crystals.

The best way to defrost grass-fed beef is slowly, in the refrigerator. Take the meat out of the freezer between 24 and 48 hours before you want to prepare it, and allow it to defrost in the refrigerator with a temperature of around 41°F. This method results in minimal compromise to texture. If you are pressed for time, ground beef and braising cuts won't suffer noticeably from an expedited defrost. Submerge the frozen vacuum-sealed package in a bowl of cold water and change the water every 30 minutes or so. A small package of ground beef will take an hour or less to defrost. A 3- or 4-pound roast will defrost in about 3 hours.

> **"Using high-quality freezers and the vast improvements in technology allow restaurants to purchase whole beef not only for special events but also on a weekly basis."**
>
> **ANDREA REUSING**
> *chef/owner of Lantern, Chapel Hill, North Carolina*

What to Ask when You're Ready to Buy the Cow

The breed of an animal, whether beef, chicken, or lamb, is often said to be what determines 80 percent of flavor and texture. It is also critical to how an animal adapts and thrives—or fails to thrive—on pasture. When buying any kind of meat, the best way to understand what you're getting is to purchase directly from the producer and ask questions about the animal's breed, age, and diet. The following tips will help you broker your first beef purchase.

Breed

There are more than 800 breeds of cattle. Across the United States, each region has a different climate and type of pasture. The breeds that thrive in each are those that are the best genetically suited to the environment and can forage efficiently on perennial plants and grasses, taking up sufficient amounts of the right nutrients. They are also the breeds that taste best.

Age

The age of an animal combined with its breed will tell you a great deal about the characteristic of its meat. Younger animals tend to be leaner. British breeds like Angus, Hereford, or Red Poll, raised on pasture between 9 and 14 months, will have veal-like qualities, whereas an 18- to 24-month-old animal will have more external fat and marbling. Continental European breeds like Charolais and Piedmontese may take longer to mature on pasture because of their size.

Diet

Grass-fed beef eat only grass and herbaceous leafy plants. They never eat grain or grain by-products and must have continuous access to a pasture during the growing season. Small ranchers unable to incur the expense of certifying their operations as "organic" may be producing a product that would qualify, but be certain to ask not only what the animals eat and if they spend their entire lives on pasture, but also what kinds of chemicals are used on the ranch.

A "finishing" diet refers to what the cattle is fed in the final period of growth before it is slaughtered. This is the crucial period when the animal's fat layer and internal marbling develop. Conventional feedlot cattle eat a predominantly grain diet (they require some roughage) through finishing; most "naturally raised" cattle are raised on pasture and finished on grain; and 100 percent grass-fed cattle are always on pasture.

Aging

Meat available through retailers is usually wet-aged, a process where large pieces of meat are vacuum-sealed immediately after they are cut to prevent moisture loss. Dry-aging is an old-fashioned method and refers to the time from when the animal is slaughtered to when the carcass is broken down into cuts. Beef purchased from farmers or ranchers who use small meat-processing plants is typically dry-aged by hanging the carcass in a walk-in cooler so that the enzymes naturally present in the meat break down muscle tissue, resulting in greater tenderness. Since it is exposed to air, the carcass loses moisture from evaporation, further concentrating its beefy flavor. The intensity of flavor increases with the length of the aging period, which might be anywhere from 10 to 28 days. Dry-aging is a more expensive process than wet-aging due to the loss of weight from dehydration and the fact that the aged carcass must be trimmed completely of its dried exterior.

ERIC YOST

White Dog Café | *Philadelphia, Pennsylvania*

Bolognese is a slow-cooked meat sauce typically used to dress tagliatelle pasta. This recipe calls for traditional ingredients and techniques with one exception. Lamb takes the place of veal or beef and gets a spicy kick from a liberal dose of red pepper flakes. The dollop of creamy pesto made with basil and ricotta that tops each tangle of noodles offsets the richness of the sauce perfectly. **SERVES 4 TO 6**

Spicy Lamb Bolognese with Basil Ricotta on Fettuccine

1 tablespoon extra-virgin olive oil

½ medium sweet onion, preferably Vidalia,
   cut into ¼-inch dice (about 1 cup)

2 cloves garlic, finely chopped

2 tablespoons fennel seed

1 tablespoon crushed red pepper flakes;
   more as needed

1 pound ground lamb

¼ cup dry white wine

6 cups crushed tomatoes
   (two 28-ounce cans)

2 tablespoons tomato paste

½ cup packed fresh basil leaves,
   coarsely chopped

½ cup loosely packed fresh flat-leaf
   parsley leaves, coarsely chopped

1½ tablespoons fresh thyme leaves,
   finely chopped

Kosher salt and freshly ground black pepper

1 pound fresh or dry fettuccine or linguine,
   cooked according to the package
   directions

Basil Ricotta (recipe on the facing page)

Heat the olive oil in a large nonreactive saucepan over low heat. Add the onions, garlic, fennel seed, and red pepper flakes. Cook, stirring frequently, until the onions are soft and translucent but not brown, about 10 minutes.

Increase the heat to medium and add the lamb. Sauté the mixture, stirring frequently, for about 5 minutes, or until the lamb is no longer pink. Add the wine and cook until most of it has evaporated, about 3 minutes. Skim off and discard any fat from the top of the mixture.

Add the tomatoes and tomato paste and reduce the heat to low. Cook, uncovered, stirring and scraping the bottom of the saucepan frequently, until the sauce has thickened, 1½ to 2 hours.

To serve, stir the basil, parsley, and thyme into the sauce. Season to taste with salt, black pepper, and more red pepper flakes, if desired. Serve over your favorite pasta topped with a dollop of basil ricotta.

Basil Ricotta

MAKES 1 CUP

½ cup firmly packed fresh basil leaves

2 tablespoons freshly grated Parmigiano-
Reggiano

1 small clove garlic

⅓ cup olive oil

½ cup fresh whole-milk ricotta

Combine the basil, Parmigiano, and garlic in the bowl of a food processor. Process until finely chopped. With the motor running, slowly add
the olive oil and process until the mixture is the consistency of pesto.
Remove the mixture to a large bowl and fold in the ricotta.

Choosing Pastured Lamb

Sheep raised for meat are often of English origin, with names that conjure up images of quaint hamlets in the countryside—Dorset, Hampshire, Cheviot, Cotswold. Heritage breeds have become popular because they require minimal care, add to genetic diversity, and expand the offering of flavors and textures. Though they're generally raised for specific purposes—meat, milk, and wool—there is some overlap of "eaters" and "knitters."

Because their nutritional needs are few, sheep can be raised, in most states, on land unsuited for any other domesticated animal. They thrive on sparse natural forage, producing meat of exceptionally high quality on a diet of grass and mother's milk. Period. Like calves, lambs destined for the commodity market start out on pasture and are finished in feedlots.

Sheep are grazing animals that belong on grass; grain isn't necessary to finish lamb, but it is sometimes used as a supplement for sheep with special nutritional needs, including pregnant ewes and ewes nursing two or more lambs. Lamb cannot be marketed as hormone-free since the meat has naturally occurring benign hormones.

The commodity market doesn't observe a strict marketing season for lamb, but if we were to identify one, it might be between the beginning of March and the end of September. The notion of spring lamb is an antiquated one.

Leaner than its grain-fed counterpart, pastured lamb is best eaten at medium rare.

ERIC STENBERG

Jack Creek Grille at Moonlight Basin | Big Sky, Montana

The popularity of grass-fed beef has helped open the door for game meats like bison and venison as healthy alternatives to commercially raised beef. Bison has a full, beefy flavor, which means that a little goes a long way. Add fresh local produce and cheese and you have a salad that satisfies for lunch or dinner. The combination of the smoky notes of the grilled steak and corn, the acidity of the shallot vinaigrette, and the salty tang of feta is delicious and memorable.

Because they are lean and muscular, game meats are best prepared slow-cooked over low heat or quickly seared over high heat. SERVES 6

Grilled Bison Flank Steak with Grilled Corn, Greens, and Roasted Shallot Vinaigrette

3 ears sweet corn

One 1½-pound bison flank steak

½ cup red wine, such as Zinfandel or
  Cabernet Sauvignon

¼ cup extra-virgin olive oil

½ teaspoon finely chopped fresh rosemary

2 small heads heirloom lettuce, such as
  'Buttercrunch,' 'Red Salad Bowl,' or
  'Speckled Trout,' roughly torn into
  bite-sized pieces

½ cup crumbled feta cheese

Roasted Shallot Vinaigrette
  (recipe on page 154)

Kosher salt and freshly ground
  black pepper

⅓ cup dried cherries

Peel back the corn husks without detaching them and gently rub as much of the silk from the cobs as possible. Pull the husks back down to cover the corn and remove the outermost layer. Soak the corn, covered in cold water, for at least 30 minutes. Place the flank steak in a shallow pan large enough for the steak to lay flat. While the corn is soaking, whisk the red wine with the olive oil and rosemary and pour over the steak to marinate for 30 minutes.

Heat a grill to high. Remove the corn from the water, shake each ear well, and grill, in its husk, over the hottest part of the fire for 4 to 5 minutes, turning several times to char the husks evenly. Continue to cook until the kernels are golden brown and tender, about 5 minutes more. Set aside and cut the corn off the cob when it is cool enough to handle.

Remove the steak from the marinade and pat dry. Put on the hottest part of the grill and grill for about 5 minutes, then turn the meat over and grill for another 3 minutes. Remove it from the heat when the meat is rare, or between 120° and 125°F. As with most meats, overcooking bison is a guarantee of tough meat. Let the meat rest for 5 to 10 minutes before slicing it on the bias into thin strips.

Gently wash and dry the lettuce. Mix the lettuce with the corn and crumbled feta, add enough vinaigrette to coat the leaves, and toss again. Season to taste with salt and black pepper and add the dried cherries. Put some of the salad on each plate and lay several slices of the grilled steak on top.

>>>

Roasted Shallot Vinaigrette

MAKES ABOUT ½ CUP

½ tablespoon unsalted butter

3 shallots, thinly sliced into rings

2 teaspoons granulated sugar

1 teaspoon whole-grain mustard

2 tablespoons red-wine vinegar

¼ cup extra-virgin olive oil

1 teaspoon finely chopped fresh thyme

Kosher salt and freshly ground black pepper

Melt the butter in a small sauté pan over medium-high heat. Add the shallots, reduce the heat, and simmer until they are evenly golden brown.

Allow the shallots to cool slightly, then put them in a blender or food processor with the sugar, mustard, and vinegar. Blend until smooth. With the machine running, slowly drizzle in the olive oil until the vinaigrette has emulsified. Add the thyme and season with salt and black pepper.

Choosing Grass-Fed Bison

Bison once roamed the North American prairies in large numbers; now fewer than 1 million are raised in the United States and Canada. Unlike cattle, bison are genetically diverse wild animals predisposed to live on the tall prairie grasses of another era. But a significant number of bison are finished on feedlots with grain, for the same reasons that domesticated livestock are—to put on weight quickly. The only advantage to confining bison to feedlots is that the resulting lack of exercise keeps the meat tender, since bison meat doesn't marble in the final stages of growth.

Grass-fed bison has a deep, distinctive, and slightly sweet flavor similar to lean beef. The meat is dark purple in color with fat that is sometimes yellow. Like grass-fed beef, bison raised on grass is higher in omega-3s and other nutrients than its grain-fed counterpart and is most delicious eaten rare and in season, usually in the fall.

TODD GRAY

Equinox | Washington, D.C

A whole roast chicken is the beginning of many good things, with leftovers somewhere close to the top of the list. If you don't have enough meat left over, roast a chicken just for this salad—it's worthy of its own bird. The combination of textures and flavors in the recipe is welcome as the weather turns cooler. After you pull the meat from the carcass, toss the bones in a pot with a coarsely chopped onion, a carrot, and some celery; cover with water, add a bay leaf, a few peppercorns, and some parsley stems, and simmer on low for a flavorful broth. SERVES 6

Amish Hand-Pulled Chicken Salad

One 2½-pound roasted chicken, cooled

1 small red onion, finely chopped

2 ribs celery, finely chopped

1 cup mayonnaise

1 cup cashews, lightly toasted and coarsely chopped

⅓ cup dried cherries, coarsely chopped

1½ tablespoons coarsely chopped fresh tarragon

Kosher salt and freshly ground black pepper

After removing the skin from the roast chicken, pull the meat from the breast and legs, tearing it into bite-size pieces. You should have about 4 cups of chicken. Add it to a large bowl with the onions and celery and toss until the ingredients are evenly distributed. Fold in the mayonnaise, stirring to coat all of the chicken pieces. Add the cashews, cherries, and tarragon and season to taste with salt and black pepper. Allow the salad to chill for 30 minutes before serving.

ADAM KEOUGH

Absinthe Brasserie & Bar | San Francisco, California

A classic French dish, coq au vin, or "rooster in wine," used to be made with tough, older birds that benefitted from braising. These days, recipes usually call for chicken or capon.

Typically made with Burgundy, variations of coq au vin using local wine exist in most regions of France. Coq au vin is often accompanied by parsley-flecked potatoes and buttered green peas. In this version, the peas go straight into the pot with the chicken, and roasted potatoes are recommended on the side. SERVES 4 TO 6

Coq au Vin

1 whole chicken, 2½ to 3 pounds

Kosher salt and freshly ground black pepper

4 tablespoons canola oil, divided

1 medium carrot, roughly chopped

1 medium onion, roughly chopped

3 cloves garlic, smashed

8 ounces cremini mushrooms, stems
  removed and reserved, and caps sliced

1 medium leek, roughly diced,
  white part only

1 rib celery, roughly chopped

3 black peppercorns

4 cups chicken stock (homemade
  or store-bought)

1 bay leaf

4 sprigs fresh thyme, divided

1 pig's foot (optional)

1 bottle Burgundy or Pinot Noir

½ cup plus 2 tablespoons unbleached
  all-purpose flour, divided

3 to 4 ounces bacon, cut into ¼-inch by
  1-inch pieces (called lardons)

1 cup pearl onions

2 tablespoons unsalted butter

1 cup fresh peas

Use a chef's knife to remove the chicken legs; then cut down the back of the chicken, separating the breasts from the backbone. You will have two breast pieces. Set aside the backbone. Wash and pat dry the chicken pieces thoroughly, then season generously with salt and black pepper. Place on a rack and cover with plastic wrap. Set in the refrigerator for later use, as long as overnight.

To make the stock in which the chicken pieces will be braised, chop the chicken back into 4 pieces, dry them well, and season with salt and pepper. Heat a large heavy-bottomed pan over medium-high heat until very hot. Add 1 tablespoon of canola oil and sear the chicken back pieces until golden brown all over, then remove to a plate and discard any remaining oil.

Add the second tablespoon of canola oil to the pan and heat until hot. Reduce the heat to medium high, add the carrots, and caramelize until light golden brown. Repeat with the onions. Add the garlic and sauté for 2 more minutes, then add the mushroom stems, leeks, celery, and peppercorns. Sauté for 3 minutes before adding the chicken stock, browned chicken back pieces, bay leaf, 2 sprigs thyme, and pig's foot, if using. Bring the mixture to a boil and reduce to a simmer. Skim any foam or impurities off the top using a ladle and discard. Simmer over the lowest possible heat for 4 hours.

Carefully strain the stock through a fine-mesh sieve and set aside, reserving the pig's foot (if used). Press gently on the chicken back pieces and vegetables to remove all of the liquid before discarding. The recipe can be completed up to this point and finished on the following day. For coq au vin made over 2 days, chill the stock once it has cooled slightly.

The following day, remove the chicken breast and leg pieces and the stock from the refrigerator.

Add the wine to a large wide nonreactive pan, and cook slowly over medium low heat until the wine is reduced by about half, about 20 minutes; set aside. Put the flour in a shallow wide bowl, dredge each of the four chicken pieces, and shake off any excess flour. Heat an ovenproof pan or Dutch oven over medium-high heat and add the remaining 2 tablespoons canola oil. Fry the chicken pieces skin side down until golden brown, making sure to brown all sides. Remove to a plate.

Add the bacon lardons to the pan and slowly cook until crisp. Remove to a paper-towel-lined plate and add the pearl onions to the pan. Sauté the onions until they're light golden brown, remove from the pan, and add the sliced mushroom caps. Sauté for about 5 minutes, then combine with the onions and reserve.

Heat the oven to 300°F.

Add the butter to the pan and melt it before adding the remaining 2 tablespoons flour and stirring continuously with a wooden spoon to make a roux. When a smooth paste is formed, add the reduced wine and thyme and bring to a boil, whisking constantly. Add the chicken stock and leg pieces, cover the pan, and put it in the oven for 50 minutes. After 50 minutes, remove the pan from the oven, add the breast pieces, and cook, covered, for another 40 minutes. Remove the pan from the oven and let the chicken rest in the pan for 1 hour. When cool, remove the herbs and chicken pieces. Separate the drumsticks from the thighs and cut the breasts into 2 pieces each for a total of 8 pieces. Add the pearl onions and mushrooms to the pan and cook the sauce until it thickens slightly. Use a fork to pull the meat from the pig's foot, if using, or pick it with your fingers. Add it with the chicken pieces and peas, to the thickened sauce. Heat everything through (about 10 minutes) and serve.

PETER DAVIS

Henrietta's Table in The Charles Hotel | Cambridge, Massachusetts

The ingredients in this marinade are ordinary staples in most kitchens, but together they work magic on a leg of lamb, giving it a crunchy, chewy, deeply caramelized crust. Served with a fresh, nutty salad of grains and beans dressed in an herby vinaigrette (that tastes lovely with the lamb), this makes for a beautiful spring meal. Roasted asparagus or braised young leeks would fill out this menu perfectly. SERVES 6 TO 8

Maple-Balsamic Roasted Leg of Lamb with Heirloom Grain and Bean Salad and Spring Chive Vinaigrette

½ cup soy sauce

½ cup balsamic vinegar

½ cup maple sugar

1 clove garlic, finely chopped

1 sprig fresh thyme

One 3½- to 4-pound boneless leg of lamb, rolled and tied

Kosher salt and freshly ground black pepper

Heirloom Grain and Bean Salad (recipe on page 160)

Chive Vinaigrette (recipe on page 160)

Combine the soy sauce, vinegar, ½ cup water, sugar, garlic, and thyme in a deep nonreactive bowl large enough to hold the lamb. Whisk the ingredients together, add the lamb, and turn over to coat with the marinade on all sides. Cover tightly with plastic wrap and marinate in the refrigerator overnight, turning at least once.

Heat the oven to 350°F and remove the lamb from the marinade to a roasting pan. Season well with salt and black pepper and roast in the middle of the oven for about 1 hour, or until an instant-read thermometer inserted in the center of the roast reaches 130° to 135°F, for rare. Remove the lamb from the pan and allow it to rest for 30 minutes before slicing.

Serve the sliced lamb on a bed of heirloom grain and bean salad and drizzle with chive vinaigrette.

>>>

Heirloom Grain and Bean Salad

MAKES 4 CUPS

1 cup cooked red quinoa

1 cup cooked farro or wheat berries

1 cup cooked French lentils

1 cup cooked heirloom beans, such as
   Appaloosa, Calypso, or Scarlett Beauty

⅔ cup Chive Vinaigrette (recipe below);
   more as needed

Kosher salt and freshly ground black pepper

Toss the grains and beans together in a large bowl, dress with some of the vinaigrette, and let sit for at least 1 hour at room temperature. Add additional vinaigrette if the salad is dry and season to taste with salt and black pepper if needed.

Chive Vinaigrette

MAKES 1⅓ CUPS

½ cup canola or grapeseed oil

½ cup extra-virgin olive oil

Juice and finely chopped zest of ½ lemon

¼ cup Champagne vinegar

¾ teaspoon kosher salt

¼ teaspoon freshly ground black pepper

3 tablespoons finely chopped fresh chives

1 tablespoon finely minced shallots

1 small clove garlic, finely minced

Whisk the ingredients well to combine.

CAROLINE FIDANZA

Saltie | Brooklyn, New York

A crosscut beef shank, also called shin bone or soup bones, is a piece of the animal's leg that you can get from a butcher or at the supermarket. Because the shank is all muscle and tendon with a marrow-filled bone in the middle, you'll want to cook this cut at a low temperature over a relatively long period of time. Prepare this dish, including the farro, the day before serving to allow the flavor of the ingredients to develop fully. Add the cooked farro to the cold broth and warm them together before serving. **SERVES 4 TO 6**

Beef Shin and Farro Soup

2 pounds meaty crosscut beef shank

Kosher salt and freshly ground black pepper

¼ cup extra-virgin olive oil, divided

5 medium carrots, peeled

3 leeks, split and rinsed

⅓ cup coarsely chopped fresh flat-leaf parsley leaves (stems reserved)

1½ cups farro, presoaked if necessary

6 scallions, thinly sliced on the bias, white and light green parts only

Pat the beef shanks dry with paper towels, then generously season with salt and black pepper at least an hour before cooking, or overnight, if you have the time.

Heat a heavy-bottomed soup pot or Dutch oven over medium heat and add 2 tablespoons of olive oil. When the oil is hot, add the shanks and brown on both sides; transfer to a plate and discard the oil.

Add the browned shanks back to the pot and cover with 10 to 12 cups of cold water. Cut 2 carrots and 1 leek in half lengthwise and add them to the pot with the parsley stems. Bring just to a boil, then reduce to a simmer and cook, covered, over the lowest possible heat until the meat on the shank is tender, at least 3 hours. Check periodically, skimming off any foam that's collected on top and adding water as necessary to keep the contents of the pot covered.

Meanwhile, cook the farro in a pot of generously salted boiling water until tender, up to 40 minutes. Drain the farro and toss with the remaining olive oil. Slice the remaining 3 carrots and the white parts of the remaining 2 leeks thinly on the bias.

When the meat is falling apart tender, remove it from the pot with a slotted spoon. Once it has cooled slightly, pull or slice the meat into bite-size chunks and add them back to the broth with the sliced carrots and leeks. Simmer until the vegetables are just cooked through, 10 to 15 minutes. Season the broth to taste with salt. Add the farro and scallions and cook to warm through, about 10 minutes. Ladle the soup into bowls and finish with a big pinch of chopped parsley and some freshly ground black pepper.

ROBERT STEHLING

Hominy Grill | Charleston, South Carolina

The pork shoulder makes up 25 percent of a hog's carcass weight and is typically divided into a top portion—the Boston butt—and bottom portion—the picnic roast. These well-exercised muscles are rich, flavorful, and inexpensive. When braised or cooked with moist heat, these large cuts of meat taste better over time.

This hearty stew is complete when garnished with fried apple and onion rings; add a poached egg on top and serve for brunch. SERVES 6

Pork Shoulder and Hominy Stew

2 tablespoons bacon fat

One 2½-pound boneless pork shoulder roast, cut into 1½-inch pieces

2 medium onions, diced (about 2 cups)

2 stalks celery, diced (½ cup)

2 cloves garlic, finely minced

1 green bell pepper, diced (1 cup)

3 cups pork or chicken stock

2 bay leaves

1 teaspoon dried thyme

1 teaspoon dried basil

Pinch of crushed red pepper flakes

1 teaspoon freshly ground black pepper

1½ teaspoons kosher salt; more as needed

4 cups whole hominy, cooked, with 1 cup of the cooking liquid reserved (or two 14-ounce cans, rinsed and drained)

¼ cup coarsely chopped fresh flat-leaf parsley

¼ cup sliced scallions, white and green parts

Heat 1 tablespoon of the bacon fat in a large Dutch oven or braising pot (5 quarts is a good size) over medium-high heat. Brown the pork on all sides, turning the pieces with tongs as you go. Remove the meat and put it on a large plate to collect any juice that it releases.

Add the remaining 1 tablespoon of bacon fat and the onions to the pot and cook over medium-high heat, stirring frequently, until the onions begin to brown slightly. Add the celery and continue to cook and stir until almost tender, then add the garlic. Cook the garlic for 2 minutes, add the bell peppers, and continue cooking until they are wilted, about 5 minutes.

Increase the heat to high and add the pork to the pot with the stock, bay leaves, thyme, basil, red pepper flakes, black pepper, salt, and cooked hominy. Bring the mixture to a simmer and cook over low heat until the pork becomes tender, about 2 hours. Add a reserved cup of hominy cooking liquid if necessary.

Season to taste with salt, if necessary (the salt content in canned hominy varies). Stir in the parsley and scallions just before serving.

AARON BURGAU

Patois | New Orleans, Louisiana

Gumbo is a Creole specialty and mainstay of New Orleans cuisine. The rich, thick stew always begins with a dark roux to which a variety of different vegetables, meats, and/or shellfish are added. Most gumbos include the holy trinity of onion, celery, and green pepper—plus garlic—as their base, and greens are sometimes added for good luck. This combination of rabbit and andouille, the heavily spiced French sausage traditional to Cajun cookery, is unbeatable. **SERVES 6 TO 8**

Smoked Rabbit and Andouille Gumbo with Greens

½ cup vegetable oil

½ cup unbleached all-purpose flour

1 medium white onion, cut into ¼-inch dice (about 1 cup)

½ red bell pepper, cut into ¼-inch dice (about ½ cup)

½ green bell pepper, cut into ¼-inch dice (about ½ cup)

1 large rib celery, cut into ¼-inch dice (about ½ cup)

2 tablespoons finely minced garlic

½ cup coarsely chopped canned tomatoes and their juice

½ teaspoon dried thyme

1 tablespoon Creole Seasoning (recipe on the facing page)

3 bay leaves

7 to 8 cups chicken stock (homemade or store-bought)

1 large bunch collard or mustard greens, stems removed and leaves coarsely chopped

½ pound andouille sausage, cut in half lengthwise and sliced ¼ inch thick

½ pound smoked rabbit or chicken meat, cut into 1-inch pieces

Kosher salt and freshly ground black pepper

Hot sauce

Cooked long-grain rice, for serving

To make the roux, heat a large heavy pot or Dutch oven over medium-high heat and add the oil. When the oil is smoking, slowly add the flour, a little at a time, stirring constantly until all the flour has been added and the roux begins to darken. After about 30 minutes, or when the roux is dark red brown, add the onions and cook, stirring constantly, until they caramelize and the roux becomes a chocolate brown color.

Add the peppers, celery, garlic, and tomatoes and continue to cook until the vegetables become soft and slightly translucent, 10 to 15 minutes. Add the thyme, Creole seasoning, and bay leaves, stir to combine, and add 7 cups of the stock. Bring the contents of the pot to a boil and add the greens. Reduce the heat and simmer for 30 minutes before adding the sausage and rabbit or chicken pieces. If the gumbo seems to be getting too thick, add the remaining cup of stock. Continue cooking for another 30 minutes, season to taste with salt, black pepper, and hot sauce, and serve over hot long-grain rice.

Creole Seasoning

1 tablespoon onion powder

1 tablespoon garlic powder

1 tablespoon dried oregano leaves

1 tablespoon dried sweet basil

1½ teaspoons dried thyme

1½ teaspoons black pepper

1½ teaspoons white pepper

1½ teaspoons cayenne pepper

1½ teaspoons celery seed

2 tablespoons plus 1½ teaspoons
  sweet paprika

Mix all of the ingredients in a bowl or combine in a food processor or blender and pulse to finely grind. Store in a cool, dark place for up to 6 months.

Choosing Sustainably Raised Rabbit

Free-range rabbits are rare because they are vulnerable to so many predators—hawks, raccoons, coyotes, and owls, to name a few. Most rabbits are raised in hutches throughout the calendar year, a production method that has been around for centuries. The mobile chicken coop/tractor model is becoming a more common method for pasturing rabbits, providing protection and continual access to fresh, new grass at the same time. Rabbit droppings are gold in a garden, particularly because they are an odorless, ready-to-use fertilizer that doesn't burn plants the way chicken manure does.

Rabbits that don't have access to pasture are usually fed an antibiotic-free diet of alfalfa.

Rabbit meat is delicate and easy to digest and is lower in fat and calories than chicken. Once stripped of its skin and fat, it tends to dry out quickly and is best served by moist cooking methods like braises and stews, which create a mutually beneficial relationship between the tender meat and a full-flavored sauce. Even the offal can be used, particularly the liver, which makes a pate almost identical in flavor to chicken liver pâté.

FRANK BRIGTSEN

Brigtsen's Restaurant | *New Orleans, Louisiana*

This grilled lamb has a gutsy mix of garlic, herbs, and mint. The addition of jalapeño gives mint jelly, lamb's long standing companion, a slight kick that accents the smoky flavor of grilled lamb chops. The recipe comes together quickly once the chops come out of the marinade, making it good for a weeknight meal. Since lamb chops are always a treat, this is also a nice dish for entertaining. **SERVES 4**

Grilled Marinated Lamb Chops with Jalapeño Mint Jelly

⅔ cup fruity red wine, such as Pinot Noir or Beaujolais

2 teaspoons minced fresh garlic

2 tablespoons plus 2 teaspoons coarsely chopped fresh oregano leaves

1 tablespoon plus 1 teaspoon coarsely chopped fresh rosemary leaves

1 tablespoon plus ½ teaspoon kosher salt, divided

1¼ teaspoons finely ground black pepper, divided

1 teaspoon freshly squeezed lime juice

1⅓ cups mild olive oil

Eight 4-ounce lamb loin or rib chops

1 teaspoon onion powder

½ teaspoon cayenne

¾ teaspoon garlic powder

½ teaspoon white pepper

½ teaspoon dry mustard

½ teaspoon rubbed sage

½ teaspoon ground cumin

½ teaspoon dried thyme

Jalapeño Mint Jelly (recipe on the facing page)

In a small glass or nonreactive mixing bowl, whisk together the red wine, garlic, oregano, rosemary, ½ teaspoon salt, ¼ teaspoon black pepper, and lime juice to combine well. Add the olive oil in a slow, steady stream, whisking constantly, until fully incorporated.

Place the lamb chops in a shallow glass baking pan and pour the marinade over the top. Cover with plastic wrap and leave in the refrigerator to marinate for 3 to 4 hours. To make the seasoning mix, combine the remaining 1 tablespoon salt, the onion powder, cayenne, garlic powder, white pepper, dry mustard, sage, cumin, thyme, and remaining 1 teaspoon black pepper in a small bowl and set aside.

When ready to cook, remove the lamb chops from the marinade, pat dry, and season on both sides with about 1 teaspoon of the seasoning mix. Heat a gas or charcoal grill to high. Grill the chops for 3 to 4 minutes per side, or to the desired temperature. Serve immediately, 2 chops per person, with jalapeño mint jelly on the side.

Jalapeño Mint Jelly

⅓ cup granulated sugar

1 tablespoon plus 1½ teaspoons finely
   chopped jalapeños, with seeds

¼ cup finely chopped fresh mint

¾ teaspoon freshly squeezed lemon juice

¼ teaspoon finely chopped lemon zest

Pinch of Kosher salt

2¼ teaspoons gelatin, dissolved in ¼ cup
   water

In a small nonreactive saucepan, combine 1¼ cups cold water, the sugar, jalapeños, mint, lemon juice and zest, and salt. Bring the mixture to a boil, reduce the heat to a simmer, and cook for 6 minutes. Remove from the heat and add the dissolved gelatin, whisking until fully blended. Strain and refrigerate.

"Vegetarianism may bypass industrial beef, but it ignores the fact that most people still want to eat meat. Grass fed offers some solutions to several problems. Since there's less of it, it becomes a special food rather than something we consume on a daily basis."

DEBORAH MADISON
Santa Fe, New Mexico

Less Is More

Using meat as a condiment is another solution. A little bit of full-flavored meat, like sausage, bacon, ham, salami, or pancetta can turn a vegetable or grain-based side dish into a hearty main course. A seasonal strata (Wild Ramp and Farmstead Cheese Strata with Roasted Tomato Wine Butter on page 268) or vegetable tart (Beet Greens and Legs Pie on page 73) is more satisfying with the addition of salty prosciutto or bits of spicy sausage.

There are also a handful of ingredients with such satisfying flavor (what the Japanese call "umami," or the fifth flavor) that they can make a dish taste meaty without adding any. When combined with vegetables, grains, legumes, or pastas, these ingredients will make you forget your dish is meatless:

- roasted or grilled eggplant (Grilled Eggplant with Roasted Red Pepper and Black Olive Salad on page 19)
- sautéed or dried mushrooms (Steamed Savory Egg Custard with Shiitake Mushrooms on page 244 and Shaved Mushroom and Onion Salad with Fried Lemons on page 33)
- Fish sauce and anchovies (Treviso Bagna Cauda with Poached Egg on page 243)
- Miso (Winter Squash Soup on page 52)
- Toasted nuts and nut butters (Nasturtium Soup with Braised Pistachios on page 42)

Reading the Labels

Shopping for meat used to be a relatively uncomplicated process; it was a matter of finding the sweet spot where the best-quality cut of meat met the best price. Until recently, that meant choosing between cuts of conventionally raised commodity beef, lamb, or pork from the supermarket butcher counter.

However, a keen awareness and interest in how our food is produced is leading a growing number of consumers to seek out more sustainable alternatives to animals raised in Confined Animal Feeding Operations (CAFOs) with antibiotics and hormones. Demand for clarity and traceability has led to frequently confusing and sometimes contradictory labeling standards for meat and eggs, full of doublespeak and loopholes.

The Food Safety and Inspection Service (FSIS) is the arm of the USDA responsible for ensuring the correct labeling and packaging of meat, poultry, and eggs. The labels as defined by FSIS are called "terms of law," which means that a producer must demonstrate that the product meets the definition in order to use it on a label. "Grass fed" is a term of law. There are also "terms of art," which are self-made claims. Producers try to persuade the FSIS that a product is what they say it is, but a signed affidavit is the only assurance that practices are adhered to.

To help navigate the current landscape of meat labels and make good choices in the absence of a comprehensive set of standards, use the guidelines that follow.

AMERICAN HUMANE® CERTIFIED
Defined by American Humane Certified
American Humane Certified's program claims to provide verifiable assurance that products carrying their label have met "rigorous, science-based welfare standards and were humanely raised throughout their life process." However, the organization supports caged production for chickens as "humane," and there are no requirements for pasture access for any species.

ANIMAL WELFARE APPROVED
Defined by Animal Welfare Approved (AWA)
Animals are raised outdoors on pasture or range on true family farms with stringent welfare standards developed in collaboration with scientists, veterinarians, researchers, and farmers. Annual field audits by this third-party certifier monitor animals from birth to slaughter.

CRATE FREE
(PORK)
No legal or regulated definition
Two types of crates are commonly used in pork production. Note that a "farrowing crate free" label doesn't mean the product is "gestation crate free" and vice versa. "Crate free" doesn't mean the animal was raised outdoors.

■ **Farrowing crate.** A cage or other strictly enclosed space in which a sow is confined to give birth and suckle her piglets. The sow's movements are restricted so that she can't turn around or have free movement. Farrowing crates are prohibited under Animal Welfare Approved (AWA) standards.

■ **Gestation crate.** A cage or stall in which a sow is confined during her pregnancy and in which her movement options are limited. AWA standards prohibit gestation crates.

FOOD ALLIANCE
Defined by Food Alliance Certified
The Food Alliance livestock certification program uses two evaluation criteria: fixed and scored inspection. Farms must comply with all fixed criteria but may become certified based on the "average" score in some areas. Food Alliance–certified products come from farmers and ranchers who provide safe and fair working conditions, support humane treatment of animals, and practice good environmental stewardship. Food Alliance is a third-party certifier.

FREE RANGE/FREE ROAMING (POULTRY)

Defined by USDA

Producers must prove to the agency that the poultry has had access to the outdoors. The type of outdoor access (pasture or dirt lot, for example), length of time birds are required to have outdoor access, and how these stipulations are verified are not legally defined and vary greatly from facility to facility. Overcrowding is common.

FREE RANGE/FREE ROAMING (SPECIES OTHER THAN POULTRY)

No legal or regulated definition

The type of outdoor access provided (pasture or dirt lot, for example), the length of time animals are required to have outdoor access, and how these stipulations must be verified are not legally defined and vary greatly from facility to facility. There is no requirement to demonstrate to the USDA that birds and animals have even had access to the outdoors, let alone any reference to other management practices. No independent third-party verification.

GLOBAL ANIMAL PARTNERSHIP (GAP) 5-STEP PROGRAM

Defined by Global Animal Partnership

GAP brings together farmers, scientists, ranchers, retailers, and animal advocates with the common goal of wanting to improve the welfare of beef cattle, pigs, and broiler chickens in agriculture. To qualify for the program, farmers must meet the basic requirements of the Step 1 level, the first and least stringent of the steps. (Dr. Temple Grandin, the renowned animal scientist, stated that in most cases, the Step 1 standards were the same as—or only marginally better—than those found in industrial farming systems.) The GAP program which started as an exclusive 2-year program at Whole Foods Markets, will eventually be adopted by other grocery retailers and restaurants.

GRAIN FED

No legal or regulated definition

While this designation implies that the animal was fed grain exclusively, a mixture of corn, soy, and other grains—many of which are genetically modified—is the industry standard feed for beef. This is usually not a positive claim since cows, sheep, goats, and bison are ruminants whose digestive tracts are designed for grass, not grains. Preventative dosing with antibiotics and hormones is intended to address the array of health problems created by a grain-based diet. With regard to poultry, grain fed implies that birds were fed a vegetarian diet without actually specifying it.

GRASS FED

Defined by the USDA

Grass fed refers to the diet of cattle, sheep, goats, and bison. Grass-fed animals—cows and bison, mostly—are sometimes referred to as "grass finished." They may or may not be organic, but they are guaranteed to have eaten nothing but grass, freshly grazed pasture, and forage during the growing season and stored grasses and forage (hay and silage) during the winter months and in drought conditions. During the growing season, grass-fed animals must have continuous access to pasture. It's useful to keep in mind that grass can be grown and harvested and transported to a feedlot, and the end result will still be eligible for a grass-fed label.

Grass-fed animals are not, by definition, necessarily free of antibiotics and hormones. But they rarely have a need for them since they're not crowded into feedlots where disease is rampant and where they're eating a grain-based diet that they're unable to digest properly.

GRASS FINISHED

No legal or regulated definition

Not to be confused with grass fed, grass finished implies that animals are fed grass and forage for an undefined period before slaughter, although they may have been given grains and other nonforage feed for the majority of their lives. The size of the operation and amount of grazeable pasture is often what dictates how much forage a grain-fed animal gets. This label does not define prohibited feedstuffs and medications.

NATURALLY RAISED

Defined by the USDA

Meat bearing a "naturally raised" label must be free of antibiotics and growth hormones and never have been fed animal by-products. The label guarantees nothing about how or where the animal was raised.

Breaking It Down

NATURAL
Defined by the USDA

This label only applies to the animal after it is slaughtered and guarantees nothing about how the animal was raised. "Natural" meat products are free of artificial ingredients or added color and are minimally processed. Minimal processing means the product was not processed in a manner that fundamentally alters it. The natural label must include a qualifying statement, like "no artificial ingredients" or "minimally processed."

NEVER, EVER
No legal or regulated definition

Meat labeled "never, ever" means that the animals were never given antibiotics or hormones. A sick animal requiring treatment is culled from the rest of the herd and sold on the commodity market once it is healthy.

NO HORMONES ADMINISTERED
Defined by USDA/FSIS

Hormones are commonly used to accelerate the growth weight of beef cattle and increase milk production in dairy cattle. If sufficient documentation is provided by the producer to show that no hormones were used in raising the animals, the agency will approve the label.

NO HORMONES ADDED
Defined by USDA

This claim cannot be used on labels for pork or poultry, since hormones are not allowed in raising either animal.

NO ANTIBIOTICS
Defined by USDA

Antibiotics are given to cattle, hogs, sheep, and chickens to prevent or manage diseases. The USDA is accountable for proper use of these claims, but there is no system in place for verification.

ORGANIC
Defined by the USDA/FSIS

Like vegetarian, the "organic" label offers no guarantees about how the animal was raised. However, it does provide the assurance that the animal was fed a diet of 100 percent certified organic, non-GMO feed, which may or may not have included grain, and received no hormones or antibiotics.

PASTURED/PASTURE RAISED
No legal or regulated definition

While this designation implies that animals were raised outdoors on pasture, there is no way to ensure if any claim is accurate since the term is not regulated or certified.

VEGETARIAN FED
No legal or regulated definition

Animals raised on a "vegetarian" diet haven't been fed meat by-products, but they aren't necessarily raised outdoors or on pasture since grain is also a vegetable.

Fresh from the Freezer

Farmer's markets, independent grocery stores and co-ops, artisanal butcher shops, ranches and farms that sell online. These outlets are among the number of fully transparent sources of sustainably raised meat that continue to grow in step with demand. One of the best ways to participate in the delights and economic benefits—to you and the farmer—of eating sustainably raised meat is to purchase a share directly from the producer and store the cuts in your freezer. Cooking your way through a quarter cow, a half pig, or a whole lamb or goat is an adventure that is gratifying on many levels, one being the sense of discovery that comes from trying new cuts and experiencing new flavors. But nothing satisfies or increases the integrity of the supply like supporting a system that honors the whole animal.

Buying fresh pastured meat and poultry from a butcher counter is a convenience and will always be more expensive than buying directly from a farmer. Real value comes from cultivating a relationship with a producer and buying from the source. This allows consumers (chefs and home cooks alike) to ask questions and make informed purchases that take into account the age and breed of an animal and how it was raised. In the case of larger animals, the buyer may have a say in how it is butchered (by completing a "cutting order") and packaged. An inventory of frozen meat is essential to ranchers and farmers as a means of extending the season and selling a whole cow in parts to a variety of users, including direct market retail and restaurants.

Freezing is the best way to preserve the flavor and quality of fresh meat and to enjoy a seasonal product throughout the year; it's no different than opening a jar of peaches, canned at the height of summer, to savor in January. So there's no need to turn up your nose at the idea. The stigma attached to frozen meat, and beef in particular, is usually connected to a single negative experience. Meat that is slaughtered in season, vacuum-packaged, and frozen at the peak of freshness has all of the attributes of the same fresh cuts of meat and is superior to any fresh meat available in the off-season. Cryovac®, a method of vacuum sealing with thick sheets of plastic, is widely used by processors. Ask to have your meat wrapped this way; the increased protection this method ensures will keep meat, frozen at the proper temperature (at or below 0°F), for up to 1 year without sacrificing flavor or texture.

Many chefs prefer to use fresh meat, but the flavor differences between fresh and frozen are unnoticed by most. The important thing to focus on is the source for the meat. There is more forgiveness when an animal is well raised, cared for, and treated humanely.

"If properly handled throughout the process, there's nothing wrong with using frozen meat. The potential drawback is in the fact that, when you buy a piece of frozen meat, you may not have any assurance that it was properly frozen, how long it's been frozen, or if it's been kept at the right temperature (0°F or below)."

DAN ROSENTHAL
President of the Rosenthal Restaurant Group, Chicago, Illinois

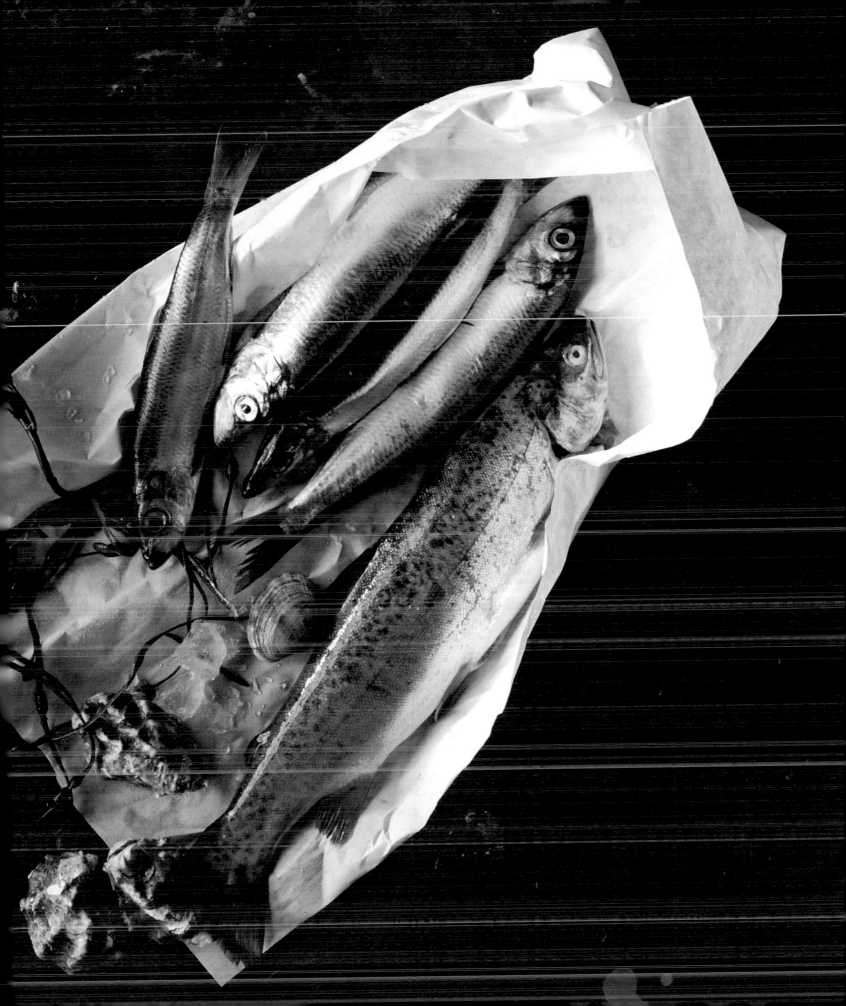

An oyster savored slowly tells the story of its life, with flavors of the ocean tides that reached over it or the salty bay or creek where it was grown. Bright red sockeye salmon from the pristine waters of Alaska's Bristol Bay feast on orange krill that turns their flesh deep red. Bluefish "blitz" in the harbors and inlets of Long Island Sound, where the bunker and eels run thick. These wild fish and shellfish are but a few examples of foods we eat that are an expression of the place they were raised. The astonishing variety of species and flavors inspires excitement among chefs and diners. For Sam Hayward, chef/partner of Fore Street in Portland, Maine, this couldn't be more true. "Atlantic pollock, which are very different from the Pacific species; Northern shrimp, sometimes called Maine shrimp; silver hake, also known as whiting; Atlantic mackerel; blue mussels: asking me which is most delicious is like asking me which of my children I love most."

Fish and Seafood

Satisfying a Global Appetite

Fish and shellfish have never been more popular, not just for their health benefits but also for the delicious diversity seafood brings to our diets. As the global appetite for seafood has resulted in dwindling stocks of many marine species, we have begun to explore others that are less commonly eaten: anchovies, mackerel, and rainbow trout are just a few. While we wait patiently for seasonal delicacies—Chesapeake Bay soft-shell crabs that peak in July and Dungeness crabs from the northern West Coast shores during the winter holidays; tiny sweet pink shrimp from the Gulf of Maine in the winter and bay shrimp from the estuaries of the Pacific Ocean in spring and summer—we dig in to more readily available species, responsibly farmed fish, and smoked, cured, and frozen fish. In some places, we must get our fill of wild oysters between September and April, but throughout the year, we can find excellent farmed versions.

The oceans have changed more in the last 30 years than in all of human history. Throughout the world, decades of intense fishing have diminished populations of species high on the food chain—the predators of the sea, including dolphins, sharks, whales, tuna, and turtles. According to the Food and Agriculture Organization of the United Nations (FAO) and a recent landmark study, 63 percent of the global fish stocks assessed are in need of rebuilding. Current global assessments of species that are overfished range between 25 percent and 72 percent of fish stocks depending on the definition used, but the common message is this: Overfishing has increased substantially since the middle of the last century.

Overfishing is just part of the problem, though. Many fish are caught using methods and gear that destroy ocean habitats, threaten other species, and pollute the waters. Acidification of the seas, fertilizer and sewage runoff from land, and

> ## "It is imperative that we support our regional fisheries. Failing to do so means losing not just local traditions and ways of life, but also a great deal of knowledge about sustainable fishing practices."
>
> **MICHAEL LEVITON**
> *chef/owner, Lumière,*
> *Newton, Massachusetts*

> ## "We're never going to save the oceans just by eating sustainable seafood. Some of the energy and attention focused on increasing our supply of resources needs to be redirected toward better utilization of existing resources."
>
> **BARTON SEAVER**
> *National Geographic Fellow, chef,*
> *and author of* For Cod and Country

rising temperatures and increasing numbers of dead zones where few species can survive are the realities of a changing climate, proof that what we do at sea and on land impacts the waters and their creatures.

Preserving Traditions and Ways of Life

Regulating wild-caught fisheries is challenging, too. In its 2011 publication *Turning the Tide: The State of Seafood,* the Monterey Bay Aquarium reports that an estimated 20 percent of the world's fish are caught illegally, a compounding factor in the overfishing equation. Enforcing rules on the high seas is a formidable task, but closer to home, successful management of regional fisheries through cooperative efforts between regulators and fishers has helped to address and control the problem of overfishing. The relationship between fishers and regulators is complex, but everyone agrees on the importance of maintaining a healthy population of fish in the sea. As consumers, we can support thoughtful management of species and local economies by purchasing domestic seafood in season and by being aware of seafood populations and their constantly changing status.

Supporting responsible forms of aquaculture is part of the answer, too. Humans have been raising fish for almost as long as they've been catching them. Chinese manuscripts dating back to the fifth century BC suggest the Chinese practiced fish culture, and Romans are known to have cultivated oysters, the first known form of aquaculture that has continued in some form to the present day. Only recently has global aquaculture production boomed into an industry that poses challenges to the environment and consumers, the same challenges linked to large-scale, land-based food production. With more natural fish populations in serious decline

and increased demand for seafood at our tables, it isn't a question of whether we should embrace aquaculture, but how we can ensure that it provides a responsible alternative that also tastes good. A wide variety of tools are available to help us do that (from certifications and labels to seafood guides), but one of the best ways to make a difference is by purchasing fish from a trusted purveyor.

Fish are one of the few remaining wild animals that we eat. When talk turns to their future and how long we will continue to enjoy them, two assessments of the health of our seas typically surface: that overzealous fishing has nearly exhausted certain species of fish and destroyed their habitats and that once-depleted populations of wild fish are beginning to show signs of recovery. The state of our seas is complicated, making both assessments often true.

Diversity, Variety, Revitalization

Ocean populations and habitats are constantly changing, making it difficult to come up with black-and-white answers to questions and choices that have many layers. Our best purchases are informed by ample information to make decisions on a case-by-case basis. What is clear is the need to preserve the diversity of our oceans and to return them to health.

From flavorful farmed sturgeon and catfish to wild Alaskan salmon and rich, oily sardines, a world of delicious sustainable seafood options awaits us, and we can explore it for many years to come, if we are careful. By viewing our ecosystem as a whole and understanding the impact of our seafood purchases, we can identify and support the species and the organizations that manage our resources thoughtfully, and by doing so advocate not just for a sustainable future for seafood, but a restorative one.

GREG HIGGINS

Higgins Restaurant and Bar | *Portland, Oregon*

Oregon pink shrimp—also known as "bay shrimp" and "salad shrimp"—come from the world's first shrimp fishery to be certified sustainable. The tiny sweet shrimp are found mostly in the estuaries of the Pacific Ocean and are plentiful between April and October. Maine pink shrimp, a cold-water variety available between December and February, or any other small, sustainably harvested shrimp make a good substitute. **SERVES 8**

Carpaccio of Chinook Salmon with Bay Shrimp and Pumpernickel

1 fresh Chinook salmon fillet, about
  1 pound, skinned and boned

¼ cup extra-virgin olive oil; more for
  garnish

1 tablespoon honey

3 tablespoons freshly squeezed lime juice

½ teaspoon hot chili sauce

8 ounces Oregon pink shrimp, marinated in
  the juice of 1 lime

½ small red onion, cut into ¼-inch dice
  (about ¼ cup)

2 hard-cooked eggs, grated

1 small bunch arugula

8 thin slices dark pumpernickel bread,
  lightly toasted

1 tablespoon lemon verbena chiffonade

1 teaspoon fleur de sel

Using a sharp slicing knife, cut thin slices of salmon on the bias. Arrange the slices in 2-ounce portions on eight separate sheets of plastic wrap, fitting a few slices together closely to create a tight circle. Cover each circle with another sheet of plastic wrap and, using light tapping motions and a smooth mallet, very gently pound the salmon until you have paper thin, plate-size rounds of carpaccio.

Combine the olive oil, honey, lime juice, and hot sauce. Fold in the marinated bay shrimp, diced onions, and grated egg. Remove the top layers of plastic wrap from the carpaccio and transfer each round to a chilled plate. Arrange a small bed of arugula leaves in the center of the carpaccio and top with some of the shrimp salad and a slice of pumpernickel toast. Garnish with a drizzle of olive oil, a sprinkle of lemon verbena, and a pinch of fleur de sel.

CHAD WHITE

Counterpoint | San Diego, California

If you've not tried them, fresh sardines are wonderful, a completely different animal than canned. This particular preparation of briny sardines shows them in their best light.

If you have the opportunity, purchase sardines directly from a fishing boat. To clean them, use a medium-stiff bristle brush to gently scrape away the scales under cold running water. To gut the sardines, make a small incision along the belly and use the tips of your finger to pull out the entrails. Rinse again under gently running cold water and pat dry.
SERVES 4

Sardines Veracruz

2 tablespoons extra-virgin olive oil

½ bunch fresh flat-leaf parsley, leaves only

2 small cloves garlic

12 fresh sardines, cleaned

Sea salt, preferably smoked

4 pieces Roasted Tomato Confit
   (recipe below)

1 cup frisée, yellow center leaves only

2 red radishes, thinly shaved

Olive Tapenade (recipe on page 180)

Combine the olive oil, parsley leaves, and garlic in a blender or food processor and pulse until smooth. Use the mixture to coat the sardines, sprinkle with smoked sea salt, and set aside until the grill is hot.

Heat the grill to high and cook the sardines for 2 minutes per side, or until their eyes turn cloudy. Put 3 sardines each on four plates and top with a piece of tomato confit. Toss the frisée with the radishes and a tablespoon of tapenade and place a small amount of salad on top of the tomato confit. Drizzle the remaining tapenade around the plates.

Roasted Tomato Confit

**MAKES 16 TO 20 PIECES, OR
ABOUT 1½ CUPS**

¼ cup extra-virgin olive oil, divided

Kosher salt and freshly ground black pepper

8 to 10 ripe plum tomatoes
   (about 2 pounds), halved

2 cloves garlic, finely minced

2 sprigs fresh thyme, leaves only

\

Put a rack in the center of the oven and heat to 300°F. Line a baking sheet with foil and spread about 2 tablespoons of olive oil evenly over the pan. Sprinkle the oil with salt and a few grinds of black pepper.

Halve the tomatoes lengthwise and use a small spoon to scoop out the seeds. Lay the tomato halves on the baking sheet, cut side up, and drizzle with the remaining olive oil. Season with salt and pepper and scatter the garlic and thyme leaves over the tomatoes. Roast for about 1 hour, turning the tomatoes over halfway through the cooking time. When the skin blisters and the tomatoes are very tender but continue to hold their shape, remove the pan from the oven and allow them to cool to room temperature on the pan. Peel off the skin and store the tomatoes in whatever oil remains in the pan. Add more oil to cover if you plan to keep them in the refrigerator for more than 2 days.

>>>

Olive Tapenade

MAKES 2½ CUPS

1 cup finely chopped green olives

1 shallot, finely chopped

3 cloves garlic, finely minced

1 tablespoon finely chopped preserved lemon

2 teaspoons freshly squeezed lemon juice

1 teaspoon crushed red pepper flakes

1 cup extra-virgin olive oil

3 tablespoons finely chopped fresh
flat-leaf parsley

3 tablespoons finely chopped fresh chives

3 tablespoons fresh thyme leaves,
finely chopped

Combine all of the ingredients and set aside.

Thinking inside the Can

With home pickling and preserving back in vogue, we need to bring back canned seafood, which offers a great opportunity to support sustainable fisheries.

Canned pink salmon is one of the best seafood products available on supermarket shelves. The largest pink salmon fishery in Alaska manages stocks responsibly, and relatively little of the fish is used as fresh product. Canned salmon is loaded with calcium and omega-3s, which are good for heart health and neurological development and low in marine toxins such as methylmercury. It makes a delicious and inexpensive substitute for canned tuna and can be turned into mouth-watering salmon cakes with the addition of a few simple ingredients and very little time.

Canned sardines and anchovies are staples in my house. I put them in braises, salads, sandwiches, and almost everything else, for the unmistakable depth of flavor and heart-healthy fatty acids they add. Eggplant stuffed with anchovy-studded ratatouille is perfect for a summer evening's meal. Canned and jarred mussels, oysters, and clams are another economical solution for heart-healthy meals that are as quick and easy as the flip of a lid. Make a mean smoked mussel chowder by adding half-and-half, celery, potatoes, herbs, and seasonings.

Canned seafood typically comprises species with high rates of productivity and a lower status on the marine food chain, both of which result in a smaller environmental impact. These species tend to be small, so they don't accumulate toxins like mercury, PCBs, and dioxins common in larger, longer-lived predatory fish. Fresh seafood is perishable and can be costly after factoring in spoilage and waste. Canned seafood is packed shortly after harvest, when it is freshest, and it keeps for months.

One of the prevailing arguments against a more sustainable food system is that "good food" is inaccessible because it costs too much. Canned seafood is available to everyone, everywhere. Pink salmon, anchovies, sardines, and bivalves like clams and oysters are among the most beneficial foods, not only for the health of our oceans but for that of ourselves and our families. So the next time you're planning a meal, or your doctor recommends eating more seafood, remember to think inside the can.

National Geographic Fellow, chef, and author of For Cod and Country, **BARTON SEAVER** *has a mission to engage us in a more sustainable food system on every level.*

WAYNE JOHNSON

Ray's Boathouse | *Seattle, Washington*

Briefly sautéed calamari finishes cooking in a warm, fresh tomato sauce brightened with the flavors of lemons, herbs, and chiles. After marinating in the sauce overnight, the pleasantly chewy rings of calamari are served with grilled bread, saffron-infused aïoli, and peppery watercress. Serve small portions to begin a meal, or add more greens and some extra bread to turn it into a satisfying lunch or light dinner. **SERVES 6 AS A STARTER OR 4 AS A MAIN COURSE**

Spicy Calamari with Tomatoes and Saffron Aïoli

¼ cup olive oil, divided

1 small onion, cut into ¼-inch dice
(about ½ cup)

2 teaspoons finely minced garlic

2 teaspoons kosher salt

2 teaspoons crushed red pepper flakes

2 cups tomato purée

2 teaspoons finely chopped lemon zest

2 teaspoons finely chopped fresh rosemary

1 teaspoon tomato paste

1 pound fresh calamari, sliced into
½-inch-wide rings

2 tablespoons finely chopped fresh
flat-leaf parsley

Saffron Aïoli (recipe on page 182)

6 pieces grilled bread

1½ cups watercress

1 tablespoon finely chopped chives

Warm 2 tablespoons of the olive oil in a nonreactive saucepan over medium high heat. Add the onions and sauté for 3 minutes, or until they are translucent. Add the garlic, salt, and red pepper flakes and cook for 30 seconds. Stir in the tomato purée, lemon zest, rosemary, and tomato paste and cook for 5 more minutes. Remove from the heat.

In another pan, warm the other 2 tablespoons of olive oil over high heat and sauté the calamari until opaque, about 2 minutes. Add the calamari to the pan with the warm tomato sauce and let it stand for 20 minutes. Stir in the parsley and put in a clean container to cool in the refrigerator.

To serve, drizzle or smear some saffron aïoli on the bottom of each of six plates. Cut the slices of grilled bread in half, crisscross on top of one another, and place over the aïoli. Divide the calamari among the plates, placing a small mound in front of the grilled bread. Put several stems or about ¼ cup watercress on top of the calamari and sprinkle with chives. Serve with additional aïoli.

>>>

Saffron Aïoli

MAKES 2 CUPS

1 large egg yolk

1 teaspoon kosher salt

⅛ teaspoon white pepper

1½ teaspoons Dijon mustard

2½ teaspoons sherry vinegar

1 teaspoon freshly squeezed lemon juice

½ cup olive oil

1 cup canola oil

½ teaspoon saffron threads

1 teaspoon finely minced garlic

½ teaspoon granulated sugar

Place the egg yolk in the bowl of a food processor or in the bowl of a stand mixer fitted with the whisk attachment. Pulse or whisk on high speed until the yolk is a pale shade of yellow. Add the salt, pepper, mustard, vinegar, and lemon juice and pulse or whisk to combine. With the food processor or mixer running, gradually add the olive and canola oils in a thin, steady drizzle. When all of the oil has been incorporated refrigerate the mayonnaise.

To finish the aïoli, place ¼ cup water and the saffron in small saucepan and bring to rolling boil. Remove from the heat, pour into a nonreactive bowl, and cool completely.

Add the mayonnaise, garlic, and sugar and whisk to combine.

> **"Flounder is an example of a mislabeled fish because flounder is a generic name often used for a wide variety of flatfishes found all over the world. Ask your supplier for the country of origin or even more specific region of origin and the Latin name of the species."**
>
> **MEGAN WESTMEYER**
> *Sustainable Fisheries Partnership, Honolulu, Hawaii*

JOSE DUARTE

Taranta | Boston, Massachusetts

Basic Peruvian seviche is made with just five ingredients and is traditionally accompanied by corn on the cob and boiled sweet potatoes. Aji amarillo is a South American hot, yellow, chile pepper typically used in Peruvian cooking. It adds excellent flavor to seviche. Aji rocoto paste is made from hot red peppers. Habaneros, which have a similarly fruity flavor, would make an acceptable though hotter substitute. Remove most of the seeds if you use one. **SERVES 6**

Summer Flounder Seviche with Littleneck Clams

1 pound fresh summer flounder

1 small red onion, halved and thinly sliced (about ⅓ cup)

½ teaspoon aji amarillo paste

½ teaspoon aji rocoto paste

Sea salt

10 to 12 key limes, juiced (about ½ cup juice)

15 freshly steamed littleneck clams, shells removed

2 sweet potatoes, cut into wedges and boiled until tender, for serving

3 ears corn on the cob, broken in half and boiled until tender, for serving

Cut the fish into bite-size pieces and combine with the onion in a large glass or nonreactive bowl. Quickly rinse both with cold water and drain well. Add the aji amarillo and rocoto pastes, and season with salt.

Add the lime juice and two ice cubes, to freshen the mixture. Toss quickly and remove the ice cubes before they have a chance to melt and dilute the mixture. Add the clams and arrange the seviche in a deep platter, surrounded by wedges of boiled sweet potatoes and pieces of freshly boiled corn on the cob.

Ten Tips for Making Better Seafood Choices

Making smart, sustainable choices when purchasing seafood is complicated, even for chefs. Jose Duarte, chef/owner of Taranta in Boston, explains: "As it is very confusing, I decided to make my own decisions based on my own research, coming to my own conclusions after learning about the source, the species, and its treatment. I also work to build relationships with producers and fishermen. By visiting a harvest location and learning about the product, I can gather enough information to provide to my customers."

As consumers, we, too, can do a certain amount of our own research, which we will undoubtedly use to reach our own conclusions. Following these tips is a good place to begin.

1 Eat lower on the food chain.

Large predators like tuna, swordfish, and Chilean sea bass are critical to maintaining the balance of the food chain, but as predators, they naturally have smaller populations than their prey species and are more vulnerable to overfishing. Because they are high on the food chain, large predators can also contain higher levels of mercury than most other seafood. Consuming species lower on the food chain, including sardines, anchovies, herring, and shellfish, reduces the risk of contamination, contributes to a better balance in the marine ecosystem, and generally leaves a smaller carbon footprint, since the capture and processing of smaller fish requires less intensive energy use.

2 Buy domestic seafood from well-managed fisheries.

The United States has some of the strictest fishery conservation regulations in the world. Fisheries that are certified by an independent third party can provide some assurance about how a fish was managed or raised, caught, and handled. If it's available, seafood from a domestic *and* local source is even better. The shorter the distance your food travels, the greater the chances are that you're supporting traditional fishing communities and getting fresher seafood that has utilized less fuel in the journey to your table.

3 Choose wild fish caught using sustainable fishing methods.

Wild fish are associated with fewer health risks than farmed fish, but they aren't perfect. Depending on the method used to catch them, certain wild species come with the added cost of damage to ocean habitats and depleting other populations of sea life.

Fishing gear used to catch bottom-dwelling species can be invasive and cause serious destruction to the more-sensitive and less-resilient ocean floor habitats that they share. Nonselective fishing methods that capture and kill other species, or bycatch, pose a threat to sea turtles, seabirds, whales, dolphins, and other creatures that are too small, too young, or otherwise not commercially valuable.

4 Think seasonally.

All animals are affected by the seasons, but the constantly changing conditions of the seas have a direct and impactful influence on seafood availability. Fish spawn at certain times of the year, grow at regular rates, and mature pretty much at the same time within a species. If a fish is caught before it reaches maturity, it doesn't have a chance to reproduce. Matching the fishing season to the time in the fish's life when it has produced the optimum number of progeny is an important step to maintaining a healthy population of that species. Wild fisheries open and close at different times of the year depending on the conditions in the water and atmosphere, the seasons when certain species are geographically available, and when the catch quotas for different fish have been met. A thoughtful supplier takes these considerations into account.

5 Seek out U.S.-farmed finfish.

The problems posed by farmed fish mirror those connected to land-based factory farms. Both industries have been charged with causing harm to the environment and to animals by dosing them with chemicals and antibiotics that become a source of health problems for those who eat them. But the aquaculture industry has improved a great deal over the last five years, and as more sustainable methods for raising fish are created, the options for safe and tasty seafood are becoming more varied. In fact, the Monterey Bay Aquarium recently gave its highest green rating to a farmed coho salmon.

The issue is more about where the fish are farmed than the species themselves. Tilapia and barramundi are two examples of finfish being produced sustainably in the U.S. but not necessarily elsewhere. The massive amounts of those species produced in China and Southeast Asia and exported to the U.S. are not sustainable products.

6 Choose farmed shellfish when it comes to aqua-culture.

Bivalves like clams and mussels rank highest when it comes to environmentally friendly aquaculture, primarily because they lead lives similar to wild shellfish and are easier to contain than fish due to their lack of mobility. Marine shellfish actually enhance water quality, and oysters provide habitat by helping to create the structure for the entire ecosystem. The filtering properties of farmed shellfish are identical to those of wild shellfish, and they are playing a significant role in helping to heal the ecosystems we've damaged. A farmed oyster can filter up to 50 gallons of water per day while creating habitat for hundreds of other species. They are also extremely nutritious.

7 Know your sources and ask questions.

Developing the same kind of good relationship with a fisherman or fishmonger that you have with the rancher or butcher who supplies your meat allows you to know what you're getting and to ask for particular kinds of fish from specific sustainable operations. You should always ask these two questions before buying: Where does the fish come from? Is it wild or farmed?

Don't assume that the answers to these questions will stay the same all year. Your purveyor may have to change sources or suggest alternatives based on availability.

8 Ask more questions.

Once you've got answers to the previous questions, you'll want to find out more.

For wild fish, ask:
- Is the population of this species healthy? Does it reproduce quickly?
- Where was the fish captured?
- Is the fishery well managed?
- How was the fish caught?
- Does the fish have any health risks associated with mercury or PCBs?
- How far did the fish travel to reach its final destination?

For farmed fish, ask:
- How was the fish raised?
- Are water pollution and escape by the fish potential problems?
- What was the fish fed? Is it carnivorous or was its diet mostly vegetarian?
- Was the fish raised with antibiotics or pesticides?
- Is there good government oversight of the fish farming industry in that area?

9 Be flexible.

There are good substitutes for most seafood species that provide alternatives out of season and when availability is low. Cooking with lesser-known species like black rockfish, amberjack, and porgy can ease pressure on widely consumed species (tuna, salmon, and shrimp are the top three). Eating a variety of fish also reduces your exposure to potential contaminants.

10 Support small-scale fisheries.

Like small-scale ranchers and farmers, small-scale fishers who use low-impact methods like hook-and-line, harpoon, and reef nets are under pressure from policies that favor industrial-scale methods. Restaurants and consumers can be an important source of support and revenue for these producers.

Chad White, executive chef of Counterpoint in San Diego, California, believes that one way consumers can help change the way seafood is harvested is by "supporting your local fishing industry. Get to know your own area by staying in touch with fishers."

JENN LOUIS

Lincoln Restaurant | Portland, Oregon

Sustainably farmed Manila clams are widely available in the Pacific Northwest, primarily in Washington State and British Columbia. Farmed clams pose little threat to the environment since they do not impair water quality or require wild fish as feed. They are generally hatched responsibly in pens, live out their lives in the wild, and are harvested with racks, which don't significantly impact bottom habitats.

Substitute littleneck or cherrystone clams for manilas, both of which must be cooked slightly longer before they open. SERVES 4

Manila Clams with Sorrel and Cream

Kosher salt

2 ounces sorrel

½ cup heavy cream

3 tablespoons extra-virgin olive oil

2 cloves garlic, thinly sliced

½ small fennel bulb, cut into ¼-inch dice
(about ¼ cup)

½ small yellow onion, cut into ¼-inch dice
(about ¼ cup)

3 sprigs fresh thyme

¼ cup white wine

2 pounds Manila clams

1 cup vegetable stock

¼ cup (½ stick) unsalted butter

Freshly ground black pepper

2 lemons

8 slices crusty bread, grilled

Prepare an ice bath by filling a small bowl with cold water and adding a handful of ice cubes.

Bring a small pot of generously salted water to a boil over high heat. Add the sorrel, quickly submerge and immediately remove it, and then transfer to the ice bath. When cool, remove the sorrel and wring it dry with a clean towel.

Coarsely chop the blanched, dry sorrel and add it to a blender with the cream. Blend until smooth and set aside.

Warm the olive oil in a medium-size sauté pan over medium heat. Add the garlic, fennel, onions, and thyme and cook over medium heat until the vegetables are translucent, about 5 minutes. Add the white wine and continue cooking until it evaporates almost completely. Add the clams, vegetable stock, ½ cup sorrel cream, and the butter, and season with salt and black pepper. Cook just until the clams open and the sauce has thickened slightly, about 5 minutes.

Serve the clams with lemon wedges and grilled bread.

LEE RICHARDSON

Ashley's Restaurant at the Capital Hotel | *Little Rock, Arkansas*

The texture of catfish reminds chef Lee Richardson of Chinese preparations. With that in mind, he combined Southern pantry items like green tomato relish and pepper jelly to create a dish that he describes as purely Southern, but one that should also be pleasing to fans of Chinese cooking. He doesn't use soy sauce or other Chinese flavors and prefers not to serve the fish with rice. Instead, he garnishes it with a coarsely chopped fried egg.

SERVES 8 AS A STARTER OR 4 AS A MAIN COURSE

Sweet-and-Sour Catfish

Two 9- to 12-ounce catfish fillets, skin on

Kosher salt

½ cup unbleached all-purpose flour

Vegetable oil, for frying

2 eggs

¼ cup Green Tomato Jam
  (recipe on the facing page)

¼ cup Red Pepper Marmalade
  (recipe on the facing page)

4 scallions, shaved on the bias or thinly
  sliced, for garnish

Trim the edges of the fillets and about ½ inch of the thinnest part of the tail, and remove any brown or gray matter from the skin side of the fish. Divide the fillets into 2-ounce pieces by cutting one portion from the head end, one from the tail end, and splitting the remainder in half lengthwise along its natural line. Season the pieces with salt and refrigerate for 1 hour.

After an hour, remove the fish from the refrigerator and individually pat dry using a paper towel. Lightly dredge the pieces in flour and shake off any excess.

Heat a frying pan containing ½ inch to ¾ inch of vegetable oil to about 350°F over medium-high heat. Cook the fish pieces on both sides until golden brown, about 2 minutes per side. Remove from the pan to drain on a paper-towel-lined plate.

Place a frying pan over medium heat, lightly coat with oil, and add the eggs when the pan is hot. Fry the eggs over easy, remove from the heat, and transfer to a mixing bowl. Add the green tomato jam and red pepper marmalade to the fried eggs and combine with a fork, breaking the whites up into small pieces and stirring the runny yolks into the jam and marmalade.

To serve, divide the mixture among either eight small plates or four large plates, placing a spoonful of jam-marmalade mixture in the center of each plate and leaving a little bit of liquid behind in the bowl. Put a piece of catfish on top and drizzle with some of the leftover liquid. Garnish with a pinch of shaved scallions.

Green Tomato Jam

MAKES ABOUT 2 CUPS

2 green tomatoes, halved and cut
  into ⅛-inch-thick slices

½ small yellow onion, thinly sliced
  (about ¼ cup)

¾ cup white-wine vinegar

½ cup granulated sugar

Combine the ingredients in a nonreactive pan over medium-high heat. Bring the mixture to a boil and reduce the heat to a simmer. Cook slowly, stirring occasionally, until the mixture has a jam-like consistency.

Remove the pan from the heat and allow to cool slightly before storing in a clean jar in the refrigerator. The jam will keep in the refrigerator for up to 3 months.

Red Pepper Marmalade

MAKES ABOUT 2 CUPS

2 red bell peppers, 3 if small

1 cup granulated sugar

1 cup white-wine vinegar

Cut the peppers in half from stem to blossom end. Remove the seeds and any white pith, and thinly slice the peppers into ¼-inch-thick strips.

Combine the pepper strips with the sugar and vinegar in a nonreactive pan over medium-high heat. Bring the mixture to a boil, reduce the heat to a simmer, and continue to cook slowly until the liquid has reduced by half.

Remove the pan from the heat and allow to cool slightly before storing in a clean jar in the refrigerator. The marmalade will keep in the refrigerator for up to 3 months.

Facts about Wild and Farmed Fish

Wild Facts

POPULATION

Although the populations of some species are precarious and/or more vulnerable due to overfishing and habitat destruction, a number of popular fish like Alaskan salmon and Pacific sablefish can be sourced from healthy fisheries. These robust populations are an indication that some fisheries are managing their resources well.

SPECIES

Fish and shellfish that grow quickly and spawn frequently are good choices for consumption because they are resilient to pressure from overfishing. Mahimahi, wahoo, anchovies, and oysters reach reproductive age long before Chilean sea bass, orange roughy, and sharks, which are slow to reach maturity and must be managed carefully if they are to survive.

CAPTURE LOCATION AND MANAGEMENT

Fishery management varies tremendously from one location to the next; populations of halibut, cod, and sole, which are healthy in the Pacific, are depleted in the Atlantic. Knowing about a particular fishery's practices, and whether its stocks are managed responsibly or are depleted, is crucial to making good decisions about purchasing.

HEALTH RISKS

Water quality also varies and is an important factor in determining whether a population of fish is associated with the health risks caused by pollution and contaminants including metals, industrial chemicals, pesticides, and microbes. Because levels vary among different types of fish, and all of the contaminants found in seafood are odorless, tasteless, and virtually undetectable to the naked eye, the FDA recommends that certain populations (primarily pregnant and nursing women as well as young children) avoid fish with high levels of mercury, including swordfish, shark, king mackerel, and Gulf of Mexico tilefish.

Farmed Facts

About 50 percent of the seafood consumed worldwide is a product of aquaculture, or fish farming, nearly two-thirds of which occurs in China. With global fisheries reaching peak harvest and some natural fish populations declining far below their potential production, the breeding, rearing, and harvesting of fish and shellfish from a variety of environments continues to gain acceptance as a responsible means of meeting the demand for seafood. Aquaculture can provide a sustainable alternative that allows wild stocks to replenish and maintain productive populations, but it can also be a source of pollution and damage to ocean habitats and their populations, especially in countries where methods are unregulated. When buying farmed fish, there are several factors to consider before making your purchase.

HABITAT

Some farmed products are held in open-water systems like sea cages and net pens located in coastal areas and inland waterways. These systems rely on the natural exchange of the water surrounding them to flush out waste, excess feed, and the chemicals sometimes used to combat disease. The volume of waste that comes from these pens, which are frequently overcrowded in order to increase profits, is the real problem.

Because they may contain more fish than the ecosystem can support, the pens can be a source of concentrated waste, parasites, and disease that can be transmitted into the wild, threatening wild sea life and creating dead zones. Open-water farming can only be sustainable if the density of fish in the pen is low and the impact on the surrounding environment is constantly monitored. These systems are susceptible to being ripped open by predators and storms, causing concern about farmed fish that are able to escape and reproduce in the wild, genetically altering those populations and competing with them for food and habitat.

Farmed mollusks, on the other hand, are filter feeders that clean the water they're raised in. Oysters, clams, scallops, and mussels are examples of responsibly farmed seafood that enhance water quality and help to heal damaged habitats, and these are good candidates for open-water systems.

Land-based tanks are closed (or semiclosed) systems that are unconnected to outside waters and eliminate almost any chance of the fish escaping. However, these tanks are associated with higher costs for processing and disposing of wastewater and the extra energy necessary to maintain a truly closed operation.

Developing systems for aquaculture farming in tandem with agriculture is becoming a more popular eco-friendly option. When done right, the systems produce very little waste since the fish waste fertilizes the plants, which in turn filter the water and return necessary nutrients back to the fish. Rice farmers in Asia have long used this method to fight the pests that harm their rice paddies by farming certain species of fish alongside the crops.

DIET

Farmed species in many aquaculture systems are fed a diet of fishmeal made from wild fish. While it takes 2 pounds of wild fish, ground into fishmeal, to produce 1 pound of farmed fish, carnivorous species, like salmon, can require up to 5 pounds of fish "food" to produce just a pound. Not only does this mean that wild species higher in the food chain have less to eat, but it creates a net loss of wild species from the sea. Making use of the scraps and byproducts of processing fish for human consumption is a far better means of supplying farmed fish with the proteins and oils they require. Currently, a vast untapped potential source of nutrition is ending up in landfills.

DISEASE AND ANTIBIOTICS

Increasing the density of fish in a system offers the same benefits and risks that overcrowding in any factory farm operation does. Greater numbers of fish may increase profits, but close quarters mean introducing stress, disease, and parasites that require treatment with antibiotics and pesticides. Antibiotic use in aquaculture has been linked to the development of resistant strains of bacteria in the populations who eat farmed seafood just as it has in overcrowded chicken, cattle, and hog operations.

SETH CASWELL

emmer&rye | *Seattle, Washington*

Lightly seared albacore tuna rubbed with a fragrant mixture of toasted coriander, herbs, and orange zest tastes even better eaten in thick slices, with spoonfuls of the tangy herb and egg condiment the French call Sauce Gribiche. Serve the tuna with fresh tender lettuce leaves and crusty bread for lunch or accompanied by herbed crackers as a starter. SERVES 8 AS A STARTER OR 4 AS A MAIN COURSE

Seared Albacore with Sauce Gribiche

1 tablespoon finely chopped orange zest

2 tablespoons grapeseed oil, divided

1 albacore tuna loin, about 1½ pounds, trimmed and portioned into three 8-ounce rectangles

Kosher salt and freshly ground black pepper

1 tablespoon coriander seed, toasted and ground

1 tablespoon finely chopped fresh cilantro

1 tablespoon finely chopped fresh flat-leaf parsley

Sauce Gribiche (recipe below)

Warm a heavy frying pan over high heat. When it is moderately warm, reduce the heat add the orange zest, and toast and stir for about 30 seconds until aromatic and lightly golden. Remove the toasted zest from the pan and set aside.

Return the pan to the stove, add 1 tablespoon of the oil, and increase the heat to high. Season the tuna pieces with salt and black pepper and, when the pan is very hot, sear the tuna for 45 seconds on each side. Immediately transfer to a plate to cool in the refrigerator. Mix the coriander, cilantro, parsley, orange zest, and the remaining 1 tablespoon of oil. Rub this mixture over the cool seared tuna and marinate overnight.

To serve, evenly slice each piece of tuna into 8. Arrange 3 slices each on eight plates, or arrange the slices on a large platter. Dollop a spoonful of sauce gribiche on each slice of tuna and serve.

Sauce Gribiche

2 hard-cooked eggs, peeled, whites and yolks separated

3 shallots, finely chopped

¼ cup sherry vinegar

2 tablespoons Dijon mustard

½ cup extra-virgin olive oil

2 tablespoons finely chopped fresh chives

2 tablespoons finely chopped fresh chervil

2 tablespoons finely chopped fresh flat-leaf parsley

2 tablespoons chopped pickled fiddlehead ferns (found at specialty markets) or cornichons

3 tablespoons capers, drained and chopped

Kosher salt and freshly ground black pepper

Press the egg yolks through a mesh sieve into a nonreactive bowl or break up and mash with a fork. Add the shallots and sherry vinegar to the yolks and whisk until well combined. Slowly drizzle in the olive oil while continuing to whisk. When the dressing is thickened, fold in the finely chopped egg whites, herbs, pickled fiddlehead ferns, and capers and season to taste with salt and black pepper. Cover and refrigerate overnight to allow the flavors to meld.

JOHN SHIELDS

Gertrude's | *Baltimore, Maryland*

Chef John Shields believes, as many of us do these days, that Mother Nature just might know best: Eating what's in season in our own regions will provide us with exactly the nutrients we require at that time of year. This recipe combines all the elements of a Maryland summer, when the blue crabs are running, the corn in the fields is ready to be harvested, and the peppers in the garden are just beginning to turn red.

SERVES 8 TO 10

Chesapeake Bay Blue Crab and Corn Chowder

¼ cup (½ stick) unsalted butter

1 medium onion, cut into ½-inch dice (about 1 cup)

1 clove garlic, finely minced

2 teaspoons finely chopped shallots

3 tablespoons unbleached all-purpose flour

1 small red bell pepper, cut into ½-inch dice (about ½ cup)

1 small green bell pepper, cut into ½-inch dice (about ½ cup)

½ small fennel bulb, cored and cut into ½-inch dice (about ¼ cup)

3 cups Crab Stock (recipe on the facing page), fish stock, or clam juice

2 medium waxy potatoes, peeled and cut into ½-inch cubes

3 cups heavy cream, heated

4 ears sweet yellow corn, husked and kernels cut off

Kosher salt and freshly ground black pepper

1 pound lump blue crabmeat, picked over for shells

Red Pepper Coulis (recipe on the facing page), for garnish

¼ cup finely minced chives, for garnish

Melt the butter in a large stockpot over medium heat. Add the onions, garlic, and shallots, and sauté, stirring frequently, until tender, about 5 minutes. Add the flour, stir, and cook for about 3 minutes, being careful not to brown the flour. Add the red and green peppers and fennel, and cook, stirring frequently, for about 2 minutes.

Add the stock, bring the mixture almost to a boil, and then reduce the heat and simmer for 10 minutes. Add the potatoes and continue to cook for 15 minutes before adding the heavy cream and corn kernels.

Simmer the chowder for 15 more minutes and season to taste with salt and black pepper. Add the crabmeat and heat gently for 5 to 7 minutes, or until hot. Add additional salt and pepper if desired, ladle into bowls, and garnish with a spoonful of coulis and the minced chives.

Crab Stock

MAKES ABOUT 1 QUART

2 or 3 cooked blue crabs, including top shells
   and cleaned bodies

1 small onion, thickly sliced

1 rib celery, coarsely chopped

1 medium carrot, peeled and coarsely
   chopped

2 cloves garlic, unpeeled

1 bay leaf

1 teaspoon whole black peppercorns

½ teaspoon dried thyme leaves

Combine the crab shells and bodies, onions, celery, carrots, garlic, bay leaves, black peppercorns, and thyme in a large stockpot with 5 cups of water. Put the pot over medium-high heat and bring to a boil. Reduce the heat to a simmer and continue to cook for 30 minutes. Using a fine-mesh sieve or a strainer lined with cheesecloth, strain the stock into a large bowl. Cool and refrigerate if not using immediately.

Red Pepper Coulis

MAKES 1 CUP

3 tablespoons olive oil

2 large red bell peppers, coarsely chopped
   (about 2 cups)

1 tablespoon finely minced garlic

¾ cup vegetable stock

2 tablespoons apple-cider vinegar

Pinch cayenne pepper

Kosher salt

Heat the olive oil in a sauté pan over medium-high heat. Add the peppers and garlic and cook, stirring frequently, for 10 minutes, or until the peppers are soft. Add the vegetable stock, vinegar, and cayenne pepper and continue to cook over medium heat until the liquid has reduced by two-thirds. Remove from the heat and allow to cool slightly.

When the mixture is slightly cooler, place it in a blender and blend until smooth. Pour through a fine-mesh sieve and season to taste with salt. Allow the mixture to cool completely, at least 1 hour, before serving.

Fresh vs. Frozen Fish and Seafood

Today's technology means frozen fish is delicious, economical, and better for fishermen and the environment than fresh-caught seafood. Fish that are flash-frozen at sea immediately after they're caught are at the peak of freshness, flavor, and nutrition.

Chef Peter Merriman agrees. "Frozen fish is the future. Storing fish when they are at their peak reduces pressure on fishermen and prevents fish from being harvested out of season. There are good ways to freeze fish at sea—nitrogen slurries, for example—and when done right, frozen fish is of excellent quality."

Fishermen who have the ability to freeze their catch on their boats can use economies of scale to consolidate processing and add value by utilizing the entire fish. It also gives them the freedom to fish in the best and safest conditions and removes the pressure of having to deliver fresh fish immediately.

Chef Sam Hayward sees a place for frozen fish in the market. "I have occasionally had frozen-at-sea (FAS) fish that was better than at least some fresh examples of the same species. From time to time, I buy FAS fish to eat at home, and much of it is better than some fish landed by trip-boats. Handling practices and the amount of time between death and processing of a fish can be the most salient point, rather than fresh vs. frozen. That said, I don't buy frozen fish for the restaurant."

While experts may be able to tell the difference between fresh and frozen seafood, most of us cannot and will be equally pleased with the quality of seafood frozen properly. Make sure that the fish you choose is labeled "fresh frozen"; retailers in most states are required to label previously frozen fish that is being sold thawed.

TOM BIVINS

CROP Bistro & Brewery | *Stowe, Vermont*

Fresh mussels steamed in ale get extra flavor from wild onions and thyme. Though these sweet, plump shellfish are a great way to start a meal, a few glasses of lager and a loaf of crusty bread for sopping up the buttery broth turn them into a meal.

A wild mussel's beard is found where the two shells meet. To remove it, pinch it between your thumb and first finger and use a side-to-side motion to tug the beard out. SERVES 4

Wild Mussels with Spring Onions, Thyme, and Lager

2 pounds wild mussels

6 wild spring onions or scallions

16 ounces lager or pale ale

2 tablespoons fresh thyme leaves

Zest of 1 lemon, coarsely chopped

Kosher salt and freshly ground black pepper

1 tablespoon unsalted butter

Loaf of crusty bread

Clean the mussels in cold water, checking to make sure their shells are tightly closed. Discard any mussels with cracked shells. If any of the mussels are open, gently tap them against the counter and discard those that don't close up. Individually scrub the mussels, trying to remove anything clinging to the outside. Wash the spring onions and trim off the root end. Thinly slice the white portion and coarsely chop the green.

Heat a large frying pan over medium-high heat. Add the lager and heat to a simmer. Add the mussels and cover, shaking the pan vigorously every 30 seconds or so. After about 2 minutes, lift the lid and add the spring onions, thyme, and lemon zest. Cover and cook for another 2 minutes; the mussels are ready when all of the shells have opened. (Discard any mussels that do not open.) Put the mussels in a large serving bowl or several individual bowls and keep warm.

Continue simmering the remaining liquid to reduce it by half, season to taste with salt and black pepper, and swirl in the butter. Pour the sauce over the mussels and serve with crusty slices of fresh bread for dipping.

JASPER WHITE

Summer Shack | Cambridge, Massachusetts

You can purchase lobster meat for this recipe, but the stew improves immeasurably if you steam the lobsters yourself, slightly undercooking them so that the meat finishes cooking in the stew without getting tough. There's no need to buy the large, expensive lobsters—small chicken lobsters are perfect for this dish.

Once you've cooked and shelled the lobsters, the stew comes together quickly. You can even make it from start to finish and keep it refrigerated for up to 2 days. **SERVES 4 AS A MAIN COURSE OR 8 AS A STARTER**

Home-Style Lobster Stew

3 live hard-shell (or 4 new-shell) chicken lobsters, about 1 pound each, or 14 ounces cooked lobster meat

¼ cup (½ stick) unsalted butter

1 small leek, white and light green parts only, cut into ¼-inch dice

½ cup diced celery root, cut into ¼-inch dice

1 small ripe tomato, peeled, seeded and diced

1 teaspoon sweet Hungarian paprika

Freshly ground black pepper

4 cups whole milk

½ cup heavy cream

Kosher salt or sea salt

1 tablespoon chopped fresh chervil or flat-leaf parsley

1 tablespoon chopped fresh chives

Put a 3- or 4-gallon steam pot fitted with a rack on a large burner. (Use an inverted colander if you don't have a rack.) Add about 1 inch of water to the pot and bring it to a rolling boil. Keep the pot covered with a tight-fitting lid and let it fill up with steam before adding the lobsters.

Place the lobsters in the steamer and replace the lid quickly. Allow 8 minutes for hard-shell lobsters and 6 minutes for new-shell (summer) lobsters. The idea is to slightly undercook the lobsters since the meat will also cook in the stew. Use long-handled tongs to transfer the lobsters from the pot to a pan or platter to cool to room temperature.

When the lobsters are cool enough to handle, remove the meat from the tails, knuckles, and claws, reserving any liquid. Cut the meat into ¾-inch chunks. Remove any roe from the female lobsters, coarsely chop it, and add it to the lobster meat. You can also pick the meat from the carcasses and the walking legs; otherwise, wrap both up and freeze them for later use.

About an hour before serving the stew, drain the chunks of lobster meat in a colander set over a bowl so they are somewhat dry; reserve the juice. Warm the butter over medium heat in a deep 10- or 12-inch frying pan, or a pan with plenty of surface area. When the butter is foamy,

>>>

add the lobster meat and roe and sizzle gently for about 1 minute. Turn the pieces over using tongs and cook for 1 minute more. The butter will take on a pinkish red color.

Remove the lobster pieces from the pan and add the leeks and celery root. Increase the heat and sauté the vegetables until they soften slightly. Add the tomatoes and cook briefly before returning the lobster meat to the pan. Sprinkle with the paprika and some freshly ground black pepper. Reduce the heat to low and cook for 1 minute more.

Add the milk and cream to the pan and heat slowly until the stew is hot but not boiling, about 5 minutes. Do not boil. Remove the pan from the heat and let sit for a minimum of 30 minutes. This resting time is crucial for the flavors to develop. If you don't plan to eat the stew within an hour, refrigerate it when it comes to room temperature. When it is completely cold, cover it with plastic wrap.

To serve, return the stew to a wide pot over low heat. Season it with salt and more pepper if needed. When it is hot—but not boiling—ladle the stew into warm cups or bowls and sprinkle with the chopped chervil or parsley and chives. Serve immediately.

ADOLFO GARCIA

RioMar | *New Orleans, Louisiana*

Black drum is a prolific saltwater fish with a large head and teeth, which come in handy for crushing the shells of the mollusks they feed on as adults. Commonly found in and around brackish waters, black drum are especially abundant along the Texas coast.

When combined with the raw fish, the citric acid in lime juice "cooks" the fish without changing its flavor, causing it to become firm, but still tender and opaque. SERVES 4 TO 6

Coconut Black Drum Seviche

1 pound black drum fillet, cut into ½-inch pieces

1 small red onion, cut into ¼-inch dice (about ½ cup)

1 small jalapeño, thinly sliced (remove the seeds for a more mild version)

½ cup freshly squeezed lime juice (from about 4 limes), or enough to completely cover the fish

Kosher salt

7 ounces unsweetened coconut milk

¼ cup coarsely chopped fresh cilantro

Combine the black drum pieces with the onions, jalapeños, and lime juice in a glass or nonreactive bowl. Season with salt and allow the mixture to sit for 2 to 3 hours, stirring after 1 hour to ensure that it is "cooking" evenly. During this time, the fish will take on the other flavors and begin to firm up.

Drain off half of the lime juice after it's been sitting between 2 and 3 hours and add the coconut milk and more salt to taste. Chill until ready to serve, up to 3 days. Add the cilantro just before serving.

**"Black drum is a wonderful, versatile fish
from our Gulf waters. When purchasing it,
look for the smaller fish sold as 'puppy drum.'
It's flaky, delicious, and almost identical to
its threatened cousin, red drum."**

STEPHEN STRYJEWSKI,
Cochon, New Orleans, Louisiana

Lesser Known Species of Fish

Fishers and chefs are bringing new species and old favorites to the market and the table in hopes of easing the pressure on overfished species. As consumers, we can do our part in helping ocean ecosystems to flourish by embracing a wide variety of less-familiar seafood, such as farmed arctic char, spotted seatrout, striped bass, and longfin squid. Some of these species are farmed, while others are wild-caught; underutilized varieties vary depending on the area of the country. Find out what's plentiful but perhaps overlooked where you live, and seek those fish out under their various names at restaurants, fish counters, and supermarkets.

Branzini (also known as European and Mediterranean sea bass) has long been popular in the Mediterranean, where Italian chefs are particularly fond of its complex flavor. Some branzini is farmed sustainably, while other operations present the environmental and health challenges of farmed salmon, and the fish are fed a diet of fishmeal rather than algae and other organic matter. The subtle flavor of farmed branzini is virtually indistinguishable from wild branzini, making it a popular choice among chefs.

Barramundi, a type of perch, reproduce quickly—females can produce millions of eggs—and are a good substitute for red snapper. In the U.S., most barramundi are raised in recirculating tanks that minimize damage to the environment. But the species is increasingly being farmed in Southeast Asia under less sustainable conditions, in net pens that are a source of concentrated waste, which pose other environmental threats.

Wreckfish are a large, long-lived species related to grouper and sea bass. They are thought to reproduce prolifically, which increases the species' resistance to fishing pressure and suggests it is possible to maintain a healthy population. Although they are found all along the East Coast, most wreckfish come from the Charleston Bump, a deep water bank on the Gulf Stream off the coast of Charleston, South Carolina, where a limited number of vessels are licensed to fish for the species using low-impact hydraulic hook-and-line mechanisms.

Sablefish (black cod), prized for its buttery flavor and fatty flesh, is in high demand in Japan, where most of the popular

---

"Wreckfish is an amazing species that feeds on mollusks and crustaceans, which give it a mild yet sweet flavor."

WILLIAM DISSEN
The Market Place Restaurant, Asheville, North Carolina

North Pacific fish goes. Found in California and along the coast up to Alaska, where it is especially well managed, sablefish has a rich oily texture that is enhanced by poaching, grilling, and pan roasting (see Miso-Marinated Sablefish on page 208). According to John Ash, "We all loved Chilean sea bass because even if you overcooked it, it was still moist and delicious. Sablefish, with all of its omega-3 oiliness, is the perfect sustainable substitute."

Arctic char is considered a good substitute for Atlantic salmon, though the fillets are thinner and should be cooked accordingly. Most of the Arctic char in the U.S. comes from farms that vary in their efforts to operate sustainably, but attempts to improve them—especially to reduce the amount of fish in their chars' diet—are under way.

Bivalves and mollusks like clams, oysters, and mussels are probably the most sustainable example of farmed seafood. They filter water, cleaning it with little input from us. Some shellfish, including scallops, continue to be hand-harvested from the wild, but during the months when they're not in season, farmed shellfish provide a delicious and sustainable alternative.

Forage fish are the small, schooling fish like sardines, herring, and anchovies that larger fish such as tuna, salmon, and cod—but also whales, dolphins, and seabirds—rely on for food. The key to avoiding a collapse of the population is to monitor the catch of these little fish, leaving enough in the ocean to feed their predators. Currently, more than one-third of the forage fish caught globally are ground for fishmeal and oil that are used to feed farmed fish and livestock. If consumers seek out these tasty species for our own enjoyment (as opposed to that of a farmed fish or a cow), we can help to create a demand which, with good management, ensures that the wild population has enough to eat and that the fishers who harvest forage fish will see a reasonable return for their catch by selling them as human food rather than fish food.

"Eating anchovies is equal to a vote for a more respectful, nutritious, and profitable use of this vast and majestic resource."

BARTON SEAVER
*National Geographic Fellow, chef, and
author of* For Cod and Country,

CINDY PAWLCYN

Cindy Pawlcyn's Wood Grill & Wine Bar | Saint Helena, California

Most halibut fishing takes place in the chilly waters of the North Pacific Ocean, where this meaty, white-fleshed fish is at its best from spring through midfall. Here, its moist texture and sweet, almost buttery flavor are captured under a cumin-dusted crust created by quickly searing the fish. It finishes cooking in a thin but intensely piquant sauce filled with Mediterranean ingredients that complement the fresh, clean flavors of the fish. SERVES 6

Tunisian Halibut with Olives, Preserved Lemons, and Capers

1¾ pounds fresh halibut steak

Kosher salt and freshly ground black pepper

1 teaspoon ground cumin

1 small fresh chile

4 to 6 baby red onions

3 tablespoons extra-virgin olive oil, divided

1 medium red onion, grated (about 1 cup)

2 medium tomatoes, halved, seeded, and grated (about 2 cups)

1 head of garlic, cloves separated

1 tablespoon tomato paste

1 teaspoon coriander seeds, ground

1 cup brine-cured olives, rinsed and drained

Flour, for dusting the fish

6 cherry tomatoes

¼ cup capers, rinsed and drained

½ preserved lemon (peel only), rinsed, drained, and cut into thin julienne

1 tablespoon chopped celery leaves, for garnish

Rinse the fish, pat dry with paper towels, and divide into 6 equal pieces. Season each piece with salt and black pepper. Sprinkle the cumin evenly over the fish. Cover and refrigerate for at least 1 hour.

Steam the chile and baby onions until almost tender, about 10 minutes. Stem, seed, and coarsely chop the hot pepper. Peel the onions.

In a deep-sided medium frying pan, heat 2 tablespoons of the olive oil. Add the grated red onions and cook over medium heat, stirring frequently, for 3 to 4 minutes, or until softened. Add the grated tomatoes and cook until the excess moisture evaporates, about 7 minutes. Add the garlic, tomato paste, ground coriander, olives, steamed chopped hot pepper, baby onions, and 1 cup water. Cover and cook over medium heat for 10 minutes. The sauce should be thin, light, and very hot.

Heat the remaining 1 tablespoon oil in a large nonstick pan over medium-high heat. Dust the seasoned fish pieces with flour and fry in the hot oil, skin side down, for 2 minutes, or until the skin is crispy. Turn the pieces over and fry on the other side for 1 minute before pouring the hot sauce over the fish. Add the cherry tomatoes, capers, and preserved lemon peel, and simmer over low heat for 1 more minute. Remove from the heat, cover, and let stand for 15 minutes before serving with the sauce. The fish will finish cooking in the receding heat. Garnish with chopped celery leaves.

MATTHEW WEINGARTEN

Sodexo | New York, New York

Triggerfish are named for the way they lock the spine on their dorsal fins when they're alarmed. They live near coral reefs in tropical areas and can be found in the Gulf states as well as in states along the Atlantic coast. A diet of nearly 100 percent shellfish gives triggerfish a subtle and slightly sweet flavor similar to crab. (This probably explains why they were once considered the fishing crew's bonus and nearly impossible to find for sale.) Substitute any firm, fresh, seasonal fish with a delicate flavor. SERVES 6

Whey-Poached Triggerfish with Asparagus

6 skinless triggerfish fillets, 5 to 6 ounces each

Kosher salt and freshly ground black pepper

2 tablespoons olive oil; more for drizzling

3 cups leftover milk whey (see Simple Farmer Cheese on page 21), or 2¼ cups water whisked into ¾ cup crème fraîche

½ bunch asparagus, thinly sliced on the bias

1 teaspoon caraway seeds

1 tablespoon fresh flat-leaf parsley leaves

1 tablespoon fresh tarragon leaves

1 tablespoon fresh dill

1 tablespoon fresh thyme leaves

Mashed potatoes, for serving (optional)

Put two sauté pans large enough to hold 3 fillets each over high heat. After about 2 minutes, or when the pans are extremely hot, season both sides of the fish fillets with salt and black pepper. Put a tablespoon of olive oil in each pan and gently place 3 fillets in each pan, leaving room between them. Sear the fish on one side until it is lightly golden, then carefully flip the fillets over and pour half of the whey into each pan. Divide the asparagus, caraway seeds, and herbs between the two pans and bring to a boil. The dish is finished at this point. The asparagus should be just cooked through, and the sweet flavor of the herbs and vegetables will have created a wonderful pan sauce. Serve as is, with a generous drizzle of olive oil over top, or over potatoes mashed with olive oil.

PETER MERRIMAN

Merriman's Kapalua | Lahaina, Hawaii

Because they are among the fastest growing and maturing fish, mahimahi (also known as dorado and dolpinfish) stand up well to fishing pressure. U.S. Atlantic pole-and-line or troll-caught are the best choices. Molokai sweet potatoes aren't available outside of Hawaii, but you can use regular sweet potatoes to make the chips for the crust. The smoky, sweet-and-sour flavors of the salsa tie the dish together and are especially good with the firm-fleshed, slightly sweet fish. **SERVES 6**

Sweet Potato–Crusted Mahimahi with Fire-Roasted Tomato-Ginger Salsa

Canola oil, for frying

1 medium-size Molokai purple sweet potato
or regular sweet potato

¼ cup panko breadcrumbs

4 teaspoons chopped fresh flat-leaf parsley

4 teaspoons chopped fresh chives

4 teaspoons finely chopped fresh oregano

1 large egg

6 skinless mahimahi fillets, about
4 ounces each

Kosher salt and freshly ground black
pepper

Fire-Roasted Tomato-Ginger Salsa
(recipe on the facing page)

Put 1½ to 2 inches of oil in a wide, deep pan and warm to 325°F over medium-high heat. Scrub the potato and slice thinly on a mandoline, leaving the skin on. Rinse the potato slices under cold water for 1 minute, then pat dry and fry in the canola oil until golden brown. Remove the chips from the oil and drain on paper towels.

When they have cooled completely, put the chips in the bowl of a food processor with the breadcrumbs and herbs. Pulse the ingredients quickly until they are finely chopped. Pour into a shallow wide, bowl and set aside.

Whisk the egg in a shallow, wide bowl with 2 tablespoons of water. Season the fish fillets with salt and black pepper. Dip one side of each fillet into the egg, then into the crumb coating.

To cook the fish, heat the oven to 450°F and warm 2 tablespoons of canola oil in a nonstick ovenproof pan over medium-high heat. When the oil is hot—but not smoking—put the fish in the pan crumb side down. Cook until the crust is golden brown, about 3 minutes. Turn the fish over and finish cooking it in the oven, about 2 minutes. Serve immediately with Fire-Roasted Tomato-Ginger Salsa under or on the side of the mahimahi, so that the sweet potato crust stays crispy.

Fire-Roasted Tomato-Ginger Salsa

MAKES 2 CUPS

2 ripe tomatoes, halved

2 jalapeños, halved and most of the seeds
removed

2 limes

3 cloves garlic, coarsely chopped

1 shallot, coarsely chopped

2 tablespoons finely minced fresh ginger

3 tablespoons red-wine vinegar

2 tablespoons Dijon mustard

2 tablespoons honey

¾ cup canola oil

Kosher salt and freshly ground black pepper

Char the tomato halves (cut side up) and jalapeños on a hot grill, under the broiler, or on the burner of a gas stove. Cut the limes in half and put on a hot grill for about 2 minutes, or until grill marks appear. Squeeze the juice from the limes for about ¼ cup.

Put the charred tomatoes, jalapeños, and lime juice in the bowl of a food processor with the garlic, shallots, ginger, vinegar, mustard, and honey. Purée until nearly smooth, then add the canola oil. Season to taste with salt and black pepper.

Shopping for Seafood

The freshest, most delicious fish is the one you hook yourself, but we mostly rely on fish markets and supermarkets with good seafood counters where fish are sold whole, as sides, or in fillets or steaks. When buying fresh seafood, get as close to the source as you can. If you live near the ocean, there may be a seafood market stocked with the local catch. Community-supported fisheries (CSF) are modeled on the agricultural equivalent, CSAs, and provide weekly shares of freshly caught fish in season to subscribers. Farmer's markets in coastal areas can also be excellent sources of information and sustainable seafood.

Eco-labels, seafood guides, online resources, and third-party certifiers also provide information about how farmed and wild fish are managed from one operation to the next. Your fishmonger should also be able to give you insight into the sustainability of specific operations and whether they are known for responsible practices. If none of these indicators are present, ask more questions or make another choice.

Finally, trust yourself. If a fish is fresh, it will have a mild cucumber-like odor. Skip anything that smells fishy or that's prepackaged. The skin of a fresh fish is shiny, with white or pink fat. (Fat that is brown or gray probably means the fish was kept too long and has oxidized. Be certain to distinguish between this and the dark meat or bloodline of a fish.) If its scales are intact, they should glisten and have a bright silvery cast. The gills should be bright red and the eyes bright and clear, with shiny dark pupils. Avoid fish with cloudy eyes. A fresh fish has firm, elastic flesh that clings tightly to the bone and springs back when pressed with a fingertip.

Every fish and shellfish has a unique flavor and texture owing to its genetics and the waters in which it swims, but most seafood species are interchangeable with at least one other variety. When a fish isn't available due to seasonality, sustainability, or price, consider trying something different.

JOHN ASH

Santa Rosa, California

Sablefish, which is also known as black cod or butterfish, is a sustainably sought fish that comes mostly from Alaska, though it is also abundant in parts of the Pacific Northwest. Marinating it in miso, the umami-rich paste made with soybeans, rice, and/or barley, is a traditional preparation, but the marinade is also wonderful slathered on other kinds of fish, chicken, and pork. Serve the sablefish with sweet pickled sushi ginger, toasted sesame seeds, and daikon sprouts. **SERVES 6**

Miso-Marinated Sablefish

¼ cup mirin

¼ cup sake wine

½ cup plus 2 tablespoons white *shiro* miso

⅓ cup granulated sugar

6 sablefish fillets, skin on, 6 to 7 ounces each

3 tablespoons canola or grapeseed oil

Pickled sushi ginger, for garnish

Sesame seeds, toasted, for garnish

Daikon sprouts, for garnish

Combine the mirin and sake in a small saucepan and bring to a boil. Whisk in the miso until smooth, then add the sugar and cook over medium heat, stirring constantly, until the sugar has dissolved. Transfer the marinade to a bowl and cool.

Pat the cod fillets thoroughly with paper towels and generously coat with marinade on both sides. Place in a nonreactive bowl or dish with any remaining marinade, cover tightly with plastic wrap, and refrigerate for at least 8 hours or overnight.

Heat the oven to 400°F. Warm the oil over medium-high heat in an ovenproof sauté pan large enough to hold the fish in one layer. When the oil is hot, scrape the excess marinade off the fish and cook the fish until lightly browned on one side, about 2 minutes. Turn the fish and place the pan in the oven until the fish is cooked through and flaky, about 8 minutes. Serve on warm plates topped with the garnishes.

How Fish Is Caught

Maintaining the ocean's ecological balance is critical to preserving its long-term viability as a source of sustainable seafood. A robust and diverse marine ecosystem is characterized by the health of its species and their surroundings. Fishing methods play an important role in maintaining both.

Dredging is a harmful, high-impact catch method that uses heavy chain-mesh scoops dragged behind fishing boats to excavate the ocean floor, usually for oysters and scallops. But anything that gets in the path of the gear as it scrapes along the ocean bottom is scooped up, too. Dredges should be used only in areas with resilient habitats, like sand or mud, and should include a device that allows some bycatch to escape.

Drift nets are a high-bycatch method of fishing the top few meters of a water column with gillnets suspended by floats. Drift nets are now illegal in many parts of the world, but they are still used on the high seas.

Gill nets are stationary nets used to catch finfish by entangling them. The nets can be weighted to hang at any level in the water column and are often anchored to sit on the ocean floor. This is a high-bycatch method that can be made more selective by restricting the size of the mesh so that it targets specific sizes of fish.

Harpooning is a method of spearing one fish at a time with a large harpoon that is typically used on large predator species. Since it doesn't disturb the ocean floor, harpooning has little effect on the habitat and doesn't usually involve bycatch.

Hook-and-line (or vertical line gear) is a low-impact catch method that uses sharp hooks attached to lines made of monofilament or other materials. Rod and reels—both fishing poles and mechanized—and handlines are two examples of this low-bycatch method. Since the gear is almost always actively tended, fish caught in error can be released quickly.

Longline fishing uses short vertical lines with hooks attached to a longer horizontal main line fed into the water from a spool on a boat. Longlines can range anywhere from several hundred yards in length with hundreds of hooks to several miles long with thousands of hooks. Longlines are usually set and allowed to passively fish for hours at a time. This high-bycatch method is known for incidental capture of seabirds, turtles, and nontargeted fish, but the fishing gear and techniques can be modified so that it's not as invasive.

Pole-and-line fishing (also called poling and pole-and-live-bait fishing) attracts schools of fish to the surface of the water with bait fixed to the end of a short pole. Fishers work close to the vessel so the ocean floor is not affected. This low-bycatch method allows for easy release if the wrong species bites.

Purse seines are large nets that circle and surround schools of fish before closing at the bottom like a purse, preventing them from diving to escape. Though it's meant to target specific varieties (Alaskan salmon is one), purse seines trap all sorts of bycatch. Purse seines can be low in bycatch if they are used to target species that school in single species groups and if contact with the seafloor is infrequent.

Reef nets are a low-impact, low-bycatch fishing method developed by Native Americans on the Pacific Coast, where they are still used to harvest wild salmon. The nets are designed to simulate a natural reef or obstacle that the salmon must swim across on its way to spawn. The method is stationary and is actively tended by fishermen who use anchored gears to pull the nets to the surface and release the fish into a live tank, where untargeted species can be identified and released unharmed.

Traps and pots are among the oldest known methods for catching certain fish and crustaceans including lobster, crab, and shrimp. The gear is passive, in that it traps certain species when they enter an enclosing device that sits on the ocean floor. The traps are usually linked to buoys that float on the surface in order to aid in locating them. Escape holes in traps and pots are often used to allow small fish or undersized crustaceans to escape.

Trawling is a high-impact, high-bycatch fishing method that drags a large wide-mouthed net through the ocean or along the floor, scooping up the fish in a particular range in the water column as the boat moves forward. Trawls should be used only in areas with resilient seafloor habitats (sand, gravel, and mud); the net should include a device that allows some bycatch to escape.

Trolling is a lower-impact fishing method in which hook-and-line gear is pulled through the water by a vessel at low speed.

"We need to continue efforts underway to perfect the selectivity of fishing gear, an acute need especially in the Northeast's groundfishing sector, with its multispecies."

SAM HAYWARD
Fore Street, Portland, Maine

MIKE LATA

FIG | Charleston, South Carolina

The sweet meat of blue crab is cherished in the South Carolina Lowcountry, where the season begins in spring and peaks midsummer. Here, the first catch of the season (called "peelers") is paired with other spring delicacies including morel mushrooms, spring onions, freshly dug fingerling potatoes, and young kale. The resulting flavors are as verdant and lively as the season they announce. SERVES 4

Carolina Soft-Shell Crabs with Wilted Young Kale, Spring Onions, and Morels

4 fresh soft-shell blue crabs

1 pound small fingerling potatoes
(10 to 12), washed and dried

¼ cup extra-virgin olive oil, divided

2 teaspoons kosher salt; more as needed

4 medium spring onions, thinly sliced
with tops reserved

1 teaspoon crushed red pepper flakes

1 large bunch (about ½ pound) young kale,
stems removed and leaves torn into
bite-size pieces

¼ cup chicken stock (homemade or
store-bought)

¼ cup (½ stick) unsalted butter, divided

8 ounces morel mushrooms, wiped
cleaned and sliced crosswise

2 lemons

Sea salt

Clean the crabs over a bowl. Using a sharp pair of kitchen scissors, cut off the face, then the tail, and finally the gills. Squeeze the center of the crab to remove the insides and pat the whole thing dry.

Heat the oven to 375°F. Toss the potatoes in a bowl with 2 tablespoons of olive oil and the salt. Arrange in a single layer on a baking sheet and bake until the potatoes are very tender and can be pierced easily with a fork, 15 to 35 minutes, depending on the size of the potatoes. Remove from the oven and set aside.

In a frying pan with a heavy bottom or a Dutch oven, heat the other 2 tablespoons of olive oil over medium heat. Add the spring onions and red pepper flakes to the pan and cook, stirring occasionally, until the onions are soft and translucent. Add the torn kale leaves and chicken stock to the pan. After 3 to 5 minutes, or when the kale has wilted, transfer the contents of the pan to a bowl and reserve.

In a nonstick frying pan, melt 1 tablespoon of butter over medium high heat until it begins to foam. Add the morels and lightly season with salt. Gently sauté the mushrooms until they are cooked through and have browned slightly. Toss them with the juice of half of a lemon and set aside.

To cook the crabs, melt the remaining 3 tablespoons of butter in a large nonstick pan over medium-high heat. When the foam begins to subside, add the crabs belly side down and cook until golden brown. Turn the crabs over and cook on the other side for a few more minutes. To see if they're done, insert a paring knife into the center of a crab. The knife will be moderately hot if the crab is ready. Remove the crabs from the pan; squeeze the other half lemon over them and set aside.

To serve, warm up the greens, potatoes, and morels. Put a mound of greens on the center of each of four plates, then top with a crab and some morels. Place a couple of potatoes next to or around the crab. Sprinkle with sea salt and serve with a wedge of lemon.

SUSAN SPICER

Bayona | New Orleans, Louisiana

Horta is a simple Greek side dish made with a medley of edible leafy greens of the sort that grow wild on hillsides in the Mediterranean. The greens vary in tenderness and bitterness according to the time of year and location in which they're grown. The combination of sweet tomatoes and slightly pungent greens harmonizes nicely with the smoky, grilled flavors of the fish. **SERVES 4**

Grilled Skin-on Striped Bass with Summer Tomatoes and *Horta*

FOR THE FISH

4 striped bass fillets, skin on,
  6 to 8 ounces each
2 tablespoons extra-virgin olive oil;
  more for the grill
Kosher salt and freshly ground
  black pepper
1 tablespoon oregano, preferably
  Mediterranean, fresh or dried

FOR THE *HORTA*

1 large head escarole, or 1 large bunch
  chard or kale (about 1½ pounds)
2 lemons, zest finely chopped and juiced
1 small clove garlic, finely minced
½ cup extra-virgin olive oil
¼ teaspoon crushed red pepper flakes
Kosher salt and freshly ground
  black pepper

>>>

PREPARE THE FISH

Brush both sides of the fish with olive oil and season with salt, black pepper, and a sprinkle of oregano. Set aside while you prepare the *horta* and tomatoes.

PREPARE THE *HORTA*

Bring a large pot of lightly salted water to a boil over high heat. Prepare the greens by cutting out the core if you are using escarole, cutting off the lower stems for chard, or removing the stems if you're using kale.

Coarsely chop the greens, add them to a big bowl of cold water, and swish around to remove the sand and dirt.

When the water comes to a boil, add the greens and cook for about 5 minutes, or until tender. While greens are cooking, combine the lemon juice and zest with the garlic in a large bowl. Slowly whisk in the olive oil, add the crushed red pepper flakes, and season to taste with salt and pepper. Thoroughly drain the greens and set them aside to cool slightly.

When the greens are cool enough to handle, squeeze any remaining water from them and add them to the lemony vinaigrette. Mix well to thoroughly coat the greens and hold at room temperature until ready to serve.

>>>

FOR THE SUMMER TOMATOES

2 medium-size ripe tomatoes (about
   1 pound), cored and cut into ½-inch dice

1 shallot, finely chopped

2 tablespoons extra-virgin olive oil

1 tablespoon red-wine vinegar

1 tablespoon coarsely chopped fresh herbs,
   such as basil, dill, or mint, or a combination

Kosher salt and freshly ground black
   pepper

FOR GARNISH

Coarse sea salt

Lemon wedges

MAKE THE SUMMER TOMATOES

In a small nonreactive bowl, toss the diced tomatoes with the shallots, olive oil, vinegar, and herbs. Season to taste with salt and black pepper.

GRILL THE FISH AND SERVE

Heat a gas grill or start the coals for a charcoal grill 30 minutes before cooking the fish. When the grill is hot, oil the grate and place the fish, skin side down, on the medium-hot part of the grill. Cook for about 5 minutes and lift the edge of the fish with a spatula to see if it is ready to turn—the skin should be crisp and the fish will release easily from the grill. Rub the grate with a bit more oil and turn the fish over to finish cooking, about 3 minutes. The fish can also be sautéed in a hot pan with olive oil using the same technique.

Put the *horta* on a serving platter and arrange the fish on top. Spoon the tomatoes over the fillets and sprinkle lightly with coarse sea salt. Serve with lemon wedges.

Sourcing Sustainable Shrimp

Shrimp is the most widely consumed seafood in the U.S., and shrimp farming is one of the fastest growing sectors of aquaculture around the globe. It is also one of the most destructive, uprooting mangrove forests that protect coastlines and raising the salinity of surrounding water and soil, damaging land for agriculture. The ecological consequences of shrimp farming are well documented, from the depletion of wild fish stocks to feed farmed shrimp to the widespread pollution from waste, antibiotics, and land-based activities that affect habitat for domestic shrimp.

When excess levels of nutrients like nitrogen and phosphorus are released from fertilizers and animal waste, they stimulate massive algae blooms downstream, which use up all available oxygen and make it impossible for marine species to survive.

As much as 90 percent of shrimp consumed in the U.S. is imported from Asia and South America, and less than 1 percent of foreign shrimp exported to the U.S. is tested for chemicals. This makes it imperative to know to how and where the shrimp were raised before you purchase them.

Shrimp has its own set of private-industry eco-labels, only a few of which appear on shrimp products found in the U.S. Some of the labels are based on immeasurable principles or guidelines, while others make no reference to sustainability. The USDA is believed to be developing standards for organic farm-raised seafood in the near future, but until then look for these labels:

■ **Global Aquaculture Alliance (GAA):** Best Aquaculture Practices (BAP)-certified shrimp do not claim to be organic and the process allows for some use of antibiotics and chemicals. This certification can also apply to processing plants, feed mills, and hatcheries, not just farms.

■ **Wild American Shrimp** indicates that the product was harvested in its natural habitat in U.S. waters. Period.

■ **World Wildlife Fund** has developed standards for farming shrimp that will soon be used for Aquaculture Stewardship Council certifications.

LINTON HOPKINS

Restaurant Eugene | Atlanta, Georgia

Perloo, a regional one-pot rice dish from South Carolina's Lowcountry, is a close relative of jambalaya. This recipe calls for Carolina Gold rice, which was the basis of the colonial and antebellum economy of the South and is enjoying a resurgence in popularity.

Georgia's wild shrimp, caught by local fishermen, are the other star of this perloo. Strong tides carry the shrimp through marshland, which acts as a natural filter, imparting the seafood with sweet flavor and its firm texture. SERVES 6

Atlantic Shrimp Perloo

30 jumbo shrimp, heads left on

½ teaspoon kosher salt

½ pound smoked bacon cut into
 ½-inch dice

1 medium yellow onion, cut into
 ¼-inch dice (about 1 cup)

3 cloves garlic, finely chopped

1 cup Carolina Gold® rice

¼ cup chopped roasted peanuts

1 small tomato, finely chopped
 (about ½ cup)

4 sprigs fresh thyme

½ cup chopped fresh flat-leaf parsley

1 bay leaf

2 tablespoons freshly squeezed lemon juice

Freshly ground black pepper

½ cup finely chopped scallions, white and
 green parts

Peel the shells off the shrimp, leaving the heads intact. Set the shrimp aside, refrigerating until ready to use. Put the shells in a pot with 3 cups of water and the salt. Bring the liquid to a boil over medium heat, reduce the heat, and boil gently for 10 minutes. Strain the shrimp stock into a 1-quart glass bowl or measuring cup and discard the shells.

Heat the oven to 325°F. Warm a Dutch oven over medium heat, add the bacon, and cook until crisp. Drain the bacon on a paper-towel lined plate and set aside. Add the onions to the bacon fat and cook for about 5 minutes, or until lightly translucent but not brown. Add the garlic and cook for 1 minute longer. Add the rice and peanuts and stir to coat with the bacon fat. Add 2 cups of shrimp stock, the tomatoes, thyme, parsley, and bay leaf. Bring to a boil, cover, and place the Dutch oven in the oven.

Bake for 25 minutes, or until the rice is tender. Remove the pan from the oven, add the shrimp, and return to the oven to bake until the shrimp are cooked through, about 5 minutes.

Remove the pan from the oven, stir in the lemon juice, reserved bacon, and salt and black pepper to taste. To serve, arrange on a platter garnished with scallions.

SAM HAYWARD

Fore Street | Portland, Maine

Sea scallops are as delicious raw as cooked. Sear them quickly in a hot cast-iron skillet, keeping the interiors cool and mostly raw so that their mild sweet flavor shines through. Scallop season in Maine runs from December through April; the other ingredients in this recipe are easy to find in the winter months. SERVES 6

Sea Scallops with Saffron and Cider

2 teaspoons fresh chervil leaves

¼ teaspoon finely chopped fresh winter savory

1 tablespoon finely chopped fresh chives

2 ounces apple-smoked slab bacon (without the rind), cut into ¼-inch dice

1 cup safflower, peanut, or grapeseed oil

Kosher salt

4 ounces celery root, peeled and cut into ½-inch dice

2 ounces firm dense winter squash, like butternut, kuri, or blue hubbard, peeled and cut into ½-inch cubes

1 medium leek, white part only, rinsed and cut into ¼-inch dice

3 tablespoons apple-cider vinegar

1½ cups dry hard cider

Large pinch of saffron threads; more for garnish

1 cup heavy cream, preferably unpasteurized

Sea salt

Aleppo pepper

½ cup baby bok choy leaves, loosely packed

1½ pounds jumbo sea scallops (U-10 to U-16), connective tissue trimmed and patted dry

Freshly ground black pepper

Combine the chervil, savory, and chives in a small bowl and set aside.

Put the bacon in a heavy-bottomed saucepan over medium-high heat and cover with the oil. Bring the mixture to a simmer, reduce the heat to very low, and continue to cook gently for 10 to 15 minutes, until the bacon is tender but not browned. Cool the bacon to room temperature in the oil, remove with a slotted spoon, and drain on paper towels.

While the bacon is cooling, bring a pan of generously salted water to a boil. Blanch the diced vegetables in the boiling salted water, then drain and refresh in cold water.

Combine the apple-cider vinegar and hard cider in a nonreactive saucepan and reduce by about three-quarters, to ½ cup. Meanwhile, add a large pinch of the saffron threads to a dry frying pan over medium-high heat until fragrant. Whisk the saffron threads and cream into the reduced cider mixture, bring to a boil, reduce the heat, and simmer until slightly thickened, about 10 minutes, whisking occasionally. Season with sea salt and a pinch of Aleppo pepper. Keep warm.

Just before cooking the scallops, combine the blanched vegetables, bacon, and bok choy leaves in a small frying pan with a little of the oil. Sauté quickly to heat through and gently wilt the bok choy. Keep warm.

Generously season the scallops with kosher salt and black pepper. Heat a large heavy-bottomed frying pan over high heat. Add 1 to 2 tablespoons oil, or enough to lightly film the bottom.

Working in batches, carefully add the scallops to the hot pan without crowding. Sear on one side for about 2 minutes, or until brown, then turn and cook for 1 to 2 minutes more on the other side. Remove from the pan to a platter and keep warm. Continue cooking the scallops in batches, making sure the pan is very hot each time and being careful not to overcook them. They should be well seared on both flat surfaces but still translucent and barely warm in the center.

To serve, divide the hot, seared scallops among six plates. Drizzle some of the saffron cream sauce around them. Sprinkle the sautéed vegetables and bacon over and around them, and garnish with a pinch of the herb mixture and a few saffron threads.

JUDI BARSNESS

Chez Jude Restaurant | Grand Marais, Minnesota

Baking fish in parchment paper, a French technique called *en papillote,* is an ideal method for cooking delicate fish since it stays moist as it steams in the packet, taking on the juices and flavors of everything inside with it. Besides being the world's easiest cleanup, cooking in parchment is a winning method that should be tried with any fish.

For this recipe, you could also use lake trout, walleye, wild salmon, jumbo sea scallops, shrimp, or any other favorite fresh fish. **SERVES 6**

Whitefish in Parchment with Lobster, Lemon, and Dill

Six 14-inch squares parchment paper

6 tablespoons (¾ stick) unsalted butter, melted

1 teaspoon finely chopped lemon zest

2 tablespoons freshly squeezed lemon juice

1 teaspoon finely chopped fresh dill

Kosher salt and freshly ground black pepper

1 each red, Yukon Gold, and blue potatoes, thinly sliced (about 6 ounces total)

6 Lake Superior whitefish fillets, 6 to 8 ounces each

6 ounces green beans, trimmed

6 baby carrots with greens, halved lengthwise

1 cup shiitake mushrooms, cleaned and halved

½ red bell pepper, julienned

6 pieces lobster claw meat (optional)

1 tablespoon finely chopped fresh flat-leaf parsley

6 fresh chive stems and flowers

Heat the oven to 450°F. Cut the parchment paper squares into heart-shaped pieces. Combine the melted butter with the lemon zest and juice, dill, and salt and black pepper to taste. Set aside.

Fold the parchment hearts in half to make a crease in the middle. Open the hearts and, using one of each variety, layer slices of potatoes close to the crease. Season with salt and pepper, place a whitefish fillet on top, and season again.

Layer a few each of green beans, carrots, mushrooms, and red pepper slices on top of the fish fillet and place a lump of lobster meat on top, if using. Drizzle each pouch with some lemon butter and sprinkle generously with chopped parsley.

Fold the left side of each parchment heart over the filling and beginning at one end, fold and crease the edges together securely so no juices escape and steam will remain within the pouch. When you reach the bottom, fold the remaining parchment under the pouch.

Place the pouches in a single layer on a rimmed baking sheet and bake for 10 to 15 minutes, or until the pouches are puffed and beginning to brown.

Remove the pouches from the oven and place one each on a plate. Garnish the top of each pouch with a crossed stem of chive flower and fresh chive. After presenting the plates, cut away the paper with a knife or scissors.

CHRIS WEBER

The Herbfarm | Woodinville, Washington

This versatile dish can be made ahead and served warm or chilled as a starter or a main course without compromising the quality and flavor of the dish.

The Herbfarm gets albacore from St. Jude, a 95-foot sustainably operated, family-owned fishing vessel based in Seattle. SERVES 8 AS A STARTER OR 4 AS A MAIN COURSE

Kombu-Cured Albacore with Salt-Roasted Potatoes and Sorrel Vinaigrette

2 pieces dried kombu kelp (large enough to wrap around the two halves of the tuna loin)

2 tablespoons sea salt; more for seasoning

1 albacore tuna loin, about 1½ pounds, cleaned and cut in half lengthwise

24 baby potatoes (3 per person for a starter or 6 as a main course), scrubbed clean

2 small Walla Walla or other sweet onions

1 tablespoon canola oil

Kosher salt and freshly ground white pepper

1 cup fresh sorrel leaves

½ cup extra-virgin olive oil

Soak the kombu in cool water for 1 hour, or until soft. Spread the kombu sheets on a clean, dry work surface and generously season with sea salt. Arrange each half of the albacore loin lengthwise on a sheet of kombu, and roll it up to completely encase the tuna. Place the loins on a rimmed baking pan and refrigerate for at least 12 hours and up to 1 day.

When you are ready to prepare the dish, unroll the loins and slice into bite-size pieces, approximately 16 slices per loin, or 32 total.

Dissolve the sea salt in 2 quarts of room temperature water. Arrange the potatoes in a pan wide enough to accommodate them in a single layer. Pour enough of the salted water over the potatoes to cover them and bring the mixture to a simmer over medium-high heat. Cook until tender, then drain off all but ¼ inch of the water and return the pan to the stove over high heat. Roll the potatoes around in the salt water until it evaporates completely and the potatoes are evenly coated in a salt crust. Remove from the heat and allow to cool.

Meanwhile, prepare the onions. Leaving the skin on, cut the onions in half from root to tip. Toss them with the canola oil, a generous pinch of kosher salt, and some white pepper; set aside for 30 minutes.

Heat the grill and char the onions on all sides until tender, about 7 minutes. Remove from the grill and allow to cool. When cool enough to handle, peel away the skin and cut the onion halves in half, from root to tip. Pull them apart into petals. Set aside 4 petals per person.

To make the sauce, place the sorrel leaves in a blender and pulse until they break down slightly. With the motor running on medium speed, slowly add the olive oil to the blender. Add a few teaspoons of water, if necessary to achieve the proper consistency, and season to taste with salt. The natural acidity of the sorrel makes the sauce vinaigrette-like.

To serve, place a spoonful of sorrel sauce in the middle of each plate, using the back of the spoon to spread it around the plate evenly. Alternate pieces of fish with the potatoes and onion petals; serve immediately.

Certification and Labels for Wild Fisheries and Aquaculture

Many certification programs and systems related to food production and distribution are under fire for green washing and blatant misrepresentation/labeling. Like the programs for produce, meat, and poultry, existing certification systems for seafood have shortcomings. Consumers who want to make the right purchasing choices are frequently confused by the lack of meaningful guidelines and inconsistent recommendations. The best answer to the question of how to assess what makes one program or label better than another is to understand as fully as possible what each one claims to measure and then make your own informed decision.

Alaska Seafood Marketing Institute (ASMI) offers independent third-party verification of the management of Alaska's major commercial fisheries based on the United Nations Food and Agriculture Organization (FAO) Code of Conduct for Responsible Fisheries (Code) and the FAO Guidelines for the Eco-labelling of Fish and Fishery Products from Marine Capture Fisheries (Guidelines).

Aquaculture Stewardship Council (ASC) is often compared to the Marine Stewardship Council. Developed by World Wildlife Fund (based on the group's extensive Aquaculture Dialogues), ASC is poised to become the best-respected aquaculture certifier around when its program comes online.

Country of Origin (COOL) is defined by the USDA. COOL labeling for seafood went into effect in 2005 for retailers of a certain size. Value-added seafood (seafood products that have been processed and prepared, like canned tuna, smoked salmon, or breaded fish fillets) is exempt, which means that more than 50 percent of seafood sold in the U.S. is sold without labels. Additionally, 90 percent of retailers, including small wholesale markets, are exempt and no mechanism for enforcement exists. Fines for noncompliance are negligible.

Food Alliance is a third-party certifier that developed its shellfish certification program in response to a request by the Pacific Coast Shellfish Growers Association (PCSGA), who wanted to supplement its own Environmental Codes of Practice. Certification applies to North American shellfish producers growing shellfish from seed to harvest in a defined area and with clear ownership of the shellfish being cultured. The program does not cover wild harvest.

Friend of the Sea (FOS) is a global nonprofit organization and certification program for sustainable seafood from wild fisheries and aquaculture.

The **Global Aquaculture Alliance (GAA)** is a leading aquaculture industry trade association and certification program. GAA's Best Aquaculture Practices (BAP) standards measure aquaculture globally using a sometimes-confusing combination of site inspections and sampling for sanitary controls, therapeutic controls, and traceability. Compliance with BAP standards is implemented by the **Aquaculture Certification Council (ACC)**, an independent certifying body that examines all stages of the aquaculture cycle, from hatchery and growth through processing. Because the two organizations collectively award certification for a number of things, it may be unclear whether it is the actual farm that is certified as sustainable or the processing plant that is certified as sanitary.

GLOBALG.A.P. is a private-sector—and not particularly well-respected—body that sets standards for agricultural products globally.

Label Rouge is an accolade given by the French government to products of superior quality, particularly in relation to taste. Scottish salmon was the first non-French food item to receive distinction in 1992, and salmon from Norway and Canada now bears the Label Rouge. Label Rouge French certification guarantees traceability of quality fish and seafood products grown in accordance with strict principles and practices with respect for fish welfare, sustainability, and the environment.

Marine Stewardship Council (MSC) operates a rigorous and widely recognized certification program for the sustainability and environmental responsibility in wild-capture seafood. The MSC's global standard for sustainable and well-managed fisheries measures the stock population of the target species and the impact harvesting has on the marine ecosystem; it also ensures the fishery has a responsive management structure in place. Fisheries are audited against this standard by independent, third-party certifiers and often undertake improvements in their fishing practices in order to gain certification. The assessment process is scientifically peer-reviewed with required involvement from outside stakeholders, such as advocacy groups and government agencies.

There are no U.S. standards for organic seafood, but several international groups including **Naturland, BioSuisse,** and **Soil Association** certify organic and allow use of their labels. Respect for the environment, respect for the animal, and guaranteed consumer safety are the main objectives of organic certification. Certification guarantees that the fish was farmed in pure clean water and that no GMOs are involved in the fish themselves or what they eat. Feed is made up of wild fish caught under quotas and organic cereals. Fish density is lower than in traditional farming and life cycle is longer, according to the natural cycle of fish in the wild. Canada also has organic standards for aquaculture, which were recently approved by the Canadian General Standards Board.

Seafood Safe is a testing program for mercury and PCBs, two of the most prevalent contaminants found in seafood today. The program informs consumers of how much seafood they can consume per month without exposing themselves to dangerous levels of these contaminants. The Seafood Safe label reflects safe consumption levels for women of childbearing age, who are the adults at the highest risk.

"Seafood eco-labels have a wide variety of standards; some can be very misleading. It's worth taking the time to dig deeper into the certification standards of an eco-label before relying on it to guide your purchases."

MEGAN WESTMEYER
Sustainable Fisheries Partnership, Honolulu, Hawaii

BRIAN RAE AND JODY ADAMS

Rialto | *Cambridge, Massachusetts*

Though it appears somewhat involved, this recipe is extremely manageable if you make the pepper stew and pesto the day before you plan to serve the dish. The stew in particular benefits from the extra time during which the flavors develop and deepen.

The stew and pesto are delicious with a variety of fish, including rockfish, black rock cod, black snapper, and sea bass. Use whatever fresh fish is available locally. SERVES 8

Pan-Seared Black Bass with Pepper Stew and Spicy Green Pesto

FOR THE PEPPER STEW

½ teaspoon coriander seeds

1½ teaspoons fennel seed

¼ teaspoon white peppercorns

2 tablespoons olive oil

1 medium onion, thinly sliced (about 1 cup)

2 cloves garlic, finely minced

2 tablespoons finely minced fresh ginger

1 rib celery, thinly sliced (about ½ cup)

2 green bell peppers, cut into thin strips (about 1½ cups)

½ bulb fennel, thinly sliced (about ¼ cup)

2 jalapeños, finely chopped

1 tablespoon finely chopped orange zest

1½ teaspoons finely chopped preserved lemon, or 1 tablespoon finely chopped lemon zest

2 stalks lemongrass, cut in half

½ bunch fresh flat-leaf parsley stems

6 sprigs fresh thyme, leaves set aside for another use

1 bay leaf

½ cup white wine

8 cups fish or vegetable stock

2 tablespoons fish sauce

Juice of 1 lime

Kosher salt and freshly ground white pepper

MAKE THE STEW

Toast the coriander and fennel seeds and white peppercorns in a small sauté pan over low heat until they become aromatic, about 5 minutes. Keep the spices moving in the pan the entire time so that they don't burn. Set aside to cool before grinding with a mortar and pestle or in a spice grinder.

Warm the olive oil in a large pot or Dutch oven over medium heat. Add the onions and cook until they soften and become translucent. Add the garlic and ginger and continue to cook until they are aromatic, about 2 minutes. Add the celery, green peppers, fennel, jalapeños, and toasted spices to the pan. Stir to combine and add the orange and lemon zest. Use butcher's twine to tie the lemongrass, parsley stems, and thyme sprigs together in a bundle. Add them to the pan with the bay leaf.

Continue to cook, stirring occasionally, until all the vegetables have begun to soften. Add the white wine, using it to deglaze the pan and loosen any small bits of vegetable that have browned and stuck to the bottom of the pan. Cook until the white wine is almost gone, then add the fish or vegetable stock. Bring the stew to a simmer, cook for 30 minutes, and add the fish sauce and lime juice. Season to taste with salt and white pepper. Remove the bay leaf and thyme stems before serving.

FOR THE BASS

8 black bass fillets, 6 to 7 ounces each, skin on

Kosher salt and freshly ground white pepper

2 tablespoons vegetable oil

2 tablespoons unsalted butter

FOR SERVING

Spicy Green Pesto (recipe below)

2 tablespoons toasted sliced almonds, for garnish

2 tablespoons torn or coarsely chopped fresh mint leaves, for garnish

2 tablespoons torn or coarsely chopped fresh basil leaves, for garnish

PREPARE AND COOK THE FISH

Season the fish on both sides with salt and white pepper. When the pan is hot, add 1 tablespoon of the oil. Place 3 or 4 fillets in the pan, skin side down. The fillets should fit in the pan in a single layer with some space left around each one. Do not overcrowd the pan; the fish will be cooked in batches. If the fish begins to curl under slightly, so that the middle is no longer touching the bottom of the pan, apply gentle pressure with a spatula.

Cook the fish on the skin side for 4 to 5 minutes or until the skin is brown. It may stick slightly but will release easily when the skin becomes crispy. Use a spatula to loosen it gently if necessary, being careful not to tear the skin.

Add 1 tablespoon of the butter to the pan and turn the fillets over to cook on the other side, about 2 minutes more. Remove the cooked fish to a clean plate and repeat the process with the remaining fish fillets, vegetable oil, and butter.

TO SERVE

Warm the stew over low heat, then stir in ¼ cup of the pesto, or slightly more to taste. Ladle some stew into each of eight shallow bowls and place a piece of fish on top. Garnish with toasted almonds and torn herbs.

Spicy Green Pesto

MAKES ABOUT ⅔ CUP

2 scallions, green tops only

1 cup loosely packed fresh basil leaves

1 cup loosely packed arugula leaves

¼ cup loosely packed fresh mint leaves

¼ cup loosely packed fresh flat-leaf parsley leaves

½ small jalapeño, finely chopped

1 large clove garlic, finely chopped

¼ teaspoon preserved lemon, or ½ teaspoon finely chopped lemon zest

Extra-virgin olive oil

Kosher salt and freshly ground black pepper

Bring a small pan of water to a boil over medium-high heat. Fill a large bowl with cold water and ice and set aside.

When the water comes to a vigorous boil, add the scallion tops and blanch them until tender, about 20 seconds. Plunge them in the ice water to stop the cooking. Bring the water back to a boil and add the basil, arugula, mint, and parsley leaves. After about 5 seconds, drain them into a colander or fine-mesh sieve and put it directly in the ice bath; drain again.

Put the blanched greens in a blender or food processor with the jalapenos, garlic, and preserved lemon or lemon zest. Pulse several times, or until the ingredients make a coarse purée. Add olive oil as necessary to loosen the mixture, and season with salt and black pepper to taste. Put the purée in a wide flat container in the refrigerator to cool. This will speed up the cooling, which will help set the pesto's bright green color.

Chefs at Home:
Favorite Ways to Prepare Fish

MIKE LATA
FIG

My current favorite way to cook fish at home is to bake it. The method plays nicely with the way I cook for my family and when done properly, yields a tender and juicy result.

I like to do the work for dinner early in the day, to create separation from the cooking process before eating. I enjoy the food more when I'm not going straight from the kitchen to the dinner table. So, I roast some potatoes, fennel, and zucchini, toss in fresh herbs and olive oil, and turn them into a casserole that will be topped with a fresh fillet later. What kind doesn't really matter. Then I go off and enjoy my day.

When I come home, I lay the fish fillets on top of the vegetables, cover them with a few slices of tomato, and pop the casserole in the oven for 15 minutes. I pour a glass of wine and casually set the table while the fish is cooking. It's ready when it flakes and has created a little juice in the pan that can be embellished with more olive oil and lemon, or an aïoli. It's easy and always delicious.

MING TSAI
Blue Ginger

Flashing fish like sashimi-grade tuna or salmon fillet with hot oil is a great way to lightly cook fish while still preserving its texture and freshness. Begin by making a curry oil. Toast curry powder, combine it with a neutral-flavored oil like canola oil, and let the oil stand for at least 4 hours or up to overnight, allowing the curry powder to settle. If you don't have time to make curry oil, use extra-virgin olive oil.

Take a 2-ounce portion of fish and loosely wrap it in plastic wrap. Using a meat pounder or mallet, gently flatten the fish to approximately ⅛-inch thickness. Unwrap the fish, season it with fleur de sel and freshly ground black pepper, and garnish with chopped chives and finely julienned ginger.

Just before serving, heat the clear portion (without any of the powder) of curry oil just until it begins to smoke and immediately spoon a tablespoon over the fish. You should hear a sizzle. Enjoy with sparkling wine or sake.

JASPER WHITE
Summer Shack

North American lobster is a great—maybe the greatest—example of a sustainable marine resource. The regulations that have been in place for many decades are successful, thoughtful, and enforceable and support both the lobster population and the small-scale lobstermen and women who depend on this resource.

Unless you can fill a pot with fresh ocean water for boiling, steaming is the best way to cook lobster. Boiling can be an unforgiving method, toughening the lobster if you overcook it. But gentle steaming leaves little room for error and results in a tender, flavorful lobster. And because it requires a small amount of water, steaming is much safer in the home kitchen than a huge pot of boiling water.

Put about an inch of water in a large pot with a tight-fitting lid and some sort of steamer rack to hold the lobsters above the water. (Improvise a rack with an inverted colander or, my favorite, a 3- to 4-inch layer of rockweed.) The pot should allow 1 gallon of space per lobster up to 1½ pounds in size and more for larger ones; ample space is essential for even cooking. Cooking time will vary according to the weight and seasonal factors.

Females take longer in the late spring and summer, when they are full of roe. It is also important to note the hardness of the shell. The new (soft) shell lobsters of summer and early fall cook more quickly than hard-shell lobsters.

JUSTIN APRAHAMIAN
Sanford Restaurant

I dip mackerel—fillets or whole fish—in breadcrumbs and broil it for 4 minutes. The oily skin gets crispy on both sides and the thin fish cooks quickly.

JUDI BARENESS
Chez Jude

I'm a big fan of cedar planking and have a well-oiled cedar board that I like to use. Most planking is done with hardwoods, but cedar works well even though it's soft. First, I soak the wood in water for an hour before baking the fish, so it won't catch fire in the oven. Then I heat the oven to 325°F and arrange the fish on the plank. Sometimes I'll put thinly sliced potatoes, carrots, and other vegetables on the board with the fish. When it's ready, the board goes on the middle rack in the oven for 8 to 10 minutes per inch of thickness. Be sure the board isn't touching the sides of the oven.

BRUCE SHERMAN
North Pond

Whether at home or the restaurant, I am particularly keen on low-temperature roasting (between 150°F and 200°F) for fatty fish like salmon and delicate fish such as halibut. It takes a bit longer to cook, but the results are magnificent. The idea is to not change the nature of the fish proteins so as to significantly change their texture. Wild salmon, which is so often overcooked, becomes luxuriously soft and rich, while less forgiving fish like halibut and arctic char are remarkably tender, moist, and nuanced.

JOHN ASH
Santa Rosa, California

I like to cook from frozen. Vacuum-sealed, single fish fillets are now available frozen in some markets. Extremely convenient, these portions are often better than their "fresh" equivalent because they're flash frozen and packaged on the boat, right after they're caught. You don't even need to defrost them before cooking.

Heat a pan (preferably nonstick) over medium-high heat. Lightly coat the pan with oil, or a combination of oil and butter, and add the fish, skin side up. Cook until browned, about 3 minutes, and flip the fish over. Season well with salt and pepper and cover to finish cooking, another 3 minutes depending on thickness. Finish cooking fillets over ½ inch thick in an oven heated to 400°F. Cook to your liking, using the tip of a knife to separate the flesh and check for doneness and keeping in mind that the fish will continue to cook after being removed from the heat.

PAUL ROGALSKI

Rouge | Calgary, Alberta, Canada

Jerk seasoning, a traditional Caribbean spice rub made with allspice berries, Scotch bonnet chiles, and a host of other herbs and spices, gets a Northwest twist in a Canadian chef's hands. This recipe, which utilizes plank cooking on cedar, is a method commonly used on the West Coast; halibut is plentiful in neighboring Alaskan waters.

Chef Rogalski likes to serve a good corn succotash with this dish.

SERVES 6

Jerked Cedar Plank Halibut

FOR THE JERK SPICE

8 scallions, white and green parts, cut into
  2-inch lengths

1 shallot

2 cloves garlic

¼ cup freshly squeezed orange juice

1 tablespoon soy sauce

1 tablespoon ground allspice

1 tablespoon ground coriander

1 tablespoon grated fresh ginger

1 tablespoon granulated sugar

1 teaspoon freshly ground black pepper

1 teaspoon ground star anise

1 teaspoon fresh thyme leaves

1 teaspoon ground cinnamon

¼ teaspoon Scotch bonnet or habanero
  pepper powder

FOR THE HALIBUT

1 cedar plank large enough to
  accommodate 6 halibut fillets

6 banana leaves

2 tablespoons sesame oil

6 halibut fillets, about 6 ounces each

Kosher salt

Combine the jerk spice ingredients in a food processor and blend until smooth. Set aside.

Soak the cedar plank in water for 2 to 3 hours and dry well before using. Cut the banana leaves the same size as the halibut fillets; they will be the under liners for the fish. Brush the banana leaves with the sesame oil.

Heat the grill to high with the lid closed for 10 minutes. Season the halibut fillets with salt and put each one on a banana leaf liner. Spread 1 tablespoon of the jerk spice on top of each halibut fillet before placing it on the cedar plank.

When the grill is hot, carefully place the cedar plank with the fish on the hottest part and close the lid. The cedar will begin to smoke. Cook the fish until it is just firm to the touch, about 10 minutes. Use a spatula to remove each piece of fish from the plank by lifting from under the banana leaf. Arrange the fish on banana leaves on a platter and carefully remove the hot plank from the grill using tongs. Plunge it in cold water to cool quickly.

Dairy and Eggs

Dairy products symbolize freshness and purity in a way that other ingredients don't, perhaps because milk is our first nourishment. Milk in its many forms is fundamental to our food culture, both as a centerpiece of numerous traditional cuisines and an essential source of protein and pleasure. And eggs? It's difficult to imagine a more perfect ingredient.

Throughout the dairy case, flavor is the best indicator of how a cow or a chicken was raised—where it lived, how it was treated, and what it ate. Animals that consume the foods their bodies evolved to process—grass for cows and bugs and worms for chickens—will produce better milk, cream, butter, and eggs. It's as simple as that. And while flavor is the most compelling reason to choose local, sustainably raised ingredients, it isn't the only measure that adds to the pleasure of our collective experience of eating. Supporting small-scale dairies and egg producers expresses a desire to bring back a way of living and eating that will help sustain us and the environment in the long term.

"Supporting small-scale dairies and egg producers expresses a desire to bring back a way of living and eating that will help sustain us and the environment in the long term."

The Scale of Commercial Production

Unfortunately, the egg and dairy industries in this country are based on models that closely resemble large-scale meat production, distinguished by similarly catastrophic flaws. A business model reliant on heavy subsidization and centralization, with an end goal of churning out more faster, forces commercial operations to raise hens in sheds so overcrowded that the birds can't move, making good health and cleanliness impossible. Egg production is subject to seasonal variations in temperature and the number of available daylight hours, so the sheds are lit with artificial lights for 23 hours a day to stimulate laying and increase egg production. But the unnatural light depresses the chickens' immune systems, causing them to get sick and need additional vaccines and antibiotics. We're left with more eggs, and they're cheap, but do we want to eat them?

The network of small family farms that once supplied local milk products has been replaced by large dairy businesses equipped to provide regional and national supplies. Whether they are raised for meat or for milk, most cattle are confined in feedlots, where they are fed grain instead of the diet of grass and forage for which they're suited. Under these unnatural conditions, and with injections of hormones or hormones added to their feed, they produce an increased volume of milk with decreased nutritional value.

The majority of commercial milk comes from Holstein cows, easily identified by their distinctive black-and-white markings. Holsteins are bred to produce enormous quantities of milk—three times as much as other breeds. Milk from

Jersey, Guernsey, and Brown Swiss, also dairy cows, has greater nutritional value and higher levels of butterfat. This butterfat, present in fatty acids, stimulates the immune system and helps to protect against disease. Even though it sounds as if it's better tasting and healthier, milk from these other dairy cows isn't as widely available as the demand for it because they don't produce in volumes that can compete with Holsteins and are viewed as being unprofitable.

Local Milk

"Organic" and "hormone free," attributes that once described dairy products of the highest quality, have become household words. Now that there are gigantic organic dairies that are remarkably similar to conventional ones, minus the feed and drugs, organic isn't necessarily the best or only choice. Chad Pawlak, President and CEO of Grass Point Farms, explains, "People so often focus on the value of organic milk. Eliminating the use of growth hormones and non-therapeutic antibiotics is indeed critical. But the cost of certified organic feed may be prohibitively expensive for some dairy farmers. What has the greatest impact on flavor, health, and the environment is how the animal is raised, the amount of pasture in its diet, and the amount of exercise that is allowed with outdoor access." "Grass fed" and "local" have become the new benchmarks for quality and traceability, securing an important place in our food-sourcing lexicon.

Traditions Reborn

The revival of American cheesemaking that began in the 1980s and 1990s paved the way for another wave of old-style dairy products made in small batches on little farms and in local independent creameries. Artisanal operations throughout the country are preserving long-standing methods and traditions by producing the simple foods that we consume daily: butter, yogurt and yogurt-based drinks, buttermilk, crème fraîche, and ice cream. Made with cow, goat, and sheep milk, the ever-expanding selection offers super fresh, complexly flavored alternatives to the flavorless dairy products we've grown accustomed to eating. The increasing availability of dairy and egg products from animals raised on pasture is evidence that consumers appreciate the difference between mass-produced food and the handiwork of these artisans.

If you have a source for good meat, your supplier will be able to point you in the direction of good eggs and dairy products; it's possible the supplier produces both items as well. Expect to pay more for high-quality products from humanely raised animals that grow more slowly and/or produce less milk or fewer eggs. Premium products come with a premium price tag that allows farmers to make a living. By supporting these sustainable producers, we are participating in a broader movement that focuses on sustainable agricultural practices, informed food choices for consumers, and connecting local producers with their customers.

'Artisanal cheese-making operations are preserving long-standing methods and traditions by producing the simple foods that we consume daily.'

FRANK STITT

Highlands Bar and Grill | Birmingham, Alabama

A cool and refreshing twist on an old favorite, this recipe features thick, local buttermilk rather than the usual sour cream or yogurt. A healthy dose of red-wine vinegar and a spoonful of 'Toy Box' or 'Sungold' tomato relish for a garnish provide just the right tang. Be sure to plan ahead when making this soup to allow enough time for the cucumbers to marinate and the soup to chill before serving. The flavors that develop are worth waiting for. SERVES 4

Chilled Cucumber-Buttermilk Soup with Tomato Relish

2 pounds cucumbers (about 10 small)

1 shallot

1 sprig fresh basil; more for garnish

1 sprig fresh dill; more for garnish

¼ cup Grenache or red-wine vinegar

Kosher salt; more as needed

¼ cup buttermilk

8 to 10 cherry tomatoes preferably 'Toy Box' or 'Sungold'

Peel the cucumbers and cut them in half lengthwise. With a small spoon, remove the seeds and discard. Slice the cucumbers into ¼-inch-thick half moons and place in a large nonreactive bowl; you should have about 4 cups. Halve and slice the shallot the same way, into thin half moons. Add to the cucumbers with the leaves from the basil sprig, torn, and the fronds from the dill sprig. Pour the vinegar over the cucumbers, sprinkle with 2 large pinches of salt, and let stand for 2 to 3 hours in the refrigerator or overnight.

In a blender or food processor, purée the mixture on high speed in two batches, adding 2 tablespoons of water to each. Process for 30 to 45 seconds and pour into a large bowl. Repeat. Whisk in the buttermilk and additional salt to taste. Add more water if the soup is too thick. Chill.

To serve, cut the cherry tomatoes into quarters and season with a pinch of salt. Divide the soup among four 6-ounce bowls, put a spoonful of tomatoes in the center, and garnish with a sprig of basil or dill.

> **"Buttermilk is a delicious, versatile, and healthy part of how I cook, and thanks to a growing number of small family dairy farms, real buttermilk is back."**
>
> **LINTON HOPKINS**
> *Restaurant Eugene, Atlanta, Georgia*

JOHN CURRENCE

City Grocery | Oxford, Mississippi

These don't puff up quite like traditional gougères, but they have all the same qualities that recommend consuming them one after the next, in close succession. The pimento cheese gives the interiors a custardy quality, flecked with red from the pimentos and green from the pickles, and a decidedly Southern flavor. Use the extra pimento cheese for sandwiches or dipping. MAKES ABOUT 3 DOZEN PUFFS

Pimento Cheese Gougères

½ cup whole milk

½ cup (1 stick) unsalted butter, cut into several pieces

1 cup unbleached all-purpose flour

½ teaspoon kosher salt

4 large eggs, at room temperature

¼ cup grated extra sharp Cheddar

1 cup Pimento Cheese (recipe on page 238)

½ teaspoon freshly ground black pepper

¼ teaspoon cayenne pepper

Heat the oven to 400°F. Line two baking sheets with parchment or lightly butter them.

Combine the milk, ½ cup water, and butter in a medium-size saucepan and bring to a boil over high heat, stirring until the butter is melted. Add the flour and salt all at once, reduce the heat to medium, and stir the mixture vigorously with a wooden spoon until it pulls away from the sides of the pan. Continue stirring for several minutes over low heat, then remove from the heat and cool for 1 minute. The dough should not brown and will be thick, smooth, and shiny.

Add the dough to the bowl of an electric stand mixer fitted with the paddle attachment. Mix on low speed for 3 to 4 minutes, or until it isn't steaming any more but isn't completely cool, before adding the eggs, one at a time, incorporating each egg before adding the next. Add the grated Cheddar and pimento cheese along with the black and cayenne peppers and mix to blend.

Use a spatula to transfer the dough to a pastry bag fitted with a ½-inch round tip and pipe 1½-inch mounds, approximately the volume of a heaping tablespoon, on the baking sheets 2 inches apart.

Bake until deep golden brown, about 17 minutes. Reduce the heat to 300°F, put a wooden spoon in the door so that it's slightly ajar, and bake for another 10 minutes.

>>>

Pimento Cheese

MAKES ALMOST 2 CUPS

1½ cups grated sharp Cheddar

½ cup grated Gruyère

2 tablespoons cream cheese

3 tablespoons mayonnaise

6 tablespoons finely chopped bread-and-butter pickles

½ teaspoon cayenne pepper

1½ teaspoons Tabasco®

7 tablespoons finely chopped pimentos

Kosher salt and freshly ground black pepper

Combine the Cheddar, Gruyère, and cream cheese in the bowl of a stand mixer fitted with the paddle attachment. Mix on low speed to combine, and then add the mayonnaise, pickles, and cayenne pepper. Mix for several rotations before adding the Tabasco and pimentos. Season to taste with salt and black pepper.

The Raw Milk Debate

Most milk is processed like any other industrially produced food. Raw milk, which is a whole, natural food, is another story. Before the industrial revolution, when dairies were small and local and milk didn't travel long distances, raw milk was the standard. Pasteurization was developed to combat real danger in the pre-industrial milk supply and distribution, making milk potentially less harmful to drink. But it is criticized for destroying likely beneficial bacteria and proteins and valuable nutrients including vitamin C and enzymes essential in helping the body assimilate milk. Some individuals choose raw milk because they find it easier to digest.

As the dairy industry plays a greater role within the mainstream organic movement, raw milk is gaining in popularity again. The potential health risks connected to the consumption of milk from commercial dairy cows are well documented, linking it to everything from allergies to sinus infections to breast and prostate cancer. Proponents believe that raw, organic milk from grass-fed cows can improve digestion, help heal autoimmune disorders, and boost overall immunity. They maintain that it has a remarkably clean track record with safety and that more harmful bacteria are found in pasteurized milk.

Like beef, not all milk is the same. The way the cow is raised, when it is milked, and how the milk is handled and processed are crucial to the quality of the end product. Think of purchasing raw milk as a process nearly identical to purchasing meat directly from the producer. The rules and regulations around the sale of raw milk are continually changing, but certain principles and considerations should always inform your purchase. Make sure you know and trust the farmer and are comfortable with the practices used. Know your family's health concerns because raw milk can pose a real threat. Practice safe production, processing, transportation, storage, and use of raw milk. And most important, continue to educate yourself. The more you know or can ask about the source, the better your assurance of getting a product that you are comfortable feeding your family.

Because raw milk is regulated on the state level, its availability and whether you want to seek it out depend on where you live.

THIERRY RAUTUREAU

Rover's | Seattle, Washington

Harissa is a fiery Tunisian sauce made from hot red chilies, garlic, coriander, and oil. It is a staple of North African cuisines but also wanders into the Morrocan pantry on occasion. This salad borrows flavors from both cuisines and results in an especially vibrant presentation if you use farm eggs with bright orange yolks.

Set aside a boiled potato leftover from another meal, and cook the eggs ahead of time to reduce the time needed for this salad. **SERVES 6**

Couscous-Currant Salad with Harissa Deviled Eggs

6 large eggs

3 cloves garlic, finely minced, divided

1 tablespoon Dijon mustard

3 tablespoons harissa, divided

¼ cup plus 2 teaspoons extra-virgin olive oil

1 small boiled potato, peeled and puréed

Kosher salt and freshly ground black pepper

1 cup couscous

½ cup currants

1 small red onion, finely chopped

1 tablespoon finely grated fresh ginger

1 teaspoon cumin seed, toasted

Zest from 1 orange, finely chopped

1 tablespoon finely chopped fresh cilantro

Citrus Vinaigrette (recipe on page 240)

Bring a saucepan of water to a boil over medium-high heat. Gently add the eggs and reduce the heat to a simmer. Simmer for 10 minutes, drain the water, and place the eggs in a bowl of ice water. After 15 minutes, or when they are cold, peel the eggs and cut them in half. Remove the yolks and lightly mash them.

Combine a third of the garlic, the mustard, and 1 tablespoon harissa in a small mixing bowl and whisk together. Slowly add ¼ cup of oil, whisking, then add the puréed potato and the egg yolks. Season with salt and black pepper to taste, transfer to a piping bag fitted with a star tip, and refrigerate the aïoli for about 30 minutes before filling the eggs.

Pipe the aïoli into the center of the egg whites and refrigerate the deviled eggs until ready to use.

Add 1¼ cups water to a saucepan and bring to a boil. Stir in the couscous and currants, cover, and remove from the heat. Allow to stand for 5 minutes.

Meanwhile, heat the remaining 2 teaspoons oil in a large nonstick pan over medium-high heat. Add the onions, the remaining garlic, and the ginger. Sauté for 3 minutes, or until the onions are tender, and then add the cumin seed and sauté for 1 minute. Fluff the couscous with a fork, stir in the onion mixture, orange zest, and cilantro. Toss with the vinaigrette and season to taste with salt and the remaining harissa.

Put the couscous salad on a platter, arrange the deviled eggs on top, and serve.

>>>

Citrus Vinaigrette

MAKES ABOUT ⅓ CUP

1 blood orange, juiced

1 lemon, juiced

1 tablespoon harissa purée

1 tablespoon argan oil (peanut, walnut, and
  hazelnut oils all make good substitutes)

1½ tablespoons capers

1 tablespoon finely chopped shallots

2 teaspoons chopped fresh chives

Kosher salt and freshly ground black pepper

Whisk the blood orange and lemon juices together with the harissa purée and oil. Add the capers, shallots, and chives, and season to taste with salt and black pepper.

Health Benefits of Milk from Pasture-Raised Dairy Cows

Whole milk and full-fat dairy products have an over-inflated reputation for being high in cholesterol and saturated fat given that they also contain large amounts of conjugated linoleic acid (CLA), an unsaturated, healthy fat with many benefits. The emphasis on quantity over quality from dairy cows has had a direct negative effect on the nutritional content of the milk from the commercial industry, the loss of CLA being the most notable.

Compared to milk from commercial dairy cows, milk from pasture-raised cows has the following:

- Five times more CLA
- An ideal 1:1 ratio of essential fatty acids (EFAs)
- More beta-carotene
- More vitamin A
- More vitamin E

The True Cost of a Dozen Eggs

Depending on where you live, $8 might be the going price for a dozen eggs at the farmer's market. Though it may seem expensive to buy pastured eggs, the true cost of feeding and raising healthy, happy hens is higher than you'd expect. In fact, several studies have shown that it costs farmers substantially more to produce one dozen pastured eggs than the prices they charge.

The most significant costs for a small operation are increased labor in the absence of mechanized feeding, collecting, cleaning, and candling (checking to see if an egg is fertile). There are also farm and marketing expenses, production costs, natural yield (which is affected by daylight and circumvented by commercial operations with artificial light), care, feeding, and housing of hens. Most farmers are able to justify the discrepancy because hens pay their keep in ways that are difficult to measure: They fertilize the soil, eat bugs and weeds, and remove undesirable seeds from the surface of the soil.

Because they are a nutrient-rich protein full of goodness and perfectly suited to many preparations, eggs should be used and treated as a precious ingredient. They're worth the extra pennies.

Breaking It Down

> **"When measured as a unit of nutrition, eggs from chickens raised outdoors are actually far cheaper than their industrial counterparts."**
>
> **ANDREA REUSING**
> *Lantern, Chapel Hill, North Carolina*

JOHN SUNDSTROM

Lark | Seattle, Washington

Bagna cauda (Italian for "hot bath") is a specialty of the Piedmont region of Italy. Made with olive oil, butter, garlic, and anchovies, it is served as a starter for dipping raw vegetables.

In this version, whole milk is added, as is the custom in certain regions. The creamy flavors and textures are slightly reminiscent of the classic French salad Salade Lyonnaise, with the saltiness of anchovies standing in for the lardons called for in the Lyonnaise. **SERVES 6**

Treviso Bagna Cauda with Poached Egg

3 heads Treviso radicchio or other assorted chicories

2 teaspoons white vinegar

6 fresh duck or chicken eggs, each cracked into a small cup or ramekin

Bagna Cauda (recipe below)

1 cup fresh flat-leaf parsley leaves

⅓ cup finely grated Parmigiano-Reggiano

Wash and trim the radicchio, tearing the largest leaves into bite-size pieces. Set aside.

Bring 2 quarts of water to a boil in a large heavy saucepan. Reduce the heat to low, so that the water maintains a slow simmer, and add the vinegar. Swirl the water with a spoon and carefully slip in each egg by tipping the edge of the cup about ½ inch below the surface of the gently simmering water. Use a spoon to lightly nudge the white toward the yolk and poach for 4 to 5 minutes, until the whites are set but the insides are still runny. Poach the eggs in two batches of 3 eggs each.

Divide the radicchio among six plates and place a poached egg on top of each. Dress generously with bagna cauda, stirring well before adding to each plate. Sprinkle with parsley leaves and Parmigiano; serve immediately.

Bagna Cauda

MAKES 1 CUP

3 cloves garlic, thinly sliced

9 anchovies, packed in oil and salt

¾ cup whole milk

Pinch of crushed red pepper flakes

¾ cup extra-virgin olive oil

Freshly ground black pepper

Combine all of the ingredients in a small nonreactive saucepan and simmer gently for 1 hour. Keep warm until ready to serve.

ANDREA REUSING

Lantern | Chapel Hill, North Carolina

Eggs from pasture-raised chickens are essential to this savory Japanese custard. Known as chawanmushi, or "tea cup steam" (a reference to the vessel and cooking method used to prepare it), the custard may contain chicken, shrimp, and/or green vegetables in addition to the mushrooms called for in this recipe.

The kombu and bonito flakes needed to make the dashi are available at Asian markets. **SERVES 6**

Steamed Savory Egg Custard with Shiitake Mushrooms

6 large eggs

2 cups Dashi (recipe on the page 246), divided

¼ cup heavy cream

2 tablespoons dry sherry, divided

Kosher salt

1½ teaspoons tamari or soy sauce

½ teaspoon toasted sesame oil

¼ teaspoon granulated sugar

Small pinch of freshly ground white pepper

20 chives, preferably Chinese, pale part trimmed off

2 teaspoons vegetable oil, preferably expeller-pressed

6 meaty shiitake mushrooms, stemmed and thinly sliced

1 shallot, finely diced

Heat the oven to 350°F.

In a medium bowl, whisk the eggs and gradually add 1½ cups of the dashi and the heavy cream. Add 1 tablespoon of the sherry, 1 teaspoon salt, tamari, sesame oil, sugar, and white pepper. Whisk well. Strain the custard through a fine-mesh sieve and divide the mixture among six 6-ounce custard cups or ramekins. Cover each with a square of foil big enough to extend 2 inches all around. Fold the foil over the rim of each cup and seal it tightly.

Put the cups in a deep baking dish and add boiling water to come about halfway up the sides of the cups. Set the pan on the middle shelf of the oven and bake for 20 to 25 minutes, until the custard has just set. Remove the pan from the oven and leave the cups in the water to cool.

While the custards bake, blanch the chives in salted boiling salt water for 20 seconds and then briefly dip in an ice bath. Drain, pat dry, and cut into 1-inch lengths.

Heat a medium frying pan over high heat. When hot, add the oil and swirl it in the pan. Immediately add the mushrooms, lower the heat to medium, and cook, tossing frequently, until the mushrooms are slightly softened and starting to color, about 2 minutes. Add the shallots, season well with salt, and cook until the mushrooms are tender, about 2 minutes. Deglaze the pan with the remaining 1 tablespoon sherry and 1 to 2 tablespoons of dashi—just enough to make a flavorful broth that will lightly coat the top of the custard. Adjust the seasoning, remove from the heat, toss with the chives, and keep warm.

Just before serving, remove the foil from the custards and top them with small piles of the sautéed shiitakes and a spoonful or two of the broth. Serve warm or at room temperature.

>>>

Dashi

MAKES 3 CUPS

5 dried black mushrooms

One 1x4-inch strip of kombu

3 tablespoons bonito flakes

Put 3 cups of water and the mushrooms in a nonreactive saucepan and bring to a simmer. Turn the heat to low, cover, and cook, at a very gentle simmer for 10 minutes. Add the kombu and continue to simmer gently for 5 more minutes. Turn the heat off and add the bonito flakes. Let steep, covered, for 8 minutes. Strain through a fine-mesh sieve.

Put an Egg on It

Follow the lead of these chefs in using eggs in some unexpected ways.

DEBORAH SCARBOROUGH, chef/owner of the Black Cat Bistro in Cambria, California, cooks farm eggs *sous vide* (French for "under vacuum"), a technique that involves cooking food sealed in airtight bags in a water bath over a longer period of time. The eggs are served on a bed of asparagus ribbons with mustard vinaigrette, bacon, fresh tarragon, and the tiniest croutons ever.

PETER DAVIS, chef at Henrietta's Table in The Charles Hotel in Cambridge, Massachusetts, uses eggs in salads, in quiches, and—his personal favorite—shirred with bacon, sausage, home fries, and cheese in a single pan.

LENNY RUSSO, chef/owner of Heartland, in St. Paul, Minnesota: "We love to poach and pickle them, but we also use them fried, as a garnish for tartare or carpaccio, and in Sauce Gribiche."

WILLIAM DISSEN, chef/owner of The Market Place Restaurant in Asheville, North Carolina, says, "We make an egg pasta when we make raviolis and other varieties of pasta. You can see the difference between the bright yellow color of the egg yolks from pasture-raised eggs and the astonishing depth of flavor they add to the completed dish."

JESSE ZIFF COOL, chef/owner of CoolEatz Restaurant in San Francisco, California: "At Flea Street, we have a special called 'Which Came First?' We put a poached egg on top of a roasted pastured chicken with seasonal vegetables, and drizzle it all with a little herb oil or butter. When you break the yolk over everything, the delicious fun explodes."

MICHAEL ANTHONY

Gramercy Tavern | New York, New York

Peekytoe is a small crab found along the East Coast and is especially abundant in the waters of Maine. Less than 1 pound each, the reddish crabs are a bycatch of lobster fishing that were routinely discarded. Delicate and fragile, peekytoe crabs cannot be shipped live, which means they must be cooked and picked by hand. Substitute any fresh crab available in your area. SERVES 4

Egg Crêpe with Crab and Pickled Ramps

2 tablespoons unsalted butter, divided

6 large eggs

3 tablespoons white soy sauce

1 tablespoon unbleached all-purpose flour

Pinch of white pepper

Vegetable oil, for coating the pan

12 wild ramps or scallions, trimmed

2 tablespoons extra-virgin olive oil

Kosher salt and freshly ground black pepper

8 ounces fresh peekytoe crabmeat

1 lemon, juiced

1 tablespoon coarsely chopped fresh tarragon

4 teaspoons Pickled Ramps (recipe below)
   or capers

Heat a grill to medium hot.

Melt 1 tablespoon of butter and set aside to cool slightly. Whisk together the eggs, soy sauce, flour, and white pepper. Add the cooled butter, whisk to combine, and strain the mixture through a fine-mesh sieve.

Lightly coat a 7- or 8-inch nonstick sauté pan with vegetable oil and place it over medium-high heat for 30 seconds, or until the oil is hot. Add ⅓ cup of egg mixture to the pan and swirl it to make a thin pancake-like sheet that covers the bottom. Cook for about 1 minute, or until set; run a heat-resistant rubber spatula around the outside of the crêpe to loosen it as it cooks. Flip the crêpe over and cook for 30 seconds more on the other side. Once the crêpe is cooked, slide it out of the pan onto a parchment-lined baking sheet. Repeat with the remaining batter.

Season the ramps or scallions with olive oil, salt, and black pepper, and place on the grill. Cook until lightly grilled, about 3 minutes.

Melt the remaining 1 tablespoon of butter in a small sauté pan over low heat and add the crabmeat. When it is warmed through, season with lemon juice, tarragon, salt, and pepper.

To serve, lay a crêpe out flat on each of four plates. Spoon warm crabmeat down the middle, from one edge to the other. Top with 3 grilled ramps and a sprinkle of thinly sliced pickled ramps. Fold in half and serve.

Pickled Ramps

MAKES 1 SCANT QUART

2 bunches small, young ramps

2 cups rice vinegar

⅔ cup granulated sugar

4 teaspoons kosher salt

¼ teaspoon yellow mustard seeds

¼ teaspoon black peppercorns

¼ teaspoon fennel seed

¼ teaspoon coriander seed

Wash the ramps and trim the root ends and some of the greens if they are tough, wilted, or unusually long. Fit the prepared ramps into a quart jar or several smaller jars and set aside.

Combine ⅔ cup water with the vinegar, sugar, salt, mustard seeds, peppercorns, fennel seed, and coriander seed in a nonreactive pot and bring to a boil. Once the sugar has dissolved, remove the pot from the heat and pour the liquid over the ramps in the jars. Allow to cool slightly, cover with a lid, and store in the refrigerator for up to 3 months.

How to Navigate Egg Labels

I t you can't buy eggs at a farmer's market or if it's winter and laying numbers are down, you may be faced with the following labels at the supermarket. With eggs, as with any other food product these days, it is important not to take the labels and certifications on the carton at face value. Even when they're relevant to the sometimes separate, sometimes overlapping issues of animal welfare and husbandry and what the animals were fed, labels have no official standards or means of enforcing them. Here are the labels you're most likely to encounter and what they mean.

AMERICAN HUMANE CERTIFIED

Defined by American Humane Certified

This certification allows both cage-free and cage-confined production systems for chickens, calling them "humane," even though an abundance of scientific evidence demonstrates that the cages are detrimental to animal welfare and nearly every major U.S. and European Union animal welfare group is opposed to them. There is no requirement for access to pasture. Forced molting through starvation is prohibited, but beak cutting is permitted.

ANIMAL WELFARE APPROVED

Defined by Animal Welfare Institute

The birds are cage free and must have continuous outdoor perching access. They must also be able to perform natural behaviors like nesting, perching, and dust bathing, and there are requirements for stocking density, perching space, and nesting boxes. Birds must be allowed to molt naturally and beak cutting is prohibited.

ANTIBIOTIC FREE

No legal or regulated definition

Chickens typically receive a steady diet of antibiotics whether they need them or not. Over time, they become resistant to the drugs. "No Preventative Antibiotics," an unregulated variation on the label, means that the birds weren't dosed regularly but may have been treated in the case of illness.

CAGE FREE

No legal or regulated definition

Cage-free eggs come from hens that aren't confined in the cages typical to the egg industry. However, the term "cage free" isn't legally regulated and the hens are usually kept by the thousands on the floor of a large barn or warehouse. The term doesn't verify that the birds had access to the outside and if so, whether it was pasture, mud, or a bare lot. Beak cutting is permitted.

CERTIFIED HUMANE/HUMANELY RAISED

Defined by Humane Society and ASPCA

This seal, sponsored by national and state humane societies and the ASPCA (The American Society for the Prevention of Cruelty to Animals), defines space requirements and bird management for humanely raised hens, but makes no claims about what they're fed.

FERTILE

No legal or regulated definition

These eggs were laid by hens that lived with roosters, meaning they were most likely not caged.

FREE RANGE/FREE ROAMING

No legal or regulated definition

The USDA has defined this claim for some poultry products, yet there are no standards for hens or free-roaming egg production. The term is unregulated but implies that hens have access to the outdoors, which isn't the same as saying they actually go outside. Because there are tens of thousands of birds in an industrial-scale facility, most never make it outside. Beak cutting and forced molting through starvation are both permitted.

Free-range systems are criticized for not addressing welfare issues like aggression, feather pecking, and cannibalism, and for offering beak trimming, or removal of the tip of the bird's beak, as a viable solution.

NATURAL

Defined by USDA

A "natural" product must contain no artificial ingredients or added color and be only minimally processed. As with meat, this label sounds good but does not refer to how an animal was raised. Natural products routinely involve confinement systems and use of antibiotic growth promoters.

NO HORMONES ADDED

Defined by USDA

The FDA banned hormone use in poultry in 1959, so this label is empty at best and misleading at worst, suggesting that other egg producers may be dosing their birds illegally.

OMEGA-3 ENRICHED

No legal or regulated definition

Algae, flaxseed, and fish oil are some of the supplements chickens are given to boost their omega-3 content. This polyunsaturated fatty acid is considered crucial to good health, but eggs aren't the most natural or efficient delivery system. For example, 3 ounces of salmon contains three times the amount of omega-3s as an enriched egg. True grass-fed pastured hens naturally have higher levels of omega-3 without dietary supplementation, but if you're interested in boosting omega-3s in your diet, eating eggs is not the most efficient way to do it.

ORGANIC/CERTIFIED ORGANIC

Defined by USDA

The USDA certifies all organic eggs. Organic eggs come from a hen whose feed is free of pesticides, herbicides, fungicides, and commercial fertilizers and contains no animal byproducts. The hens have never been given antibiotics, are cage free, and have access to the outdoors, whether or not they choose to venture out. Forced molting through starvation and beak cutting of organic birds are both permitted.

PASTURED/PASTURE RAISED

No legal or regulated definition

You probably won't see this label on a supermarket carton of eggs, but farmers selling eggs may use it to explain how they care for their birds. Pastured birds, like other pastured animals, range freely, sampling grass, grubs, and bugs. For some operators, keeping birds on pasture is only logistically possible with a smaller flock since it has to be moved when the birds eat the grass down. Farmers supplement pastured birds' diets with grain, corn, or soy for calories and fat.

UNITED EGG PRODUCERS CERTIFIED

Defined by United Egg Producers

The majority of U.S. commercial battery bird operations use this meaningless certification in marketing to customers. It indicates that the operations comply with the voluntary program, which permits routine cruel and inhumane factory farm practices and guarantees nothing more than that the company's caged hens are given food and water. Hens are confined in battery cages that don't have to provide any more than 67 square inches per bird—less area than a sheet of 8½ x 11-inch paper—and beak cutting is permitted.

VEGETARIAN/VEGETARIAN DIET

No legal or regulated definition

"Vegetarian" is another misleading label that, on its face, sounds desirable but doesn't address the living conditions of the birds. Chickens are natural omnivores who, given the choice, would spend hours outdoors, happily digging and scratching for bugs and grubs, so a vegetarian diet actually means that the chickens didn't go outdoors. It also means their feed contained no animal byproducts, like beef tallow or fish meal.

ERIC WARNSTEDT

Hen of the Wood | *Waterbury, Vermont*

Like homemade pasta, gnocchi (Italian for "dumplings") are a treat that require some extra time and effort. Since this particular version freezes well, consider making a whole batch and tucking some away.

Here, the gnocchi are made with goat milk cheese and plenty of young herbs, then tossed with shell peas, tarragon, and lemon zest, flavors redolent of spring. Let the seasons be your guide as you prepare these throughout the year; the combinations are endless. MAKES ABOUT 120 DUMPLINGS; SERVES 4 AS A MAIN COURSE OR 6 TO 8 AS A STARTER, WITH AN EQUAL AMOUNT OF DUMPLINGS LEFT FOR THE FREEZER

Goat Cheese Gnocchi with Spring Peas and Tarragon

FOR THE GNOCCHI

1 heaping tablespoon Dijon mustard

2 tablespoons finely chopped soft fresh herbs, including basil, tarragon, flat-leaf parsley, and chives

1 cup grated aged goat cheese

8 large eggs

1½ cups (3 sticks) unsalted butter

2 tablespoons kosher salt, divided

4 cups unbleached all-purpose flour

FOR FINISHING THE DISH

1 tablespoon unsalted butter, divided

1 tablespoon extra-virgin olive oil, divided

Kosher salt

2 cups freshly shelled, blanched peas

1 shallot, finely diced

1 tablespoon finely chopped fresh tarragon

1 lemon

Parmigiano-Reggiano, for serving

Combine the mustard, herbs, and goat cheese in a small bowl. Crack the eggs into a measuring cup; this will make it easy to add them slowly and without any bits of shell. Set both aside.

Add 3 cups of water to a large pot over medium-high heat with the butter and 1 tablespoon salt. Bring the mixture to a boil, stirring until the butter is melted. Add the flour all at once, reduce the heat to medium low, and stir the mixture vigorously with a wooden spoon until it pulls away from the sides of the pan. Continue stirring for several minutes, then remove from the heat and cool for 1 minute. The dough should not brown and will be thick, smooth, and shiny.

Add the dough to the bowl of an electric stand mixer fitted with the paddle attachment, along with the mustard and cheese mixture. Without washing it, fill the saucepan with water, add the remaining 1 tablespoon of salt, and bring to a boil.

Mix the dough on low speed for a few seconds and begin adding the eggs from the measuring cup, carefully adding just one at a time and incorporating it completely before adding the next. The whole process will take about 4 minutes.

Fit a pastry bag with a ¾-inch tip, fill it with about one-quarter of the dough, and twist it so that the dough is compact and sitting in the bottom of the bag.

Once the water is boiling, with one hand holding the bag and the other a small sharp knife, squeeze the bag and twist, cutting the dough at 1-inch intervals as it comes out of the bag. It will become less awkward with practice. Try to make about 20 dumplings in each round.

>>>

When the dumplings float, give them a few more seconds before removing them from the water with a slotted spoon onto a baking sheet; this allows them to cool quickly. They will be delicate while they're warm but will become more durable as they cool. Continue to refill the pastry bag and boil the dumplings in batches until the dough is gone. Remove the dumplings from the baking sheet as they cool, to avoid stacking them, or use a second baking sheet.

Set aside as many dumplings as you want to use immediately and put the rest in a zip-top freezer bag or another container for the freezer. Approximately 15 dumplings per person are the right amount for a main course, or 8 to 10 for a starter.

To serve the gnocchi, add ½ tablespoon butter and ½ tablespoon olive oil to a 12-inch sauté pan over high heat. Just as the butter is beginning to brown and smell nutty, add about 30 dumplings to the pan. Do not crowd the pan, as this may cause sticking. Toss the gnocchi in the pan occasionally so that they brown evenly. Season with salt, add 1 cup of peas, and half of the shallots. Toss the pan to keep the contents moving and to warm the peas. Add 1½ teaspoons tarragon and a squeeze of lemon juice and divide between two bowls or four small plates. Repeat to make a second batch. Serve and pass freshly grated Parmigiano at the table.

> **"Most people are familiar with fresh, unripened goat milk cheeses—those of the tangy, spreadable variety. Aged goat cheese offers its own nuance, with rustic barnyard flavors and aromas of wet hay."**
>
> **MATT JENNINGS**
> *Farmstead, Providence, Rhode Island*

Milk: It's Not Just from Cows

Once upon a time, choosing milk meant deciding between whole, skim, 1 percent, and 2 percent butterfat content—all from commercial dairy cows. Today, there are a staggering number of alternatives to homogenized, pasteurized milk from factory farms, as well as some compelling reasons to explore them. Individuals with lactose intolerance and digestibility issues have long tried to find something as smooth, creamy, and unctuous as cow milk for their coffee and cereal. Some alternatives lack calcium, milk's most important health benefit, but milk is not the only food item rich in the mineral.

No matter what kind of **cow milk** you purchase, make sure it's free of rBST (recombinant bovine somatotropin) and rGBH (recombinant bovine growth hormone), artificial growth hormones used to boost milk production in dairy cattle. These highly controversial chemicals have been found to leave residue in milk and are largely unstudied for their effects on humans.

Goat and sheep milk are easier to digest than cow milk and more nutritionally compatible with our needs. They aren't widely accepted—or available in this country, but are worth seeking out for the wide range of essential nutrients they have to offer, some of which are lacking or present in lower levels in cow milk. Both goat and sheep milk have more calories than cow milk and higher levels of butterfat, but they are lower in saturated fat and contain more protein, vitamins, and minerals.

Kefir is fermented raw milk, or raw milk that has been inoculated with bacterial cultures in much the same way that yogurt is. After it sits for a day or two, it becomes slightly effervescent and, like yogurt, a little sour.

Soy milk used to be the best and most readily available alternative to cow milk, but numerous other options are available now. Actually, with soybean farming under attack for its undesirable environmental impact and the fact that most soybeans are genetically modified, soy has shifted from being perceived as healthy to a product that should be avoided unless it is organic and/or made with non-GMO soybeans. Soy milk also tends to contain unhealthy amounts of sugar, particularly in the flavored versions.

There are loads of other **dairy alternatives** for individuals with allergies or sensitivities to dairy products. Milk made from rice, oats, hemp, coconut, almonds, and other nuts are all easy to find, and each has its selling points. Some are a good source of protein and offer additional health benefits, while others work especially well in cooking and baking. Some just plain taste better. The best way to figure out which one is for you is to read the labels and sample them.

Breaking It Down

SARAH STEGNER AND GEORGE BUMBARIS

Prairie Grass Café | Northbrook, Illinois

Like those in a traditional *tortilla española*, the potatoes for this frittata are simmered in olive oil, adding incomparable tenderness and flavor. The creamy tang of goat cheese and bright flavor of the fresh herbs turn this humble staple into something special. Spicy homemade sausage, roasted root vegetables, or a simple green salad make it a meal.

SERVES 6 TO 8

Goat Cheese Frittata with Potatoes and Herbs

1½ pounds russet, Yukon Gold, or other starchy potatoes

1½ cups olive oil

1 small onion, cut into ½-inch dice (about ½ cup)

2 tablespoons chopped fresh flat-leaf parsley

2 tablespoons finely chopped fresh chives

2 tablespoons finely chopped fresh thyme

Kosher salt and freshly ground black pepper

10 large eggs, lightly beaten

4 ounces fresh goat cheese

Peel the potatoes, cut in half lengthwise, and slice ¼ inch thick. Put the potatoes in a wide sauté pan and cover with the olive oil (they should be completely covered). Bring to a simmer over medium heat and cook the potatoes, occasionally lifting and turning them, until they are tender but not brown, about 20 minutes. Remove the potatoes from the pan to a colander set over a bowl to drain. Reserve the oil for further use.

In a 10-inch nonstick sauté pan, add 2 tablespoons of the reserved olive oil and the onions. Cook over medium-high heat, stirring frequently, until the onions are almost translucent. Whisk the herbs and a big pinch of salt and black pepper with the eggs and add the mixture to the pan along with the potatoes.

Stir frequently until the eggs begin to cook, then shake the pan and allow the bottom of the eggs to set over medium heat. After about 2 minutes, add the goat cheese in spoonfuls, evenly distributing it over top of the eggs and potatoes. Gently shake the pan to settle the goat cheese and prevent the frittata from sinking. Cook until the eggs are almost set, about 3 more minutes.

Slide a spatula along the edges and underneath the frittata. Place a large plate over the pan and, with one hand holding the frying pan handle and the other on top of the plate to keep it steady, quickly turn the frying pan over. The frittata should drop onto the plate.

Place the pan back on the burner and add just enough of the reserved oil to cover the bottom and sides of the pan, about 2 tablespoons. Let the pan warm for 30 seconds, then slide the frittata into the pan. Use a spatula or fork to gently tuck in the sides and continue cooking over medium-low heat until the eggs are just set, about 3 minutes.

Remove the frittata from the pan by sliding a spatula underneath it; hold the pan at an angle and slide the frittata onto a plate. Cool slightly and cut into 6 or 8 wedges. Serve at room temperature.

Categories and Types of Cheese

The categories and types of cheese produced in this country are vast and growing.

Types of Cheese

Artisanal, farmstead, and specialty cheesemakers use milk or cream from a buffalo, cow, goat, or sheep (or a blend) as well as a variety of techniques to come up with an almost infinite number of choices. Because many cheeses fit into more than one category, knowing how they are made helps demystify the process of selecting from all of those cheeses. The following list, while not comprehensive, includes cheeses found in most regional markets and identifies their most basic and recognizable characteristics.

Artisan cheeses are produced in small batches, primarily by hand. Because their production focuses specifically on the tradition and art of cheesemaking, artisan cheeses rely on as little mechanization as possible and can be made from all types of milk.

Farmstead cheeses are made with milk from the farmer's own herd or flock, on the farm where the animals are raised. Often the cheesemaker is the person who raises the animals. This situation provides complete control over the quality of the animals and their lives and, consequently, the milk they produce. And since it doesn't have to travel, the milk is as fresh as it gets. Farmstead cheeses are usually made in relatively small batches, often by hand.

Specialty cheeses are produced in limited quantities, to highlight unique natural flavor and texture profiles. They are made from all types of milk.

Categories of Cheese

Fresh unripened cheese is what you get when you separate the liquid whey from the milk solids. It might take the form of cottage cheese, mascarpone, ricotta, fromage blanc, or quark. Because it is perishable, fresh cheese can be given an extended shelf life by further manipulating and aging the curds.

When making **aged cheese**, the curds are drained a second time using heat, pressure, or both and formed into the desired shape. Then the cheese is ready to be aged, a process that not only takes time into consideration but also temperature, humidity, and mold—the ambient mold in the aging room and any that is added to the cheese itself.

During the aging process, the cheese is closely monitored and turned regularly so that it ages evenly. Other techniques are applied that affect the sort of rind that the cheese produces.

Natural-rind cheeses have rinds that are self-formed during the aging process, which takes place in a controlled environment over a period of time. Sometimes the wheels are wrapped, stacked, or rubbed with dry ingredients to encourage drying and compression. Cheddar, Parmigiano-Reggiano, and Manchego are aged natural-rind cheeses.

Washed-rind cheeses are surface-ripened by curing—or washing—the rind throughout the aging process. Salted brine, whey, beer, brandy, wine, or other alcohol are all used, though the liquid varies by region. The washing process helps keep the rind moist and impart flavor to the cheese. *B. linens* bacteria cause the complex flavor and sticky, reddish crust created during this process. Washed-rind cheeses are often those we refer to as "stinky," including Époisses, Munster, and Taleggio. Best Baa

Dairy (Ontario, Canada), Bleu Mont Dairy (Wisconsin), and Consider Bardwell Farm (Vermont) are all recognized for making excellent washed-rind cheeses.

Soft-ripened or bloomy-rind cheeses ripen from the outside in. Downy white and flexible on the outside, with soft, creamy interiors that are even runny at room temperature, these cheeses are always consumed within a month or two of when they're produced. They fit in somewhere between fresh and *affine* (cured cheeses), and they lose moisture and begin to harden as they age. Bloomy-rind cheeses are inoculated with a friendly mold that breaks down and softens the interior of the cheese, creating the oozy texture prized in a ripe Brie or Camembert-style cheese. From Mt. Townsend Creamery's Seastack (Washington) to Green Dirt Farm's Woolly Rind (Missouri) to Old Chatham Sheepherding Company's Hudson Valley Camembert Square (New York), award-winning soft-ripened cheeses are being made across the country.

Blue cheeses have distinctive blue-green veining that is created when the mold added during the cheesemaking process is exposed to air. The mold (*Penicillium roqueforti*) provides flavor ranging from mild to pungent, and blue cheeses can be made in many styles, Roquefort being the most common. Rogue River Blue® from Oregon's Rogue Creamery, Spring Day Blues from Spring Day Creamery in Maine, and Billy Blue® from Carr Valley Cheese in Wisconsin have all received awards from the American Cheese Society.

Raw-milk cheese is the designation reserved for cheeses made with milk that is unadulterated, or hasn't been heated to more than 100°F. (This is the temperature where hundreds of varieties of bacteria thrive and interact with the milk, imbuing it with deeper, more complex flavor.) In the United States, the FDA requires that any raw milk cheese be aged at least 60 days, to reduce the risk of foodborne illnesses associated with unpasteurized milk. For that reason, most young cheeses, both domestic and imported, are made with pasteurized milk.

BRUCE SHERMAN

North Pond | Chicago, Illinois

Ramps, also known as wild leeks, are spring's first legitimate edible offering in many parts of North America. Similar in appearance to purple-tinged scallions with stout onion-like bulbs, their unique garlicky flavor is available for a short window of time, less than a month in early spring. Try a combination of cultivated leeks and garlic the rest of the year.

SERVES 6 TO 8

Wild Ramp and Farmstead Cheese Strata with Roasted Tomato Wine Butter

FOR THE STRATA

2 cups whole milk, divided

¾ cup heavy cream

5 tablespoons extra-virgin olive oil, divided

8 cups cubed (1-inch) French bread
   (about 8 ounces)

1 small bunch spinach (about 6 ounces),

1 bunch ramps, trimmed

4 large eggs

1½ cups sheep or cow milk ricotta cheese

1½ teaspoons kosher salt

½ teaspoon white pepper

¼ teaspoon nutmeg

Dash of Tabasco sauce

¾ cup grated Alpine-style raw milk cheese,
   farmstead cheese, or Gruyère

½ cup grated Parmigiano-Reggiano

3 tablespoons coarsely chopped fresh
   flat-leaf parsley

2 tablespoons chopped fresh
   chervil leaves (optional)

>>>

MAKE THE STRATA

In a large bowl, whisk together 1¼ cups milk, the cream, and 3 tablespoons olive oil. Add the bread cubes and soak for 15 to 20 minutes.

In a small sauté pan, wilt the spinach in 1 tablespoon of olive oil over medium heat. When it's cool enough to handle, coarsely chop the spinach and set aside. Using the same pan, heat the last tablespoon of olive oil and wilt the green tops of the ramps. Remove from the pan to cool and add the minced ramp bulbs to the pan. Sauté until barely translucent, then add to the spinach along with the chopped ramp greens.

Crack the eggs into a bowl, separating the last one and adding the yolk to the other eggs; save the egg white for another use. Add the remaining ¾ cup milk, the ricotta, salt, white pepper, nutmeg, and Tabasco and whisk vigorously until the custard is smooth and homogeneous. Add to the bowl with the soaked bread cubes, mixing gently to distribute without breaking up the cubes of bread. Carefully fold in the spinach and ramps, grated cheeses, parsley, and chervil, if using. Pour into a buttered 3-quart casserole or a 9x13x2-inch pan, cover with plastic wrap pressed directly onto the surface of the bread, and chill overnight.

Heat the oven to 325°F. Bake the strata for 30 to 40 minutes, or until the top is crusty golden brown, the edges have pulled away from the pan slightly, and a skewer inserted in the center comes out clean.

>>>

FOR THE ROASTED-TOMATO WINE BUTTER

2 teaspoons vegetable oil

1 shallot, finely minced

8 to 10 ripe plum tomatoes (about
    2 pounds), cored and coarsely chopped,
    or ripe heirloom tomato scraps

2 sprigs fresh thyme

2 cloves garlic, crushed

1 bay leaf, fresh if available

1 teaspoon granulated sugar

⅔ cup white wine, such as
    Sauvignon Blanc

½ teaspoon kosher salt; more as needed

4 to 5 tablespoons unsalted butter, cubed
    and chilled

1 tablespoon finely chopped fresh
    basil leaves

Freshly ground black pepper

FOR THE SALAD

2 cups baby arugula leaves

2 tablespoons extra-virgin olive oil

1 tablespoon aged balsamic vinegar

1 pint ripe cherry tomatoes, preferably
    'Sungold' or other heirloom variety

4 sprigs fresh Opal or Genovese basil,
    leaves only, torn

3 ounces thinly sliced prosciutto

Parmigiano-Reggiano, for shaving

MAKE THE ROASTED TOMATO WINE BUTTER

In a small nonreactive pot over medium heat, cook the shallots in the olive oil until very soft and translucent. Add the tomatoes, thyme, garlic, bay leaf, and sugar and increase the heat to high to "roast" the tomatoes. After they release their liquid, over the next 2 to 3 minutes, reduce the heat and simmer the liquid until it reduces by two-thirds, about 10 minutes. Add the wine and ½ teaspoon of salt, bring to a boil, and simmer on low heat to reduce by two-thirds, 10 to 12 minutes. Strain the mixture through a fine-mesh sieve and discard the solids; about ½ cup of tomato broth should remain.

Put the tomato broth in small pot and bring to boil; boil gently until the liquid is reduced by half, about 6 minutes. Whisk in the chilled butter cubes one at a time, emulsifying each one before adding the next. After whisking in all of the butter, add the basil and season to taste with additional salt and black pepper.

MAKE THE SALAD

Toss the arugula with the olive oil and balsamic vinegar. Add the cherry tomatoes and torn basil leaves. Garnish the salad with prosciutto and shaved Parmigiano-Reggiano.

FOR SERVING

Spoon 2 to 3 tablespoons of the tomato butter in the center of each plate and top with a piece of warm strata. Divide the salad among the plates.

JEFF JACKSON

Lodge at Torrey Pines | *La Jolla, California*

Cooking methods for fresh corn vary geographically, but most would agree that this one, southern in origin, is one of the "right" ways. Get corn from the field into the pan as quickly as possible, since it converts its sugars to starch once picked.

The key to this recipe is leaving the corn in the pan only as long as it takes to warm it through. Crème fraîche and basil add richness and bright notes not usually found in the traditional preparation. SERVES 6

Creamed Corn with Basil

8 large ears corn, husked

2 to 4 tablespoons crème fraîche or
heavy cream

2 tablespoons unsalted butter

1 large shallot, finely chopped
(about ¼ cup)

1 teaspoon kosher salt

¼ teaspoon black pepper

2 to 3 tablespoons fresh basil chiffonade

Find a large wide bowl that's shallow enough that you can run a knife from one end of an ear of corn to the other when it's standing upright. Stand the shucked corn cob with the stem end of the cob resting on the bottom of the bowl. Holding the cob steady, use a sharp knife and make long downward strokes to separate the kernels from the cob. Transfer to another bowl and set aside.

Use the back of the knife to make the same scraping motion against the cobs, to extract any remaining corn pulp. You should get at least ¾ cup of corn pulp from 8 cobs. If not, add 2 tablespoons of crème fraîche. Transfer the pulp to a blender and purée with 2 tablespoons crème fraîche until smooth.

Place a large heavy frying pan over medium-high heat and add the butter. When it has melted, add the shallots and cook, stirring occasionally, until softened, 3 to 4 minutes. Add the corn kernels and stir to coat with butter and combine with the shallots. Add the corn purée, 1 cup water, salt, and black pepper. Simmer, uncovered, stirring occasionally, until the kernels are just tender, 3 to 4 minutes. Stir in 2 tablespoons of basil and add more to taste.

MATT PALMERLEE

former chef of Farm 255 | *Atlanta, Georgia*

This recipe brings out two completely different sides of cauliflower, creating flavors and textures that simultaneously contrast and complement one another. The creamy custard, mild and slightly sweet, with a hint of nutmeg, relies on dairy and eggs to boost the subtle flavor of the cauliflower, so this is a good place to use eggs with bright orange yolks and the freshest milk and cream you can find. SERVES 4

Cauliflower Custard

FOR THE CUSTARD

2 tablespoons unsalted butter, melted

2 cups cauliflower florets (about 8 ounces)

2 large eggs

⅓ cup heavy cream

⅓ cup whole milk

½ cup grated Grana Padano

½ teaspoon kosher salt

¼ teaspoon freshly grated nutmeg

Dash of cayenne pepper

FOR THE ROASTED CAULIFLOWER

2 cups cauliflower florets (about 8 ounces)

1 tablespoon extra-virgin olive oil

2 anchovy fillets, finely chopped

Zest of 1 lemon, finely chopped

Kosher salt and freshly ground
   black pepper

1 cup arugula

MAKE THE CUSTARD

Position a rack in the center of the oven and heat the oven to 350°F. Lightly brush four 6-ounce ramekins or individual ovenproof dishes with the melted butter and place in a baking pan large enough to hold them comfortably. Set aside.

Bring a pot of generously salted water to a boil over high heat. Add the cauliflower and cook until very tender when pierced with a knife, 8 to 10 minutes, depending on the size of the florets. Drain the cauliflower in a colander, pat dry with a clean towel, and purée the florets in a food processor until almost smooth.

In a large bowl, whisk together the eggs, cream, milk, Grana Padano, salt, nutmeg, and cayenne pepper. Add the cauliflower purée and whisk well. Divide the mixture evenly between the ramekins. Pour enough boiling water into the baking pan to come halfway up the sides of the ramekins.

Bake until the custards are set and a small sharp knife inserted in the centers comes out clean, about 35 minutes. Carefully remove the ramekins from the pan to a cooling rack. Increase the oven temperature to 425°F.

MAKE THE ROASTED CAULIFLOWER

In a large bowl, toss the cauliflower with the olive oil, anchovies, and lemon zest. Spread out in a single layer on a baking sheet and roast until the cauliflower caramelizes slightly and becomes tender, 12 to 15 minutes, depending on the size of the florets. Season to taste with salt, if needed, and black pepper.

TO SERVE

Run a sharp knife around the inside edges of the ramekins and unmold onto plates by placing a serving plate on top of a ramekin and inverting it. Lay a few leaves of arugula around the base of the custard and top with roasted cauliflower florets.

Who Decides the Price of Milk?

The dairy industry is complex and tied to an illogical pricing model that is based on the value of butter and a 40-pound chunk of Cheddar sold on the Chicago Mercantile Exchange. The connection? Milk is worth no more to a plant than the value of the finished product, minus the cost of making it. As the demand for butter and cheese changes, so does the value of milk. Farmers have no control over milk prices, which can change drastically compared to the farmer's fixed production costs. Dominated by a handful of large companies that buy and sell milk, the dairy industry is subject to the price manipulations of these players. Neither the price the farmer gets nor the farmer's cost of production are taken into consideration when milk is priced for the consumer market. As a result, small dairy farmers are struggling to break even as milk prices continue to decline.

For dairy farmers, one of the keys to staying solvent is keeping production costs low. Raising cattle on pasture is one of the most effective ways to increase profitability since feed is a dairy farmer's single biggest expense (up to 60 percent). Pastured animals pass on additional savings by reducing the need for paid labor; eliminating seed, fertilizer, or pesticides costs; and saving on fuel, oil, and repairs for equipment.

BRIAN ALBERG

The Red Lion Inn | *Stockbridge, Massachusetts*

This rich pudding is excellent with roast chicken or a perfectly grilled steak, but it also stands alone when served with assertive greens dressed with a lively vinaigrette.

Look for a local blue cheese like Berkshire Blue on the East Coast, Rogue River Blue in the West, or Buttermilk Blue and Maytag Blue if you're in the middle of the country. The quality of the eggs and dairy ingredients is key to this recipe. Any variety of bread works here, from whole grain to baguette to brioche. SERVES 6

Blue Cheese Bread Pudding

4 tablespoons (½ stick) unsalted butter,
  at room temperature, divided

1 small sweet onion, finely diced

1 small sprig fresh rosemary, finely chopped

4 large egg yolks

1½ cups heavy cream

Kosher salt and freshly ground black pepper

1 loaf bread, cut into ½-inch cubes
  (about 8 ounces)

8 ounces high-quality blue cheese, crumbled

Heat the oven to 350°F. Grease an 8x8x2-inch square baking dish with 2 tablespoons of butter, or divide among 6 ramekins.

Melt the remaining 2 tablespoons of butter in a small sauté pan over medium heat. Add the onions and rosemary and sauté slightly until the onions are lightly caramelized, about 15 minutes. Set aside to cool.

Combine the egg yolks, cream, and a pinch each of salt and black pepper in a large bowl and whisk together. Add the bread cubes and toss so that the pieces soak up equal amounts of custard. Fold in the onions and blue cheese.

Pour the custard into the baking dish, or divide it equally between the ramekins. Cover the baking dish(es) with foil and bake for approximately 35 minutes for a large dish, or 20 minutes for individual dishes. Remove the foil and continue to cook, uncovered, for another 15 to 20 minutes for a large dish, or 10 minutes for individual dishes. Allow to cool slightly before serving.

"The local food movement has traveled into the pantry with a renewed interest in local and heritage grains. When you buy *real* bread made with good grains and plenty of love, there is no need to waste a crumb."

PIPER DAVIS

Grand Central Baking Company, Portland, Oregon

Cheese Is Seasonal

Cheese made from organic milk isn't a bad place to begin, but a good cheesemaker will source the best milk possible by either raising the animals him- or herself or by developing a personal relationship with a dairy farmer. Whether the milk is organic might be beside the point. Because cheesemakers and cheesemaking facilities are often located on or near their dairy farmer and source of milk, it's easy to stay informed about what the animals are eating, how they're treated, and what their milk tastes like at different points in the calendar year. Commercially produced cheeses don't have noticeable fluctuations in flavor because they're made from the milk of cows who are fed a diet of grain and hay that doesn't vary from one season to the next.

Chad Pawlak of Grass Point Farms in Thorp, Wisconsin, explains: "Grass-fed artisan dairy products have confirmed flavor, chemistry, and physical differences in products made with milk from pastured cows. Dairy cows in green pastures, grazing on lush, tender pasture grasses for their forage and nutrition, produce a different type of milk. Grazing involves a complete food cycle—from building healthy soil, nurturing green pasture grasses, and allowing cows to harvest their own feed at their own pace.

Dairy products produced from grass-based milk possess both sensory and culinary advantages."

Artisan cheeses are typically made with milk from pasture-raised animals. Seasonal changes in the grazing diet of these animals affect their milk, resulting in a cheese that has the potential to taste slightly different each time you buy it. The nuances are a result of variations in the milk's flavor, butterfat content, and color as well as a host of other factors: the age of the cheese and where it has ripened, the weather, and the fact that it's handcrafted by individuals who bring uniqueness to it.

Mike Gingrich, founder and owner of Uplands Cheese Company in Dodgeville, Wisconsin, controls some of those variables by using only the milk his pasture-grazed cows produce between May and mid-October to make their award-winning Pleasant Ridge Reserve®. The Alpine-style farmstead cheese is made the same day with raw milk from the morning's milking. The herd is grazed on a diet of 80 percent fresh pasture and 20 percent grain and is moved daily to ensure a supply of fresh grass and to preserve the distinctive flavor of summer pasture in each location.

REGINA MEHALLICK AND ERIN KEM

R Bistro | Indianapolis, Indiana

Rhubarb, with its sweet-tart tang and rosy hue, is the pastry chef's asparagus—one of the early but certain signs that spring has arrived. Unapologetically astringent in its raw form, rhubarb stewed with sugar becomes a silky pink sauce that makes gorgeous ice cream. Served with thick buttermilk biscuits flavored with cardamom and orange zest and topped with strawberry-rhubarb compote, it takes on new proportions.

MAKES 1 QUART ICE CREAM AND 8 BISCUITS

Rhubarb Ice Cream Shortcake with Strawberry-Rhubarb Compote

FOR THE RHUBARB ICE CREAM

½ cup half-and-half

1 cup heavy cream

3 large egg yolks, beaten

¾ cup granulated sugar, divided

Pinch of kosher salt

1 pound (about 8 stalks) rhubarb, diced

1 orange, juiced

FOR THE SHORTCAKES

2 cups unbleached all-purpose flour

¼ cup granulated sugar

½ teaspoon baking soda

1 tablespoon baking powder

½ teaspoon kosher salt

1 teaspoon ground ginger

½ teaspoon ground cardamom

Zest of 1 orange, finely chopped

½ cup plus 2 tablespoons (1¼ sticks)
  unsalted butter, cold, cut into small pieces

¾ cup buttermilk

Milk or cream, for brushing

>>>

MAKE THE RHUBARB ICE CREAM

In a medium saucepan, scald the half-and-half and cream over medium-high heat until bubbles form around the edges of the pan.

In a large bowl, whisk the egg yolks with ¼ cup sugar and salt until pale and smooth. While whisking, slowly pour the scalded cream mixture into the egg yolks, then return the warmed egg mixture to the saucepan. Stir the mixture constantly over medium heat with a wooden spoon or heatproof spatula, scraping the bottom as you stir, until the mixture reaches 175°F and coats the spoon or spatula. Remove from the heat. Pour the custard through a fine-mesh sieve into a clean bowl and cool in an ice bath. Chill for 2 to 3 hours.

Meanwhile, put the rhubarb (you should have about 3 cups) in a non-reactive saucepan with the remaining ½ cup sugar, ½ cup water, and orange juice. Cover and cook over low heat until the rhubarb releases its juices, about 5 minutes. Uncover and increase the heat to medium high. Cook, stirring frequently, until most of the water evaporates and the rhubarb has a soft, jam-like consistency, about 20 minutes. Strain off the liquid and reserve. Mash the solids, cool, and stir into the chilled ice cream base, adding enough reserved liquid to restore the pink color.

Freeze the mixture in an ice cream maker according to the manufacturer's instructions.

MAKE THE SHORTCAKES

While the ice cream is freezing, make the shortcakes. Heat the oven to 425°F. In a large bowl, whisk together the flour, sugar, baking soda, baking powder, salt, ginger, cardamom, and orange zest. Add the cold butter pieces and rub them with the flour using your fingertips until the mixture resembles coarse meal.

>>>

FOR THE STRAWBERRY-RHUBARB COMPOTE

11 ounces (8 to 9 stalks) rhubarb, trimmed, peeled, and diced

¼ cup granulated sugar

6 ounces ripe strawberries, hulled

Slowly add the buttermilk, mixing with a fork just until combined. Do not overmix. Turn the dough out onto a lightly floured work surface and gently pat or roll to a ½- to ¾-inch thickness. Cut 8 biscuits using a floured 3-inch biscuit cutter. Arrange the biscuits on a baking sheet lined with parchment and lightly brush the tops with milk or cream. Bake for 10 to 12 minutes, or until golden brown. Cool on wire rack.

MAKE THE STRAWBERRY-RHUBARB COMPOTE

Place the diced rhubarb, 1 tablespoon water, and sugar in a medium-size heavy saucepan over medium-high heat. Cover and bring to a boil. Reduce the heat and gently simmer until the rhubarb is tender, stirring once or twice, 10 to 15 minutes. Remove the pan from the heat.

Slice the strawberries lengthwise, ⅛ inch thick, and add to the rhubarb. Shake the pan to distribute and allow the sauce to cool to lukewarm.

TO SERVE

Split the biscuits and spoon some compote on the bottom half of each. Top with rhubarb ice cream and a bit more compote. Rest the top half of the biscuit alongside.

PHOEBE LAWLESS

Scratch Baking | Durham, North Carolina

The carrots that begin showing up at farmer's markets in early spring—especially the smaller heirloom varieties—add surprising natural sweetness to custard fillings like this one. This tart is a lovely way to make use of local produce at a time of year when rhubarb and other harbingers of spring have yet to make an appearance. SERVES 8 TO 10

Vanilla Carrot Cream Tart

FOR THE TART DOUGH

½ cup confectioners' sugar

½ teaspoon kosher salt

6 tablespoons (¾ stick) cold unsalted butter, diced into ½-inch cubes

1 large egg

1 tablespoon heavy cream

1½ cups unbleached all-purpose flour

FOR THE FILLING

3 medium carrots, peeled and sliced into ½-inch-thick coins (about 1½ cups)

⅔ cup heavy cream

½ vanilla bean

2 large eggs

1 large egg yolk

⅓ cup granulated sugar

Pinch of kosher salt

1 cup buttermilk

Combine the confectioners' sugar, salt, and butter in the bowl of a food processor. Pulse several times until the mixture resembles small pebbles. Add the egg and heavy cream and pulse again. Add the flour all at once and pulse in bursts until the dough begins to come together. Scrape the dough out onto a clean, lightly floured work surface.

Working quickly and using the heel of your hand or a dough scraper, smear the dough across the floured surface a little at a time to incorporate the butter. This French technique, called *fraisage*, is the key to a tender, flaky crust.

When all of the dough has been smeared, gather it together in a mass and gently form a flat disk that's 1½ inches thick. Wrap tightly with plastic wrap and chill for at least 1 hour or freeze for up to 1 month. If using the dough right away, after an hour, remove the dough from the refrigerator and allow it to sit out for 10 to 15 minutes, to make it easier to roll.

On a lightly floured work surface, roll the dough into a 14- to 15-inch circle that's ¼ inch thick. Fold the dough in half and carefully lay it in a 10-inch tart pan with a false bottom and fluted edges. Lightly press the dough into the corners and fold the outer edge of the pastry into the sides, pressing to create an even wall that extends just beyond the top of the pan. Pinch off excess pastry and reserve the extra dough. Prick the shell with a fork and freeze for at least 15 minutes.

>>>

To make the filling, combine the carrots and heavy cream in a small nonreactive saucepan. Split the vanilla bean half, scrape the seeds, and add them to the pan along with the pod. Simmer the mixture, covered, over low heat until the carrots are soft, about 20 minutes. Cool completely, remove the vanilla pod, and purée with an immersion blender or in a regular blender until very smooth.

In a medium bowl, whisk the eggs, egg yolk, sugar, and salt until well combined. Add the cool carrot purée and buttermilk. This mixture can be made and refrigerated 2 days ahead.

Heat the oven to 325°F. Bake the tart shell for 15 to 20 minutes, or until the bottom is lightly golden. If the dough begins to bubble up, use a clean dry towel to gently press the it down.

Pour the filling into the partially baked shell and then bake for 30 to 40 minutes, or until the edges puff slightly. The tart will be jiggly in the center and appear to be underbaked—this is okay. Cool at room temperature for 30 minutes, then chill until set, about 2 hours.

Remove the tart from the pan and serve at room temperature the day it is baked or chilled the following day.

> ## "Ice cream in late-harvest flavors like sweet corn, roasted pumpkin, or celery with candied ginger are different and delicious ways to incorporate unexpected ingredients into desserts."
>
> **JENI BRITTON BAUER**
>
> *Jeni's Splendid Ice Creams, Columbus, Ohio*

MICHEL NISCHAN

The Dressing Room Restaurant | *Westport, Connecticut*

An angel food cake's structure comes almost entirely from the protein in its vast quantity of egg whites, so it is a good candidate for experimentation with alternative flours. This version substitutes a combination of brown rice flour and almond meal for the cake flour, resulting in a cake that's gluten free. The recipe is also delicious (and equally gluten free) made with a blend of heirloom ingredients from the Southern larder including Carolina Gold® rice flour, sea island pea flour, and almond meal. MAKES ONE 12-INCH CAKE; SERVES 10 TO 14

Angel Food Cake with Pear and Apple Compote

1½ cups brown rice flour

½ cup almond flour

2½ cups superfine or baker's special sugar, divided

2¼ cups egg whites (from 15 to 16 large eggs)

1 teaspoon kosher salt

2 teaspoons cream of tartar

Unsalted butter, for serving

Pear and Apple Compote (recipe on page 274)

Heat the oven to 350°F and place a rack in the lowest position. Whisk together the rice flour, almond flour, and 1 cup of sugar. Set aside.

In a clean dry bowl of a stand mixer, combine the egg whites, salt, and cream of tartar and beat together until foamy using the whisk attachment. Gradually increase the mixer speed and continue to beat the whites until they have thickened and increased in volume. Slowly beat in the remaining 1½ cups sugar, a little at a time, until the meringue holds soft peaks.

Using the whisk from the mixer or a balloon whisk, gently fold in the flour-sugar blend ½ cup at a time, just until incorporated. Spoon the batter into an ungreased 12-inch-round angel food pan and gently tap the pan on the counter to settle the batter and remove any large air bubbles.

Bake the cake for 45 to 60 minutes, making sure not to open the oven during this time. When done, the cake will be deep golden brown and spring back when pressed lightly.

Remove the cake from the oven and invert the pan onto the neck of a bottle or funnel. Suspend the cake upside down as it sets and cools, at least 2 hours. When it is cool, run a small paring knife around the edges of the pan to release the cake. Turn it out onto a plate.

To serve, warm a little bit of butter in a small sauté pan and brown slices of angel food cake on both sides until they are golden and slightly crisped. Spoon the warm compote on top.

>>>

Pear and Apple Compote

MAKES ABOUT 7 CUPS

4 firm ripe pears, peeled, quartered,
and cored, preferably Bosc

4 apples, peeled, quartered, and cored,
preferably a firm slightly tart variety
such as Pink Lady or Cortland

½ cup (1 stick) unsalted butter

¼ cup honey

1 cup brown sugar

Cut the pear and apple quarters into ½-inch-thick slices and set aside.

Melt the butter in a large sauté pan over medium-high heat, then add the honey, brown sugar, and apple and pear slices. Reduce the heat slightly and continue to cook for 3 to 5 minutes, tossing the fruit to coat it well.

"Egg yolks left over from meringues or angel food cake never go to waste in my kitchen. I use them in many desserts that call exclusively for yolks—crème brûlée, homemade ice cream, or sabayon."

JENNY MCCOY

Cissé Trading Company, New York, New York

WALDY MALOUF

Beacon | *New York, New York*

Almonds and stone fruits are natural companions for good reason: They're related. The soft kernel in the middle of the fruits' pits looks, smells, and tastes like almonds. If apricots aren't available, try this recipe with plums, peaches, nectarines, or whatever looks best at the market.

This country-style cake gets its light, delicate texture and moist creaminess from ricotta cheese. Moscato, a fragrant dessert wine, reduces and combines with the juice from the roasted apricots, giving the dessert an intense perfume and elegance. **MAKES ONE 10-INCH CAKE; SERVES 12**

Almond Ricotta Cake with Moscato-Roasted Apricots

FOR THE CAKE

½ cup cake flour; more for the pan

½ cup almond flour

1 teaspoon baking powder

¾ cup (1½ sticks) unsalted butter, melted and cooled; more for the pan

½ cup ricotta cheese

1 cup granulated sugar

1 teaspoon pure almond extract

Pinch of kosher salt

4 large eggs

FOR THE ROASTED APRICOTS

1⅔ cups (375 ml bottle) Moscato or other white dessert wine

½ cup plus 2 tablespoons granulated sugar

1 teaspoon freshly squeezed lemon juice

6 to 8 ripe apricots (about 1 pound), halved and pitted

2 tablespoons unsalted butter, cut into pieces

Whipped cream or vanilla ice cream, for serving (optional)

MAKE THE CAKE

Heat the oven to 350°F. Butter and flour a 10-inch cake pan lined with parchment paper. Set aside.

In a small bowl, whisk together the cake flour, almond flour, and baking powder. Combine the butter, ricotta cheese, sugar, almond extract, and salt in the bowl of a stand mixer. Using the whisk attachment, beat at medium speed for 5 minutes. Add the eggs one at a time, mixing until fully incorporated after each addition. Fold the dry ingredients into the batter.

Scrape the batter into the prepared pan and bake for 30 to 35 minutes, until a tester inserted into the center of the cake comes out clean. Cool completely before removing from the pan.

PREPARE THE APRICOTS

Increase the oven temperature to 500°F. In a nonreactive saucepan over medium heat, combine the Moscato, ½ cup of the sugar, and the lemon juice. Bring the mixture to a simmer, stirring until the sugar has dissolved. Simmer until the liquid is reduced and syrupy, 12 to 15 minutes.

>>>

Meanwhile, roast the apricots. Spread the apricot halves in a single layer, cut side up, on a baking sheet with a rim. Dot the fruit with the butter and sprinkle with the remaining 2 tablespoons of sugar. Roast until the fruit begins to brown, 8 to 10 minutes. Pour the Moscato syrup over the apricots and return them to the oven for 10 minutes, or until they are tender.

TO SERVE

Cut wedges of the cake and garnish with apricots, a drizzle of Moscato syrup, and lightly whipped cream or vanilla ice cream, if desired.

"If you're thinking about making your own cheese, ricotta is one of the easiest to start with. The homemade version has a wonderfully creamy texture and more nuanced flavors than most commercial brands."

VITALY PALEY
Paley's Place, Portland, Oregon

DEREK WAGNER

Nicks on Broadway | *Providence, Rhode Island*

Panna cotta is a classic Italian dessert made with milk and cream, lightly sweetened with sugar, and thickened with gelatin. It doesn't contain eggs but has the silky smooth qualities of custard, especially if you use just enough gelatin to hold its shape on a plate.

Panna cotta lends itself to many variations, including the addition of buttermilk, crème fraîche, or yogurt for part of the cream. Because the list of ingredients is short, high-quality milk and cream make a noticeable difference. SERVES 6

Cocoa Panna Cotta with Blackberries, Cherries, and Cocoa Clove Cookies

FOR THE PANNA COTTA

1 tablespoon vegetable oil, for the ramekins

4 cups heavy cream

¼ cup whole milk

½ cup granulated sugar

1 cup unsweetened cocoa powder, (natural or Dutch processed)

¼ teaspoon kosher salt

1 vanilla bean, split and scraped

(or 1 teaspoon pure vanilla extract)

One ¼-ounce package (2½ teaspoons) powdered gelatin

FOR THE COOKIES

2 cups unbleached all-purpose flour

1 cup unsweetened cocoa powder, (natural or Dutch processed)

1 teaspoon baking soda

1 teaspoon cream of tartar

¼ teaspoon kosher salt

½ teaspoon ground clove

1 cup (2 sticks) unsalted butter, at room temperature

1½ cups (6 ounces) confectioner's sugar

1 large egg

>>>

MAKE THE PANNA COTTA

Lightly oil 6 small ramekins and set aside.

Add the cream, milk, sugar, cocoa powder, salt, and vanilla bean, if using, to a medium saucepan and bring to a simmer. Whisk to combine over low heat, until the sugar dissolves completely and any cocoa powder lumps are incorporated.

In a separate bowl, sprinkle the gelatin over ¼ cup water and let stand for 5 to 10 minutes. Add to the warm cocoa cream mixture, whisking until the gelatin is completely melted.

Strain the mixture through a fine-mesh sieve into a pitcher, add the vanilla extract if using instead of a vanilla bean, and divide among the ramekins. Refrigerate for at least 4 hours or overnight.

FOR THE COOKIES

Sift the flour, cocoa powder, baking soda, cream of tartar, salt, and clove together and set aside. Using a stand mixer with the paddle attachment, beat the butter and confectioners' sugar together on medium speed until smooth, creamy, and lighter in color, about 3 minutes. Add the egg, scrape down the sides of the bowl, and mix to combine. Add the dry ingredients and mix just until they disappear into the dough. Form the dough into 2 logs and chill for at least 2 hours.

Heat the oven to 350°F. Line a baking sheet with parchment. Using a sharp or serrated knife, slice the dough into ¼-inch-thick slices and place them about 1 inch apart on the baking sheet. Bake for 15 to 18 minutes, rotating the pan halfway through the baking time. The cookies will be set around the edges and firm to the touch.

>>>

FOR THE FRUIT

3/4 cup pitted dark cherries

1/4 cup blackberries

2 tablespoons granulated sugar

2 tablespoons freshly squeezed lemon juice

1 teaspoon pure vanilla extract

Fresh mint leaves, preferably chocolate
mint, torn

MAKE THE FRUIT

Combine the cherries and blackberries with the granulated sugar, lemon juice, and vanilla extract. Add several torn chocolate mint leaves.

To serve, run a sharp knife around the edge of each panna cotta and unmold onto a plate by placing a serving plate on top of a ramekin and inverting it. Garnish with the fruit and cookies.

"There's nothing like the silken, sweet flavor of farm-fresh cream. At our restaurant, we like to use local cream to soften the flavors and make our food richer, without making it heavier."

KATE JENNINGS

Farmstead, Providence, Rhode Island

The Evolution of American Cheese, and Twelve Cheeses Not to Be Missed

The American cheese revolution has been nothing less than a revelation. Though original and farmstead cheeses are really just coming into their own in this country, the best have uncanny similarities to the European icons. They express regionally distinct terroir and heritage; honor the natural, seasonal grazing habits of milk-giving; are made at or close to the source; are raw and/or organic milk cheeses (to the extent that U.S. law allows); and value the craft of cheesemaking over volume of production.

And all are in stark contrast to what we once called "American cheese."

Cheese is a living food and, as a manifestation of terroir, the best way to discover it is to taste the varietals in your area, seasonally if possible. Here are 12 original American cheese you should try before you die:

1 Uplands Cheese Company's Pleasant Ridge Reserve®, an Alpine-style farmstead cheese made from raw cow milk in Dodgeville, Wisconsin.

2 Rogue Creamery's Rogue River Blue, a handcrafted, blue-veined cheese made from raw cow milk in Central Point, Oregon.

3 Vermont Butter & Cheese Creamery's Bonne Bouche®, an aged, geotrichum-rinded cheese made from pasteurized goat milk in Websterville, Vermont.

4 Meadow Creek Dairy's Grayson, a semisoft, washed-rind cheese made from raw cow milk in Galax, Virginia.

5 Jasper Hill Farm's Winnimere, a washed-rind cheese made from raw winter Ayrshire cow milk in Greensboro, Vermont.

6 Cowgirl Creamery's Red Hawk, a triple-cream, washed-rind cheese made from Straus Family Farm organic cow milk in Point Reyes Station, California.

7 Carr Valley Cheese Company's Cave Aged Marisa, a natural-rind cheese made from sheep milk in La Valle, Wisconsin.

8 Shelburne Farms' Clothbound Cheddar, an English-style, aged farmhouse cheese made from cow milk in Shelburne, Vermont.

9 Mozzarella Company's Hoja Santa, a fresh, wrapped cheese made from goat milk in Dallas, Texas.

10 Capriole Farmstead Goat Cheese's Wabash Cannonball, a French-style surface-ripened cheese made from goat milk in Greenville, Indiana.

11 Vermont Shepherd's namesake, Vermont Shepherd (Verano), a natural-rind cheese inspired by cheeses of the French Pyrenees, made from raw sheep milk in Putney, Vermont.

12 Vella Cheese Company's Dry Monterey Jack, an aged cheese made from cow milk in Sonoma, California.

ROBIN SCHEMPP *is founder and president of Right Stuff Enterprises.*

DEBORAH SCARBOROUGH

Black Cat Bistro | Cambria, California

White chocolate doesn't contain cocoa solids; it is a combination of sugar, dairy solids, and some sort of fat, often cottonseed oil. A good-quality white chocolate will list cocoa butter, which imparts the chocolatey flavor, as the fat.

The basil syrup in the recipe can be replaced by tossing the sliced strawberries with some granulated sugar and bruised basil leaves. The berries will take on the subtle flavor of the basil as they macerate, creating a flavorful juice that takes the place of the liquid provided by the syrup. SERVES 8

White Chocolate Mascarpone, Strawberries, and Basil in Phyllo

6 sheets phyllo dough (12x17 inches), thawed

¼ cup (½ stick) unsalted butter, melted; more for the pan

2 tablespoons granulated sugar

1 cup finely chopped white chocolate or white chocolate chips

1 cup mascarpone

1 cup heavy cream

2 tablespoons Marsala

2 pints fresh strawberries

2 to 3 tablespoons micro basil or basil chiffonade

Basil Syrup (recipe on the facing page)

2 tablespoons Reduced Balsamic Syrup (recipe on the facing page; optional)

Heat the oven to 350°F. Unroll the phyllo sheets and cover them completely with a piece of plastic wrap and a lightly dampened towel. Do not leave the phyllo uncovered as it dries out quickly, causing it to crack and fall apart when handled.

Remove one sheet of phyllo from the stack. Beginning at the edges, use a soft-bristle brush to coat the entire sheet with melted butter. Sprinkle with a teaspoon of sugar and repeat with a second sheet of phyllo. Continue layering the buttered phyllo sheets, sprinkling each one with sugar, until you've used all 6. Cut the rectangle into 8 smaller rectangles, 4¼ by 6 inches each.

Carefully press the rectangles into a lightly buttered muffin tin or 8 lightly buttered ramekins. Bake for 10 to 12 minutes, or until the phyllo cups are light golden brown around the edges. Remove from the oven, arrange the cups on a sheet pan, and return to the oven to brown the bottoms of the shells, approximately 3 more minutes. The phyllo cups can be made the day before you plan to serve the dessert.

To make the white chocolate mascarpone, add the white chocolate to a bowl that fits snugly over a saucepan containing 1 to 2 inches of barely simmering water. (The bottom of the bowl should not come into contact with the water in the saucepan.) Place the bowl over the water. Stir the chocolate occasionally, using a clean dry spoon, until it has almost melted. The remaining heat will take care of any small unmelted lumps.

Remove the bowl from the water bath and let the chocolate cool until it is barely warm and still pliable. In the bowl of an electric mixer, whip the mascarpone and cream together until soft peaks form. Add the Marsala and continue to whip until the mixture holds stiff peaks. Add the melted white chocolate, whipping the mixture until just blended. The mascarpone cream can be made about 4 hours in advance and kept refrigerated.

Before serving, wash, stem, and slice the strawberries. To serve, place a phyllo cup on each plate, spoon or pipe in some white chocolate mascarpone, top with sliced strawberries, drizzle with basil syrup (if desired), and top with either micro basil or basil chiffonade. Drizzle with a tiny bit of balsamic reduction as well if you like.

Basil Syrup

MAKES ABOUT 1 CUP

½ cup water

1 cup granulated sugar

1 teaspoon cornstarch

1 medium bunch fresh basil, leaves removed
  (about 2 cups loosely packed)

Put the water in a small saucepan over medium heat. Add the sugar and cornstarch and cook, stirring occasionally, until the sugar dissolves. Pour the warm syrup into a blender, add the basil leaves, and blend until the basil is finely chopped but not completely puréed. Let the syrup sit for 10 to 15 minutes before straining out the basil solids with a fine-mesh sieve or through a coffee filter.

Reduced Balsamic Syrup

MAKES ¼ CUP

1 cup balsamic vinegar

1 teaspoon honey

Put the balsamic vinegar in a heavy-bottomed nonreactive saucepan over medium-high heat. Stir in the honey and reduce the heat to a simmer. Maintaining a steady low simmer, slowly reduce the mixture until it loses more than half of its original volume, about 40 minutes. Continue to cook, watching closely. When the mixture appears thick and syrupy, after 10 to 15 more minutes, remove the reduction from the heat and cool slightly. Store in a sealed container in the refrigerator.

What's Next

The availability and accessibility of responsibly produced, delicious food will continue to change—whether it's because of a growing market for local and sustainable ingredients, new distribution systems, changes to the industrial food system, climate change, new public policies, and concerns we haven't yet imagined. The choices we make today may not be the same we'll make in five years or even in five weeks.

Looking back over the last 20 years, the food landscape has changed dramatically. What has not changed, though, are our mission and the principles that guide Chefs Collaborative member chefs in making their daily purchasing decisions. I hope that you find these principles as helpful and inspirational as I do.

Eat well,

Chef Michael Leviton

About Chefs Collaborative

MISSION STATEMENT

Chefs Collaborative works with chefs and the greater food community to celebrate local foods and foster a more sustainable food supply. The Collaborative inspires action by translating information about our food into tools for making knowledgeable purchasing decisions. Through these actions, our members embrace seasonality, preserve diversity and traditional practices, and support local economies.

STATEMENT OF PRINCIPLES

- Food is fundamental to life, nourishing us in body and soul. The preparation of food strengthens our connection to nature. And the sharing of food immeasurably enriches our sense of community.
- Good food begins with unpolluted air, land, and water, environmentally sustainable farming and fishing, and humane animal husbandry.
- Food choices that emphasize delicious, locally grown, seasonally fresh, and whole or minimally processed ingredients are good for us, for local farming communities, and for the planet.
- Cultural and biological diversity are essential for the health of the earth and its inhabitants. Preserving and revitalizing sustainable food, fishing, and agricultural traditions strengthen that diversity.
- By continually educating themselves about sustainable choices, chefs can serve as models to the culinary community and the general public through their purchases of seasonal, sustainable ingredients and their transformation of these ingredients into delicious food.
- The greater culinary community can be a catalyst for positive change by creating a market for good food and helping preserve local farming and fishing communities.

VISION

As a result of our work, sustainability is second nature in the greater culinary community.

Seafood Guides for Wild and Farmed Species

In additional to eco-labels and certifications, seafood guides can help inform the choices of consumers when buying seafood in a restaurant or retail store. The first condensed wallet-size guide appeared in 1999, when the Monterey Bay Aquarium released its Seafood Watch guide. It was adopted quickly as "the" source and many organizations followed suit with their own guides and comprehensive online resources, often using information from the Monterey Bay Aquarium. Since our fish come from sources around the world, international guides are included.

AUSTRALIAN MARINE CONSERVATION SOCIETY SEAFOOD GUIDE is Australia's first online resource for consumers who want to make sustainable seafood choices. The tool offers insight into the sustainability of more than 100 seafood species commonly found at fish markets, restaurants and supermarkets, including canned seafood.

BLUE OCEAN INSTITUTE GUIDE TO OCEAN FRIENDLY SEAFOOD originated a comprehensive seafood analysis and ranking methodology to create its guide. The quantitative approach evaluates a number of criteria for both wild and farmed fish. Point values are assigned and averaged to determine a final ranking for each species, which is used to generate a color linked to sustainability.

ENVIRONMENTAL DEFENSE FUND SEAFOOD SELECTOR pulls information directly from the Monterey Bay Aquarium Seafood Guide but distinguishes itself from other guides though its work with troubled fisheries to improve management and conservation, which in turn improve ratings.

MARINE CONSERVATION SOCIETY (UNITED KINGDOM) GOOD FISH GUIDE and MCS's online resource, called Fishonline, are designed to help consumers identify fish more resilient to fishing pressure from well-managed sources that are caught using sustainable methods that minimize damage to wildlife and habitats.

MONTEREY BAY AQUARIUM SEAFOOD WATCH is a tool that was created to illustrate that our oceans were showing serious signs of distress and provide consumers with guidance for sourcing seafood without adding to the problem. Less than 15 years later, more than 40 million guides have been distributed and the app has been downloaded more than 1 million times.

NOAA FISH WATCH is the National Oceanic and Atmospheric Administration's science-based resource for providing information around making smart sustainable seafood choices. The U.S. seafood products it profiles are harvested according to strict regulations that are intended to help keep fish populations and their habitats healthy and vibrant.

THE SOUTH CAROLINA AQUARIUM'S SUSTAINABLE SEAFOOD INITIATIVE is primarily a chef-oriented education program but also provides a great deal of information on their website. The primary focus is on seafood products local to the southeast U.S., but the organization also provides information on other domestic seafood.

URI SUSTAINABLE SEAFOOD INITIATIVE is a collaborative effort between the Rhode Island Sea Grant Program and the University of Rhode Island's College of Environment and Life Sciences to provide an independent and objective source of information and research on the sustainable seafood movement. It does not issue its own recommendations.

WORLD WILDLIFE FUND SEAFOOD GUIDE The WWF doesn't include U.S. fisheries in its guide, but it is a good resource for learning about imported products from Europe, Asia, and Africa.

Contributing Chefs

HUGH ACHESON, Five and Ten Restaurant, Athens, Georgia; *www.fiveandten.com*

JODY ADAMS AND BRIAN RAE, Rialto, Cambridge, Massachusetts; *www.rialto-restaurant.com*

BRIAN ALBERG, The Red Lion Inn, Stockbridge, Massachusetts; *www.redlioninn.com*

MICHAEL ANTHONY, Gramercy Tavern, New York, New York; *www.gramercytavern.com*

JUSTIN APRAHAMIAN, Sanford Restaurant, Milwaukee, Wisconsin; *www.sanfordrestaurant.com*

JOHN ASH, Santa Rosa, California; *www.chefjohnash.com*

DAN BARBER, Blue Hill at Stone Barns, Pocantico Hills, New York; *www.bluehillfarm.com/food/blue-hill-stone barns*

JEREMY BARLOW, Tayst, Nashville, Tennessee; *www.taystrestaurant.com*

JUDI BARSNESS, Chez Jude Restaurant, Grand Marais, Minnesota; *www.chezjude.com*

RICK BAYLESS, Frontera Grill, Chicago, Illinois; *www.fronterakitchens.com*

GREG BEST, Holeman and Finch Public House, Atlanta, Georgia; *www.holeman-finch.com*

TOM BIVINS, CROP Bistro & Brewery, Stowe, Vermont; *www.cropvt.com*

FRANK BRIGTSEN, Brigtsen's Restaurant, New Orleans, Louisiana; *www.brigtsens.com*

AARON BURGAU, Patois, New Orleans, Louisiana; *www.patoisnola.com*

JACKSON CANNON, The Hawthorne, Boston, Massachusetts; *www.thehawthornebar.com*

SETH CASWELL, emmer&rye, Seattle, Washington; *www.emmerandrye.com*

ASHLEY CHRISTENSEN, Poole's Diner, Raleigh, North Carolina; *www.poolesdowntowndiner.com*

JESSE ZIFF COOL, Cool Eatz Restaurants, San Francisco, California; *www.cooleatz.com*

ANN COOPER, Food Family Farming Foundation, Boulder, Colorado; *www.foodfamilyfarming.org*

ROB CORLISS, ATE (All Things Epicurean), Nixa, Missouri; *www.7ate9.biz*

ALISON COSTELLO, Capuchin Soup Kitchen, Detroit, Michigan; *www.cskdetroit.org*

JOHN CURRENCE, City Grocery, Oxford, Mississippi; *www.citygroceryonline.com*

PETER DAVIS, Henrietta's Table in The Charles Hotel, Cambridge, Massachusetts; *www.henriettastable.com*

PIPER DAVIS, Grand Central Baking Company, Portland, Oregon; *www.grandcentralbakery.com*

WILLIAM DISSEN, The Market Place Restaurant, Asheville, North Carolina, *www.marketplace-restaurant.com*

JOSE DUARTE, Taranta, Boston, Massachusetts; *www.tarantarist.com*

CHRIS EDWARDS, The Restaurant at Patowmack Farm, Lovettsville, Virginia; *www.patowmackfarm.com*

CAROLINE FIDANZA, Saltie, Brooklyn, New York; *www.saltieny.com*

SONJA J. FINN, Dinette, Pittsburgh, Pennsylvania; *www.dinette-pgh.com*

ADOLFO GARCIA, Rio Mar, New Orleans, Louisiana; *www.riomarseafood.com*

TODD GRAY, Equinox, Washington, D.C.; *www.equinoxrestaurant.com*

JOHN HALL, Canela Bistro, Sonoita, Arizona; *www.canelabistro.com*

GORDON HAMERSLEY, Hamersley's Bistro, Boston, Massachusetts; *www.hamersleysbistro.com*

SAM HAYWARD, Fore Street, Portland, Maine; *www.forestreet.biz*

Contributors

GREG HIGGINS, Higgins Restaurant and Bar, Portland, Oregon; www.higginsportland.com

DAVID HIRSCH, Moosewood Restaurant, Ithaca, New York; *www.moosewoodrestaurant.com*

PETER HOFFMAN, Back Forty, New York, New York; *www.backfortynyc.com*

LINTON HOPKINS, Restaurant Eugene, Atlanta, Georgia; *www.restauranteugene.com*

TODD HUDSON, The Wildflower Café and Coffee House, Mason, Ohio; *www.wildflowercafeandcoffeehouse.com*

JEFF JACKSON, Lodge at Torrey Pines, La Jolla, California; *www.lodgetorreypines.com*

MATT JENNINGS, Farmstead, Providence, Rhode Island; *www.farmsteadinc.com*

STEVE JOHNSON, Rendezvous in Central Square, Cambridge, Massachusetts; *www.rendezvouscentralsquare.com*

WAYNE JOHNSON, Ray's Boathouse, Seattle, Washington; *www.rays.com*

HELENE KENNAN, Bon Appétit Management Company, Mountain View, California; *www.bamco.com*

ADAM KEOUGH, Absinthe Brasserie & Bar, San Francisco, California; *www.absinthe.com*

DOLAN LANE, clarklewis, Portland, Oregon; *www.clarklewispdx.com*

GREG LAPRAD, Quiessence, Phoenix, Arizona; *www.quiessencerestaurant.com*

MIKE LATA, FIG, Charleston, South Carolina; *www.eatatfig.com*

PHOEBE LAWLESS, Scratch Baking, Durham, North Carolina; *www.piefantasy.com*

MICHAEL LEVITON, Lumière, Newton, Massachusetts; *www.lumiererestaurant.com*

JOSH LEWIN, Beacon Hill Bistro, Boston, Massachusetts; *www.beaconhillhotel.com/bistro*

JENN LOUIS, Lincoln Restaurant, Portland, Oregon; *www.lincolnpdx.com*

KENNETH MACDONALD, Sleeping Lady, Leavenworth, Washington; *www.sleepinglady.com*

DEBORAH MADISON, Founding chef of Greens, San Francisco, California; Santa Fe, New Mexico; *www.deborahmadison.com*

BARRY MAIDEN, Hungry Mother, Cambridge, Massachusetts; *www.hungrymothercambridge.com*

EVAN MALLETT, Black Trumpet, Portsmouth, New Hampshire; *www.blacktrumpetbistro.com*

WALDY MALOUF, Beacon, New York, New York; *www.beaconnyc.com*

HUGO MATHESON, The Kitchen, Boulder, Colorado; *www.thekitchencommunity.com/the-kitchen-boulder*

TONY MAWS, Craigie on Main, Cambridge, Massachusetts; *www.craigieonmain.com*

PETER MCCARTHY, EVOO, Cambridge, Massachusetts; *www.evoorestaurant.com*

JENNIFER MCCOY, Cissé, New York, New York; *www.jennymccoy.com*

REGINA MEHALLICK AND ERIN KEM, R bistro, Indianapolis, Indiana; *www.rbistro.com*

PETER MERRIMAN, Merriman's Kapalua, Lahaina, Hawaii; *www.merrimanshawaii.com*

MARC MEYER, Cookshop, New York, New York; *www.cookshopny.com*

TORY MILLER, L'Etoile, Madison, Wisconsin; *www.letoile-restaurant.com*

MARY SUE MILLIKEN, Border Grill, Santa Monica, California; *www.bordergrill.com*

KIM MÜLLER, Foodcraft, Santa Fe, New Mexico; *www.foodcraft.biz*

MICHEL NISCHAN, The Dressing Room Restaurant, Westport, Connecticut; *www.dressingroomrestaurant.com*

BRADLEY OGDEN, Lark Creek Restaurant and Group, San Francisco, California; *www.larkcreek.com*

VITALY PALEY, Paley's Place, Portland, Oregon; *www.paleysplace.net*

MATT PALMERLEE, former chef of Farm 255, Athens, Georgia; *www.farm255.com*

CINDY PAWLCYN, Cindy Pawlcyn's Wood Grill & Wine Bar, Saint Helena, California; *www.pawlcynsgrill.com*

GREG PERRAULT, June, Portland, Oregon; *www.junepdx.com*

JAY PIERCE, Lucky 32 Southern Kitchen, Greensboro, North Carolina; *www.lucky32.com/greensboro.htm*

ODESSA PIPER, Roslindale, Massachusetts; *www.odessapiper.com*

MONICA POPE, T'afia, Houston, Texas; *www.tafia.com/*

NORA POUILLON, Restaurant Nora, Washington D.C.; *www.noras.com*

THIERRY RAUTUREAU, Rover's, Seattle, Washington; *www.thechefinthehat.com/rovers*

ANDREA REUSING, Lantern, Chapel Hill, North Carolina; *www.lanternrestaurant.com*

JONAH RHODEHAMEL, Oliveto Restaurant and Cafe, Oakland, California; *www.oliveto.com*

LEE RICHARDSON, Ashley's Restaurant at the Capital Hotel, Little Rock, Arkansas; *www.capitalhotel.com/Ashleyswebsite*

PAUL ROGALSKI, Rouge, Calgary, Alberta, Canada; *www.rougecalgary.com*

LENNY RUSSO, Heartland, Saint Paul, Minneapolis; *www.heartlandrestaurant.com*

STEVEN SATTERFIELD, Miller Union, Atlanta, Georgia; *www.millerunion.com/site*

DEBORAH SCARBOROUGH, Black Cat Bistro, Cambria, California; *www.blackcatbistro.com*

MICHAEL SCELFO, Russell House Tavern, Cambridge, Massachusetts; *www.russellhousecambridge.com*

ROBIN SCHEMPP, Right Stuff Enterprises, Waterbury, Vermont; *www.rightstuffent.com*

JIMMY SCHMIDT, Morgan's in the Desert, La Quinta, California; *www.morgansinthe-desert.com/morgans-in-the-desert*

MICHAEL SCHWARTZ, Michael's Genuine Food & Drink, Miami, Florida; *www.michaelsgenuine.com*

BARTON SEAVER, National Geographic Fellow, Washington D.C.; *www.bartonseaver.org*

ADAM SEGER, Nacional 27, Chicago, Illinois; *www.n27chicago.com*

BRUCE SHERMAN, North Pond, Chicago, Illinois; *www.northpondrestaurant.com*

JOHN SHIELDS, Gertrude's, Baltimore, Maryland; *www.johnshields.com/restaurant/rest/gertrudas.html*

ANA SORTUN, Oleana, Cambridge, Massachusetts; *www.oleanarestaurant.com*

SUSAN SPICER, Bayona, New Orleans, Louisiana; *www.bayona.com*

SARAH STEGNER AND GEORGE BUMBARIS, Prairie Grass Café, Northbrook, Illinois; *www.prairiegrasscafe.com*

JOHN AND JULIE STEHLING, Early Girl Eatery, Asheville, North Carolina; *www.earlygirleatery.com*

ROBERT STEHLING, Hominy Grill, Charleston, South Carolina; *www.hominygrill.com*

ERIC STENBERG, Jack Creek Grille at Moonlight Basin, Big Sky, Montana; *www.moonlightbasin.com*

FRANK STITT, Highlands Bar and Grill, Birmingham, Alabama, *www.highlandsbarandgrill.com*

CRAIG STOLL, Delfina, San Francisco, California; *www.delfinasf.com*

ETHAN STOWELL, Staple and Fancy Mercantile, Seattle, Washington; *www.ethanstowellrestaurants.com/stapleandfancy*

STEPHEN STRYJEWSKI, Cochon, New Orleans, Louisiana; *www.cochonrestaurant.com*

JOHN SUNDSTROM, Lark, Seattle, Washington; *www.larkseattle.com*

PATTIE TAAN, Farmhouse Inn, Forestville, California; *www.farmhouseinn.com*

BILL TELEPAN, Telepan Restaurant, New York, New York; *www.telepan-ny.com*

ARAIN VITALE, KASK, and David Shenaut, Oregon Bartenders Guild, Portland, Oregon; *www.grunerpdx.com/kask.htm*

DEREK WAGNER, Nicks on Broadway, Providence, Rhode Island; www.nicksonbroadway.com

BRUCE WALLIS, At Sara's Table Chester Creek Café, Duluth, Minnesota; *www.astccc.net*

ALAN WALTER, International House Hotel, New Orleans, Louisiana; *www.ihhotel.com*

ERIC WARNSTEDT, Hen of the Wood, Waterbury, Vermont; *www.henofthewood.com*

CHRIS WEBER, The Herbfarm, Woodinville, Washington; *www.theherbfarm.com*

MATTHEW WEINGARTEN, Sodexo, New York, New York; *www.sodexousa.com*

CHAD WHITE, Counterpoint, San Diego, California; *www.gabardineeats.com*

JASPER WHITE, Summer Shack, Cambridge, Massachusetts; *www.summershackrestaurant.com*

ERIC YOST, White Dog Café, Philadelphia, Pennsylvania; *www.whitedog.com*

Contributing Experts

CARRIE BALKCOM,
American Grassfed Association

ED DOYLE,
Real Food Consulting

BARRY ESTABROOK,
www.PoliticsofthePlate.com

PAUL FEHRIBACH,
Big Jones

MIKE GINGRICH,
Uplands Cheese Company

ANDREW GUNTHER,
Animal Welfare Approved

CLIFFORD HATCH,
Upinngil Farm

FRED KIRSCHENMANN,
Leopold Center

RICHARD MCCARTHY,
Market Umbrella

GARY NABHAN,
Southwest Center of the University of Arizona

BILL NIMAN,
BN Ranch

NICOLE HAHN NIMAN,
BN Ranch

CHAD PAWLAK,
Grass Point Farms

BOB PERRY,
University of Kentucky College of Agriculture

TOM PHILPOTT,
Mother Jones

GLENN ROBERTS,
Anson Mills

ELI ROGOSA,
Heritag Grain Consevancy

DAN ROSENTHAL,
Rosenthal Restaurant Group

JOHN ROWLEY,
John Rowley & Associates

MARIA SPECK,
www.mariaspeck.com

JENNIFER SMALL,
Flying Pigs Farm

MING TSAI,
Blue Ginger

MEGAN WESTMEYER,
Sustainable Fisheries Partnership

WILL WILLIS,
Bully Boy Distillers

Vegetables, Fruits, and Other Edible Plants

Anson Mills, *www.ansonmills.com*
Baer's Best Beans, *www.baersbest.com*
Cayuga Pure Organics, *www.cporganics.com*
Food Alliance, *www.foodalliance.org*
Local Harvest, *www.localharvest.org/csa*
Non-GMO Project, *www.nongmoproject.org*
Phipps Ranch, *www.phippscountry.com*
Rancho Gordo, *www.ranchogordo.com*
Slow Food USA®, *www.slowfoodusa.org*

Meats and Poultry

American Grassfed Association,
  www.americangrassfed.org
American Humane Association,
  www.americanhumane.org
American Livestock Breeds Conservancy,
  www.albc-usa.org
Animal Welfare Approved,
  www.animalwelfareapproved.org
Certified Humane, *www.certifiedhumane.org*
Food Alliance, *www.foodalliance.org*
Global Animal Partnership,
  www.globalanimalpartnership.org

Fish and Seafood

Alaska Seafood Marketing Institute,
  www.alaskaseafood.org
Aquaculture Stewardship Council,
  www.asc-aqua.org
Blue Ocean Institute, *www.blueocean.org*
Bristol Bay Regional Seafood Development
  Association, *www.bbrsda.com*
Cape Cod Commercial Hook Fishermen's
  Association, *www.cchfa.org*
Environmental Defense Fund,
  www.edf.org/seafood
FishWise, *www.fishwise.org*
Food and Agriculture Organization of the United
  Nations, *www.fao.org/fishery*
Food and Water Watch,
  www.foodandwaterwatch.org
Friend of the Sea, *www.friendofthesea.org*
Global Aquaculture Alliance, *www.gaalliance.org*
Marine Conservation Society, *www.mcsuk.org*
Marine Stewardship Council, *www.msc.org*

Monterey Bay Aquarium, *www.mbayaq.org*
Natural Resources Defense Council,
  www.nrdc.org
New England Aquarium, *www.neaq.org*
NOAA, *www.nmfs.noaa.gov*
Oceana, *www.oceana.org*
Ocean Conservancy, *www.oceanconservancy.org*
The Pew Charitable Trusts, *www.pewtrusts.org*
Save Bristol Bay, *www.savebristolbay.org*
Save Our Wild Salmon, *www.wildsalmon.org*
Seafood Choices Alliance, *www.seafoodchoices.org*
Seaweb, *www.seaweb.org*
Shedd Aquarium, *www.sheddaquarium.org*
South Carolina Aquarium, *www.scaquarium.org*
Trout Unlimited, *www.tu.org*
URI Sustainable Seafood Initiative,
  www.seagrant.gso.uri.edu/sustainable_seafood
World Wildlife Fund, *www.worldwildlife.org*
Worldwatch Institute, *www.worldwatch.org*

Eggs and Dairy

American Cheese Society, *www.cheesesociety.org*
Best Baa Dairy, *www.bestbaa.com*
Bleu Mont Dairy
Capriole Goat Cheeses, *www.capriolegoatcheese.com*
Carr Valley Cheese, *www.carrvalleycheese.com*
Consider Bardwell Farm,
  www.considerbardwellfarm.com
Cowgirl Creamery, *www.cowgirlcreamery.com*
Grasspoint Farms, *www.grasspoint.com*
Green Dirt Farm, *www.greendirtfarm.com*
Jasper Hill Farm, *www.cellarsatjasperhill.com*
Meadow Creek Dairy, *www.meadowcreekdairy.com*
Mt. Townsend Creamery,
  www.mttownsendcreamery.com
Mozzarella Company, *www.mozzco.com*
Old Chatham Sheepherding Company,
  www.blacksheepcheese.com
Rogue Creamery, *www.roguecreamery.com*
Shelburne Farms, *www.shelburnefarms.org*
Spring Day Creamery, *www.springdaycreamery.com*
Uplands Cheese Company, *www.uplandscheese.com*
Vella Cheese Company, *www.vellacheese.com*
Vermont Butter and Cheese Company,
  www.vermontcreamery.com
Vermont Shepherd, *www.vermontshepherd.com*

Liquid/Dry Measures

U.S.	Metric
¼ teaspoon	1.25 milliliters
½ teaspoon	2.5 milliliters
1 teaspoon	5 milliliters
1 tablespoon (3 teaspoons)	15 milliliters
1 fluid ounce (2 tablespoons)	30 milliliters
¼ cup	60 milliliters
⅓ cup	80 milliliters
½ cup	120 milliliters
1 cup	240 milliliters
1 pint (2 cups)	480 milliliters
1 quart (4 cups; 32 ounces)	960 milliliters
1 gallon (4 quarts)	3.84 liters
1 ounce (by weight)	28 grams
1 pound	454 grams
2.2 pounds	1 kilogram

Oven Temperatures

°F	Gas Mark	°C
250	½	120
275	1	140
300	2	150
325	3	165
350	4	180
375	5	190
400	6	200
425	7	220
450	8	230
475	9	240
500	10	260
550	Broil	290

Numbers in **bold** indicate pages with photos